JOB REDESIGN

Job Redesign

Critical Perspectives on the Labour Process

Edited by
David Knights,
Hugh Willmott,
David Collinson

Gower

Published by
Gower Publishing Company Limited,
Gower House,
Croft Road,
Aldershot,
Hants GU11 3HR,
England

Gower Publishing Company,
Old Post Road,
Brookfield,
Vermont 05036,
U.S.A.

British Library Cataloguing in Publication Data

Knights, David
   Job redesign.
   1. work design
   I. Title   II. Willmott, Hugh
   III. Collinson, David
   658.3'06   T60.8

   ISBN 0 566 00883 1
   ISBN 0 566 00885 8 Paperback

Phototypesetting by The Castlefield Press, Moulton, Northampton
Printed in Great Britain by Biddles Ltd, Guildford, Surrey

Contents

List of Contributors

John Child is Professor or Organizational Behaviour at the University of Aston. His current research is on the introduction of new technologies and cross-national comparisons of organization.

David Collinson has conducted research into shopfloor culture in the engineering industry and industrial relations in the printing industry. At present he is engaged in research on the recruitment process.

Rod Coombs is Lecturer in the Department of Management Sciences at UMIST. He is researching the economics of technological change and its relationship to long-term trends.

Bryn Jones's recent publications have concerned latest developments in work organisation and automation in metal machining industries. He is currently writing a book on work opportunities and controls arising from the computerisation of metalwork manufacturing.

John Kelly is Lecturer in Industrial Relations, LSE. Publications include *Autonomy and Control at the Workplace, Scientific Management, Job Redesign and Work Performance* and *Steel Strike*.

Craig Littler is the author of *The Development of the Labour Process in Capitalist Societies* and *Class at Work: the Design, Allocation and Control of Jobs* (with Graeme Salaman).

Tony Manwaring is a Research Officer of the Labour Party. He formerly researched the British motor industry and recruitment practices.

Harvie Ramsay is Lecturer in the Department of Industrial Relations, Strathclyde. He is currently working on labour responses to multinational corporations and on the impact of new technology.

Michael Rose is Senior Lecturer, Bath University. He is author of *Computers, Managers and Society, Industrial Behaviour, Servants of Post-Industrial Power?* and *Reworking the Work Ethic*.

David Knights is Lecturer in Management Science, UMIST. He has conducted research into sales activities and workplace industrial relations, and on equal opportunity for racial and ethnic minorities and sex discrimination in recruitment. His publications include *Managing the Multi-Racial Workforce* and *The Theory and Practice of Management Control*.

Stephen Wood is Lecturer in Industrial Relations, LSE. He is editor of *The Degradation of Work?* and *Industrial Relations and Management Strategy* (with K. Thurley) and author of *Redundancy* (with Ian Dey).

Hugh Willmott is Lecturer in the Management Centre, University of Aston. He is currently engaged in a joint research project on Corporatism and the Accountancy Profession.

1   Introduction

In recent years, there has been a renaissance in the study of job
redesign. During the 1960s and early 1970s, knowledge of job redesign
and the restructuring of work was guided by a concern to ameliorate
human relations at work or to improve the quality of individuals'
working lives. In general, the focus was on the individual employee in
relation to the job task, the work group and the style of managerial
supervision. Underlying this interest in job redesign was a concern to
render work both more productive and humanly satisfying by
removing unnecessary obstacles to the development of 'good' employee
relations and worker motivation. Only comparatively recently has this
dominant, conventional perspective been challenged by less prescriptive studies. Fundamental to this new perspective is a belief that job
redesign, both in theory and in practice, cannot be adequately understood independently of an appreciation of the historical and politico-
economic contexts in which it has developed and been applied.

More specifically, the emergent critical perspective on job redesign
has questioned the view that the redesign of jobs *in practice* is primarily
motivated by a humanistic ideology of improving job satisfaction and
the quality of working life. Characteristic of this approach is an implicit
scepticism about widespread claims that job redesign can provide a true
reconciliation of the 'needs' of individuals (employees) and the 'needs'
of organisations (employers). For what such claims assume is that the
interests of employees can be made entirely compatible with a system of
production in which a minority of owners and controllers appropriate a
disproportionate share of the material and symbolic benefits in society.

Conventional Job Redesign in Theory and Practice
Conventional wisdom in the area of job redesign is infused by a managerialist or technicist orientation to work organisation. This is perhaps
most evident in classical approaches to the organisation of work, such as
those advocated by Taylor (1911) and Fayol (1949). However, despite

an overt concern for human values and the well-being of employees, more recent 'behavioural' perspectives on work organisation and managerial behaviour associated with the schools of 'human relations' (Barnard 1938; Mayo, 1949) 'neo-human relations' (Herzberg 1958; McGregor 1960; Davis and Cherns 1975) have responded to the managerially defined problems of low motivation and morale associated with highly simplified tasks and impersonal, hierarchical forms or organisation. Certainly, many advocates of job redesign – such as those closely associated with the earlier years of the Quality of Working Life movement – contrived to appear independent of management. Like Taylor before them, they promoted the idea that job redesign was politically neutral because it would increase the satisfaction of both individual and organisational 'needs'.

Based upon theories of motivation that abstract the individual from history and the structure of social relations, the conventional wisdom of job redesign stresses the social or self-actualising needs and expectations of individuals. On this basis, a number of alternative suggestions for designing or redesigning jobs have been developed and applied. Amongst these are job rotation, job enlargement, job enrichment, quality circles, the creation of 'autonomous work groups', the introduction of consultation and 'participation' schemes. These techniques, which offer a solution to the managerial problems of depressed employee morale and performance, constitute the theory and practice of established perspectives on job redesign. In this way, an elective affinity has existed between managers employed to rationalise work organisation and the humanistic concerns of behavioural scientists.

Clearly, many behavioural scientists working in the area of job redesign were, and continue to be, genuinely concerned with the welfare of the individual employee. Their *primary* objective has not necessarily been to increase efficiency and productivity. Rather, it has been to limit or reverse the dehumanising and degrading tendencies of the detailed division of labour in contemporary organisation. Provoked by their abhorrence of jobs designed so as to eliminate the possibility of human self-expression, these humanistic approaches identified elements of irrationality in the contemporary organisation of work. Far from simply reflecting a highly efficient technical means of production, the prevailing design of jobs and organisation of work was seen to have undermined the productive performance of labour.

Committed to the dual programme of improving job satisfaction and worker performance, many advocates of job redesign established themselves as change-agents determined to convince *managers* of the value of redesigning jobs. As individuals, managers may conceivably share the change-agent's moral concern to humanise the workplace. However, in playing out the organisational role of manager, such concerns are 'indulged' only in so far as they can be expected (or, preferably, *demonstrated*) to make an instrumental contribution to corporate performance and survival. As a consequence, if he or she is to make any progress in attaining the objective of improving employee welfare, the change-agent is obliged to develop techniques that appeal to and accommodate the more immediate interests of management.

Whether as a result of political acumen or self-interested pragmatism, the idealism associated with humanistic programmes for redesigning work has gradually given way to packages having more direct appeal to the commercial interests of management. This trend has been underlined by the realities of economic recession that have reduced the attractiveness of subscribing to job redesign techniques and strategies because they are 'progressive', 'fashionable' or 'humanising' independently of their demonstrable commercial benefits. Increasingly, 'soft', high-sounding moralising on job redesign has given way to a 'hard nosed' pragmatism dictated by managerial perceptions of conditions in the marketplace.

A New Wave in Job Redesign Research
Almost coincident with the growing scepticism amongst managers concerning the commercial value of human relations strategies of job redesign has been a renaissance of interest amongst more detached and critical academics in the field of work organisation and restructuring. Influenced by the post-Braverman (1974) revival of industrial sociology, and to a lesser extent by radical critiques of social psychology, the new wave of job redesign research has taken a more critical view of the theory and practice of job design. Characteristics of this alternative approach is a scholarly concern to describe and to provide an explanation of the process and politics of work organisation and the redesign of jobs. The primary interest in developing prescriptions for humanising reforms or increased productivity has been replaced by an interest in understanding why job redesign occurs and in developing *radical* critiques of the theories and practices associated with job redesign (cf. Kelly 1982; Wood 1982).

The present volume is representative of the new wave of interest in the redesign of jobs. Each of the papers makes a contribution to the task of analysing the social, political and economic conditions and consequences of job design. Common themes underlying this collection of papers are, firstly, a concern to extend analysis beyond the 'closed system' boundaries of the organisation in which jobs are redesigned, and, secondly, a desire to move away from narrowly deterministic or overly voluntaristic accounts of work reorganisation. In elaborating these themes, the papers penetrate more deeply into the conditions and consequences of how work is, and also broaden the debate on how it might be, organised. More specifically, the papers illuminate the internal and external processes that underpin and transform the organisation and restructuring of work. Accordingly, conventional perspectives that have focused exclusively upon the psychological health of the individual at the point of production have been largely abandoned. In their place a framework has emerged that advances an explanation of the redesign of jobs in terms of structural factors – such as advances in new technology, changes in product and labour markets and the restructuring of corporations as a result of international developments. Within this perspective these structural factors provide the context against which managerial attempts to improve the cooperation, flexibility and productivity of labour are conceived and executed. All but two of the papers collected together in this volume were selected from the first Aston-UMIST annual conference on the 'Organisation and Control of the Labour Process' (1983). These further papers were added in order to present a more rounded appreciation of the conditions and consequences of the redesign of work.

In the first paper Craig Littler examines the development and international diffusion of Taylorism and Fordism and identifies their specific economic, technical and social limits. He notes how, against a background of international competition intensified by the world recession, the inherent inflexibility of mass assembly technology (Fordism) and an extreme division of labour (Taylorism) resulted in some demand for a redesign of jobs in the 1970s. Coinciding with the pressure to render the organisation of labour more flexible, there emerged a lobby of academics and consultants proselytising programmes of 'job enrichment' – such as quality circles – for humanising the workplace. The particular value of Littler's paper is that it begins to fill out the theoretical vacuum that exists in the job redesign literature between heavily deterministic accounts of the history of management control, on the one hand (e.g. Braverman 1974; Edwards 1979), and over-voluntaristic assumptions of consensus in the labour process evident in conventional work humanisation programmes, on the other (e.g. Bennis 1966; Argyris 1970).

The theme of seeking to avoid explanations of job redesign and its effects either as a simple extension of capitalist domination or as evidence of liberal-pluralist democratic gains is also a main theme of the contributions of John Kelly and Harvie Ramsay. Kelly examines socio-economic developments in electrical engineering where companies redesigned jobs in the mid-1960s and mid-1970s in circumstances in which labour problems were almost negligible. In doing so, he rejects the crude labour process assumption that job redesign is a necessary consequence of the implicit contradiction, and explicit conflict, between capital and labour. Instead, he argues that the redesign of jobs is not simply a reflection of management's preoccupation with *control* as part of the process of extracting surplus value from labour. Nor, he suggests, is job redesign adequately understood as a development that evolves principally in response to labour problems stemming from the 'alienation' of the mass production line. Kelly urges that an explanation be sought through an analysis of the fluctuations in product and labour markets. But, in addition, he argues that the substitution of a market analysis for the more narrow explanation of job redesign in terms of labour-capital contradictions at the point of production is also unsatisfactory. Rather, he recommends an examination of specific cases of job redesign in relation to the complex contradictions that emanate from discontinuities and disjunctions within and between the circulation of capital and the cycle of production and exchange.

Ramsay's paper follows a parallel line of development. He is no less sceptical of the Marxist view that job redesign secures advantages for management than he is of the pluralistic belief that both sides gain from the change in the restructuring of work processes. Drawing upon empirical material from two recent case studies, it is concluded that the role of pay incentives has been underplayed in evaluations of job enrichment and participation schemes. In support of this argument, Ramsay observes how tighter labour markets generated by the recession have resulted in the abandonment of those schemes that were seemingly designed principally to secure managerial legitimacy. It would, however, be a mistake to deduce from Ramsay's paper that the erosion of commitment to employee participation and job enrichment has eliminated managerial interest in the redesign of jobs. As noted already, intensified competition has created production demands (e.g. product differentiation, elasticity of supply) which necessitate much greater degrees of labour flexibility.

This theme is explored from different angles in the following two papers. First, Michael Rose and Bryn Jones observe how the comparative weakening of formal trade union power caused by present reductions in the demand for labour and the erosion of job security does not automatically or necessarily result in a decimation of workplace bargaining institutions at the plant level. Equally significant is their finding of an absence of any comprehensive industrial relations strategic planning incorporating work reorganisation and job redesign schemes. Changes were discovered to take place on an *ad hoc* basis and were frequently initiated and developed by managers from outside the personnel or industrial relations sphere. Unions at plant level were also found to have no coherent strategy to work reorganisation and simply responded to management proposals in terms of the specific contingencies of the local situation. These findings challenge both labour process and strategic-contingency theories of control and resistance. For despite the divergent politics of these two theoretical approaches they each attribute to management and/or labour a rationality and intentionality which in everday practice was not found to be sustained. In failing to recognise the limited and *ad hoc* character of practical decision-making, Rose and Jones argue that such theories are in danger of producing teleological explanations. Thus, when certain quasi-random practices have the consequence of enhancing management control or labour resistance, it is mistakenly theorised as the cause rather than merely an unintended outcome of those practices.

John Child agrees with Rose and Jones that managerial strategy lacks any overall uniformity. But, in contrast, he perceives it to be more confrontational and to result from increased competition. His case studies reveal how new technology has been especially important in redesigning jobs and rendering labour more flexible. Much, however, is shown to depend upon the character of both internal and external labour and product markets. After examining various examples of job redesign in relation to the development of new technology, Child argues that managerial strategies for the control of risk and uncertainty involve job redesign and labour as only *one* possible minor aspect of the cycle of production, exchange and capital accumulation as a whole. He also suggests that technology is developing rapidly to the point where labour will become a much less significant cost or risk to the employer. It is anticipated that future managerial strategies will necessarily reflect these changes together with their effect on both product and labour markets. Nonetheless, as Child's preliminary investigations indicate, there will remain occupationally organised groups (e.g. the professions) as well as those closely involved in managing new technology (e.g. computer staff) whose labour is likely to increase in significance in respect of the management of the labour process.

The paper contributed by Rod Coombs also explores the connection between technological innovation and job redesign. To this end, he employs an analytical-historical perspective to isolate distinct phases of the mechanisation of the production process. Distinguishing between primary, secondary and tertiary forms of mechanisation, he demonstrates their links with the economic cycle as reflected in the theory of long waves. In Coombs's analysis, the present proliferation of job redesign strategies is attributed to the intensified competition which accompanies a downswing in the economic cycle. Tertiary mechanisation continues but the advantages of secondary mass production technologies become more vulnerable as long production runs have to be sacrificed in the face of extreme product-differentiated competition. The common thread running through all these strategies, whether they be based on technical or organisational change, is that they reduce labour costs at the same time as they improve its flexibility. Coombs also takes note of the evolution from primary mechanisation, involving the transformation of products, through secondary mechanisation, which allows for the transfer of products along a conveyor belt or other mechanical device, to the more recent computer based production control systems of tertiary mechanisation. Some statistical correlations are identifiable that link the proliferation of these progressive forms of mechanisation to a point of recovery in the downturn of the longwave economic cycle. However, the fact that each phase of development is associated with a completely new production technology makes it almost impossible to predict precisely its job features.

The remaining two contributions from Tony Manwaring and Stephen Wood, and David Knights and Dave Collinson, take us back to the labour process at the point of production. Manwaring and Wood draw attention to the importance of tacit skills even in the most routinised of jobs. Regardless of how sophisticated the technology or mechanised the production, they observe that there will be some dependence upon its tacit skills, as long as labour is an integral part of the process. In this perspective, job redesign schemes are seen to reflect not only technological advances in production systems but also the recognition that an optimising of their productive efficiency depends upon securing the co-operation of labour. After characterising tacit skills as grounded in the practical knowledge that develops through the routine repetition of specific tasks, the authors present some empirical examples to illustrate their argument. Quotations from a number of workers engaged in jobs considered to require personnel of almost sub-normal intelligence are interpreted as revealing certain highly specific skills which are taken for granted and only fully acknowledged when they become crucial in resolving a production crisis. In common with other contributions, the paper steers a course between the crude determinism of some labour process theory and the simplistic belief in value-consensus characteristic of much managerial psychology.

In the final paper, Knights and Collinson focus upon the impact on workplace relations of the relaxation of management control. As one specific variant on the approach to job redesign, they observe how the introduction of targets and bonuses allows for a relaxation of direct management control as workers voluntarily sanction one another in a complex system of self-organised consent to meet a given set of production demands. Comparing a recent case study of a motor vehicle plant with the work of Burawoy (1979), they conclude that although 'making out' or achieving targets does develop into a social game, the consent it generates may be highly superficial and precarious. This is because the socially organised character of the consent can easily obscure the deep-rooted economic instrumentalism and polarised conflict which underlies most workers' conditional commitment to production targets. As a system of developing the interdependent and co-operative character of the social organisation of production, the relaxation of management control is only partially successful in so far as it relies on target and bonus incentives that reflect and reinforce the economistic self-interests of workers.

Overall, the papers collected in this volume offer an alternative to conventional approaches that favour a comparatively narrow, prescriptive and often psychological view of job redesign. By developing a more detailed analysis of the organisation of work, this alternative perspective neither advocates nor reflects a naive faith in the humanistic and/or productive virtues of job redesign. In seeking a measure of detachment from the moralising ideals of liberal-humanism no less than the purely commercial interests of management, the papers share a concern to illuminate the conditions, content, complexities, contradictions and consequences of job redesign programmes and practices. Their aim is to understand and explain job redesign as a medium and outcome of the political, economic and social forces that intersect within the organisation and control of the labour process in late capitalist society.

References

Argyris, C. (1970), *Intervention Theory and Method*, Reading, Massachusetts: Addison-Wesley.

Barnard, C.I. (1938), *The Functions of the Executive*, London: Oxford University Press.

Bennis, W.G. (1966), *Changing Organisations*, New York: McGraw-Hill.

Braverman, H. (1974), *Labor and Monopoly Capital*, New York: Monthly Review Press.

Burawoy (1979), *Manufacturing Consent: Changes in the Labour Process under Monopoly Capitalism*, Chicago: University of Chicago Press.

Davis, L.E. and Cherns, A.B. (1975), *The Quality of Working Life*, London: Free Press.

Edwards, R.C. (1979), *Contested Terrain*, London: Heinemann.

Fayol, H. (1949), *General and Industrial Management*, London: Pitman.

Herzberg, F. (1958), *Work and the Nature of Man*, London: Staples Press.

Kelly, J.E. (1982), *Scientific Management, Job Redesign and Work Performance*, London: Academic Press.

Mayo, E. (1949), *The Social Problems of an Industrial Civilisation*, London: Routledge and Kegan Paul.

McGregor, D. (1960), *The Human Side of Enterprise*, New York: McGraw-Hill.
Taylor, F. (1911), *Principles of Scientific Management*, New York: Harper and Row.
Wood, S. (ed.) (1982), *The Degradation of Work?*, London: Hutchinson.

2 Taylorism, Fordism and Job Design[1]

Craig R. Littler

Introduction

This paper summarises some of my work on the significance and influence of Taylorism (see Littler 1978, 1982), and develops some ideas on Fordism and assembly-line production. In sections 3 and 4 there is a consideration of the diffusion and limitations of Taylorism and Fordism as forms of job design, leading on in section 5 to an account of some of the new forms of job design propagated in the 1970s and 1980s.

In general, these new ideas of job design and work organisation had a very limited influence: they remained the peddled gospel of a few avant-garde consultants. But history suggests that the succeeding decade (the 1980s in this case) may be the period of the widespread take-up of managerial innovations. Two interlinked factors reinforce this potentiality – the continuing economic crisis of the 1980s plus the pressures of Japanese competition. Clearly the 1980s, like the 1930s, will spur some employers to take the path of wage cuts (there have been several examples of this), an extension of work hours in some form, or an imposition of straightforward labour intensification involving no attempt at work reorganisation. Clearly mass unemployment has shifted economic power to the employers such that they can force through previously unacceptable changes amidst a climate of fear and uncertainty about jobs. But there is a limit to what can be achieved by economic coercion. In particular it ignores the changing nature of competition. In many areas price has ceased to be the predominant factor in exchange and non-price factors, such as design, reliability and quality, have assumed a larger significance. But emphasis on quality rather than the velocity of throughput means that reluctant acquiescence has to give way to active cooperation. Of course, for some employers, automation and robots appear to offer a solution – but not enough of one. The crisis of Fordism is neatly exemplified by the present dilemma of Ford Europe. Faced with the large productivity gap between its European plants and Japanese manufacturers, Ford set up its 'After Japan' programme, which as the headlines announced was a contradictory mix of robots, job cuts, a union struggle *and* an attempt to engage the enthusiasm and willingness of the workers (see *The Guardian*, 11 June 1980).

The present Ford (and Fordist) dilemma illustrates the essential tension in the capital/labour relationship – a tension between the need to regulate and dominate the production process versus the need to maximise the creativity and reliability of wage labour. This paper revolves around fundamental elements in the history of this contradiction.

(1) Taylorism

Some writers treat Taylorism as a global concept, almost as a phase of capitalism.[2] I prefer to use 'Taylorism' in a more limited sense as one form of labour rationalisation or systematic management. This implies two things: first, that there is a distinction between Taylorite rationalisation and other forms, and secondly, that the influence of Taylorism over job design and managerial strategies needs to be demonstrated in particular cases.

It is now commonly accepted that Taylorism means both a set of ideological assertions and a system of management practices. The ideological components of Taylorism (the managerialist view of labour, the opposition of 'science' and traditional human judgement, etc.) are well-known and do not require analysis here (see Littler 1982; Rose 1975: 54–9). As a set of practices I find it useful to analyse 'scientific management' in terms of three general categories: job design principles, the structure of control over task performance and the implicit employment relationship. (For the full details of this analysis see Littler 1982: 50–62.) This chapter focuses its attention largely upon issues of job design and redesign.

From a job design perspective, Frederick Taylor's scheme of so-called 'scientific management' rests upon the principle of the division of mental and manual labour. In addition, Taylorism involved:

(a) a general principle of the maximum decomposition of work tasks;
(b) the divorce of direct and so-called 'indirect' labour, by which was meant all setting up, preparation and maintenance tasks; and
(c) the minimisation of the skill requirements of any task leading to minimum job-learning times.

In general, Taylor argued that the full possibilities of scientific management 'will not have been realized until almost all of the machines in the shop are run by men who are of smaller calibre and attainments, and

who are therefore cheaper than those required under the old system'
(Taylor 1903: 105).

The application of these principles in practice can be clearly seen in
the British Bedaux Archives. For example in the mounting section of a
firm (Henry Hope and Sons) producing metal windows and doors, the
Bedaux engineers comment that:

> Our observations reveal that the utilization of labour is low, due entirely to
> the responsibility carried by each of the operatives . . . each mounter is
> responsible for the collection and distribution of work from the paint dump,
> and in each and every case the transportation of frames is carried out by the
> mounter. For instructions concerning the type of fittings required, and the
> like, the mounter is compelled to seek information from a reference book,
> and consequently, the collection of fittings from the stores immediately
> follows. While all this is done the remaining member of the gang is held up
> awaiting the results of his mate's investigations.

The consultants go on to assert that this combination of tasks 'is beyond
the purpose for which the mounters have been employed, and also a
case which could be performed by cheaper labour or preferably
mechanized'. Having thus set out Babbage's Principle,[3] they continue:

> We always consider that in hand operations, simplicity of process is the
> keynote of economy, and in the case of mounting simplicity of mounting is
> interchangeability of parts. If it is possible to obtain interchangeability when
> the fittings are produced within commercial limits then the operation
> becomes semi or unskilled instead of skilled, or assembly instead of fitting.
> (Bedaux Archives, Henry Hope & Sons, F.16, R.4, 17 Oct. 1932).

In general, throughout this case study the Bedaux consultants
advocated job fragmentation, the divorce of direct and indirect labour
and labour cheapening.

I have sought to exemplify the Taylorite principles of job design
partly because some writers, notably Kelly (1982), have argued that
Taylorism is *not* based on the detailed division of labour (pp. 19–29).
However, though Taylorism *definitionally* and in its purest form
involves deskilling, this does not imply that all elements of the labour
process (the division of labour, the structure of control and the employment relationship) have to change simultaneously. It is possible for
these elements to vary independently such that a Taylorised structure
of control is implemented without systematic job fragmentation.

If we define Taylorism carefully, then it is possible to contrast it to
other forms of work organisation – the limited wave of labour rationalisation between 1890 and 1914 based on ideas developed in the British
armaments industry; the systematic rationalisation entailed by
Fordism in which flow production required the redesign of the whole
factory (see section 2); and the bureaucratisation of the employment

relationship involving institutionalised career systems, as in the post office and railways.

This contrast with other forms of work organisation raises the question of the extent of the influence of Taylorism. My answer to this question is complex, so I will baldly state my conclusion and then proceed to qualify it: in general the direct and indirect influence of Taylorism on factory jobs has been extensive, such that in Britain job-design and technology-design have become imbued with a neo-Taylorism. However, there was no direct simple line of influence, so it is necessary to add several qualifications:

(a) In Britain there was a time-lag of influence. Indeed pre-1914 the employers rejected 'American methods of management'.
(b) Because of this time-lag, it was *neo*-Taylorite systems which were eventually introduced, especially the Bedaux system. This combined Taylorism with the First World War fatigue studies and some elements of industrial psychology.
(c) The Bedaux system was probably the most important channel for the spread of Taylorite ideas in Britain, but there were other channels, notably the transfer of American mass production industries associated with the emergence of multinationals. This included Ford's (see section 2).
(d) There continued to be significant worker, supervisor and managerial resistance to Taylorism resulting in an uneven adoption, even within the mass production industries.
(e) There is the curious paradox that despite the influence of Taylorism on job design, it did not succeed as a managerial *ideology* in Britain, unlike the USA. This paradox arose from the timing and context of implementation.

(For the details of these arguments see Littler 1982.)

Not all economies accepted Taylorite ideas of job design. A different pattern is exemplified by Japan. In Japan, partly because of the timing and rapidity of industrialisation, no extensive tradition of industrial craftsmanship was ever established. Instead Japanese factories depended on a tradition of work teams incorporating managerial functions and maintenance functions, associated with few staff specialists. In contrast to the prescriptions of Taylorism, job boundaries were relatively few, allowing considerable job flexibility.

But in the United States, and more slowly in Britain, Taylorism, with its underlying principles of job fragmentation, tight job boundaries, and the separation of mental and manual labour, became the predominant ideal for job design. However, in practice, there are limits to the division of labour implied by Taylorism. As Adam Smith realised, the division of labour depends on the desired volume of output, which, in turn, depends on the extent of the market. If a certain piece of work involved ten operations it would not be economical to employ a specialised, detailed worker for each operation if the total volume of output required only the time of one person. Thus, decomposition of tasks and Taylorite principles depend on mass markets, mass production and the velocity of throughput.

(2) Fordism and Assembly-line Technology

This linkage of the division of labour and mass markets was realised clearly by Henry Ford. He largely established, captured and maintained a mass market for automobiles between 1908 and 1929, when the last of over 15 million Model-T cars rolled off the assembly line. By that date the USA had about 80% of the cars of the entire world, a ratio of 5.3 people for every car registered at a time when cars were a comparative luxury in Britain (Flink 1975: 67 and 70).

According to Meyer (1981), Fordism as a model of production worked out by Ford between 1908 and 1913 had four basic elements:

(a) standardised product design;
(b) the extensive use of new machine tool technology;
(c) flow-line production; and
(d) the implementation of Taylorism in relation to work processes.

The key to understanding the factory operations of Ford lies in the standard design of the Model-T car. An observer in 1917 refers to a case where the Ford engineers changed the appearance of the hood and fenders, and goes on to record that 'The first month saw production curtailed by 50% and it was nearly three months before the entire organization could be geared up for the stipulated work.' (Porter 1917). Thus, even apparently minor changes in design can cause a shutdown of many months or the replacement of all tooling whilst managers and workers rediscover the most efficient way to produce or assemble the new product.

But Ford's industrial expansion was associated with, as both effect and cause, significant changes in the design and construction of machine tools. Up to the end of the nineteenth century most machine tools were still general-purpose machines which relied on a repertoire of skills by the operator. But the emergent automobile industry, adding to the impact of the bicycle industry, sparked a new and intense phase in the design and specialisation of machine tools. New design features made them semi-automatic with special controls to change or reverse speeds. There was a rapid development of special jigs and fixtures which simplified the setting-up operations and controlled the tolerances of work. Essentially the machines were designed to run continuously at high speeds once they were set up. The widespread use of specialised machines in workshops was associated with a new division of labour based on a distinction between the 'set-up man' whose job consisted of starting the machines' operations and de-bugging it, and the semi-skilled machine tender whose only tasks were to feed the machine and remove the finished pieces. By 1914 about 15,000 machines had been installed at the new, vast Highland Park plant and company policy was to scrap machines as fast as they could be replaced by improved types.

However, the greater perfection of machine tools does not indicate the qualitative shift represented by Fordism. As Bright asks: 'How do collections of machines evolve into the production line and the line into an integrated, highly automatic sequence? What is the essential principle?' (1958: 15). The answer is that Ford perfected the flow-line principle of assembly work. This meant that instead of workers moving between tasks, the flow of parts is achieved as much as possible by machines (conveyors and transporters) such that assembly workers are tied to their work position and have no need to move about the workshop. A crucial consequence of this is that the pace of work is controlled mechanically and not by the workers or supervisors. Thus instead of the increasing automaticity of *individual* machines, there is a shift towards the mechanisation of a larger span of the manufacturing cycle including transfer processes.

Associated with the new fixed-speed moving assembly lines were an accelerated division of labour and short task-cycle times. Ford pushed job fragmentation to an extreme. For example in 1922, Henry Ford records a survey of jobs in his plants:

> The lightest jobs were again classified to discover how many of them required the use of full faculties, and we found that 670 could be filled by legless men, 2637 by one-legged men, two by armless men, 715 by one-armed men, and ten by blind men. Therefore, out of 7882 kinds of job . . . 4034 did not require full physical capacity.

> (Ford 1922: 108)

Having developed a new industrial technology based on the flow-line principle and extreme job fragmentation, Ford found that control of the production process was not equal to the control of the workforce. Worker rejection of the new work processes were expressed in high rates of turnover, absenteeism and insufficient effort. For example, the head of Ford's employment department in 1913 cited a figure of $38 to train up a new worker; a small amount, but with an annual turnover of more than 50,000 workers (i.e. 400%) the total cost was two million dollars (Russell 1978: 40; also Meyer 1981).

The control techniques developed by Ford in response to these worker problems serve to mark off Fordism from Taylorism. One of Taylor's close associates asserted that he did not 'care a hoot what became of the workman after he left the factory at night, so long as he was able to show up the next morning in a fit condition for a hard day's toil' (Copley 1915: 42). But Ford went outside the factory gates in an attempt to re-mould working-class culture in accordance with industrial discipline and efficiency. The broad outlines of the Five Dollar Day and the Americanisation programme are well-known and are analysed in detail in Meyer (1981). But in this paper I wish to focus more on job design principles.

The effects of the introduction of the assembly line at Fords on productivity and profits is indicated by the fact that it reduced the labour content of chassis assembly from 12½ hours to 2 hours 40 minutes (Flink 1975: 77). In relation to job cycle times, the effects were significant but not so dramatic. Abernathy (1978: 137–9) estimates that in 1908–9, when assembly depended on non-specialised teams, the average task duration was around 514 minutes. By 1913, the chassis were stationary and specialised teams, such as axle teams etc., moved from chassis to chassis completing their allotted tasks. This high degree of specialisation resulted in the most dramatic drop in job cycle time – down to 2.3 minutes. The new moving assembly line in 1914 further cut task duration to around 1.19 minutes, and task duration and the division of labour have remained at this relatively stable level since the assembly line was first introduced. However, the assembly line tended to capture and freeze the *existing* levels of job specialisation and fragmentation, rather than causing a complete re-organisation. It was the initial processes of job specialisation which created the opening, the potential, for the later mechanisation of transfer processes.

The obvious profit-generating advantages of job specialisation, fragmentation and flow-line production resulted in Ford's competitors imitating his success and installing moving assembly lines themselves. The factors which fuelled the diffusion of Taylorism and Fordism are considered in the next section.

(3) Diffusion of Taylorism and Fordism

At least for the mass production industries, Taylorism and Fordism became the predominant ideals for organising work in the USA, Britain and many other economies. Two things helped the spread of the ideas and techniques. Firstly, the interwar years were characterised by the internationalisation of technology. In the newer industries, such as electrical engineering, chemicals and vehicles, this was particularly true. For example, one of the largest electrical engineering companies in the USA was Westinghouse Electric. This corporation became a strong advocate of Taylorism, time study and systematic job analysis. In 1924 Westinghouse concluded a technical exchange agreement with Siemens, one of the two largest German electrical firms, leading to the influence of Westinghouse management methods in German factories. Similarly, Mitsubishi Electric of Japan had a similar agreement with Westinghouse in the 1920s. The managing director of Mitsubishi went to the USA to study Westinghouse techniques and became a strong advocate of Taylorite time and motion studies (Levine and Kawada 1980: 264).

Taylorism and Fordist techniques had of course to be adapted to the labour markets, economic conditions and culture of the receiving society. But one mechanism allowed direct transplants. The diffusion of American management and job design techniques was assisted by the mechanism of the multinational corporation. Ford established subsidiaries in Britain, Germany and other countries, as did Ford's main competitor – General Motors. Ford first moved to Britain as early as 1911 when the company bought an old car plant in Manchester and in 1930/31 built the Dagenham factory which was the first major Ford plant outside of the USA. Ford's example was followed by General Motors who took over Vauxhall in 1925. When the General Motors take-over occurred the corporation radically reorganised the existing factory. All machines on the shopfloor were organised on the flow-line principle and assembly was done on moving tracks. Each department and assembly area was coordinated to produce one component every twenty minutes (Lewchuk 1983: 96).

The multinational corporation allowed not only the transfer of technique and machinery but of people, who brought with them an extensive knowledge of details and general orientations to mass production. For example, General Motors brought over a small pool of American engineers who could train British engineers in the new techniques.

There were still, of course, differences between companies. Citroen of France started an assembly line for its first postwar model as early as 1919 and, lacking qualified engineers, the company later hired American engineers and brought them to Europe. The Austin car company in Britain introduced moving assembly lines between 1922 and 1925 at the Longbridge plant, whilst Morris Motors, perhaps the leading British car firm in the interwar years, delayed the re-organisation of manufacturing methods until 1934 (Fridenson 1978).

Japan imported nearly all its cars until the late 1920s, but the direct influence of the American multinationals was felt there as well. Ford established a factory in Yokohama in 1925, followed by General Motors who set up a plant in Osaka in 1926. The 1931 Automobile

Manufacturing Enterprise Law established tariff barriers around the fledgling Japanese industry and set limits on production by Ford and General Motors. By 1939 both companies were forced to close their factories and the workers and technicians formed the core of Toyota (Levine and Kawada 1980).

The Japanese case underlines another point about the diffusion of Fordism: in Japan in the 1930s motor vehicles were seen largely as *military* vehicles. Mass production methods were seen as a precondition of military success. In other words, one factor fuelling the takeup of Taylorism and Fordism was the awareness of a link between mass production and a war economy: as Sabel points out, 'a state that did not foster mass-production industry invited defeat on the battlefield as well as in the market' (1982: 44).

Given this combination of forces underlying the processes of diffusion, by the mid-1930s Taylorite techniques had spread across Europe whilst Fordism and the moving assembly line had penetrated the largest car firms and spread to other industries such as electrical engineering.

(4) The Limits of Taylorism and Fordism
Even within the principles and practice of Taylorism and Fordism there are limits to job fragmentation and the transfer of skills to specialised machinery. First, there are the economic limits which I have already discussed – the decomposition of tasks depends on the velocity of throughput. Second, there are technical limits. For example, in an engineering factory assume that a given piece of work involves several operations such as planing, milling, turning, drilling and so on. These various operations can be economically separated as the volume of throughput increases, each task being assigned to one man, or a group of men, who do nothing else. Thus, a worker may be assigned to drill a specific hole in each piece of metal. If the volume of work increases further, then a drilling fixture or jig may be used and the work of drilling may be further subdivided by employing one man to put the parts to be drilled into the fixture and take them out again after the operation, and the other man doing the drilling and nothing else. This is an example of the divorce of direct and indirect labour discussed above. But without the further development of machining technology (which has not occurred until recently) it is difficult to subdivide either of these functions further no matter how big the market and the volume of output. In other words, the division of labour can be carried down to certain fundamental operations beyond which it must wait upon a transformation of the technology (see, Coombs, chapter 7 in this volume).

This combination of technical constraints and limits set by the nature of the market has clearly resulted in a restricted diffusion of mass production. Excluding continuous process industries, in 1969 the major mass production industries in the USA were limited to six – automobiles, household appliances and houseware, radio and TV, photographic equipment, toys and sporting goods and watches and clocks. This meant that only 25% (by value) of US industrial production of durable goods was mass production, whilst the remaining 75% was still produced by means of batches (Lund 1978). The percentages for Britain are similar.

If the above proportions are correct, then they have surprising implications for work experience. In 1982 of the 20.4 million labour force in Britain, only 5.6 million were in manufacturing industry. Therefore only about one-quarter are likely to be in a factory concerned with mass production (i.e. 1.4 million) and the number of direct workers on the line may only be half that number, say 0.7 million (see Gallagher 1980).[1] Of course, Taylorite methods may still be applied in non-mass production factories, but the popular image of assembly-line technology as typical of factory work is a misleading image.

Within the enterprise, Taylorism and Fordism carry coordination and control costs. As the division of labour is extended, coordination measures must accompany such extension; for example production planning, supervision and monitoring and inspection procedures. This is not just a practical, managerial question but also a sociological question related to the development of industry. Early industrialisation in most economies, including Britain, depended on the use of existing forms of group or cultural solidarity and subordination, such as the family and kin ties. Later patterns of work organisation, in eliminating such forms, left employers with stark and critical problems of harnessing labour's creative and productive powers. However, formal structures of control cost money and tend to offset gains from an extended division of labour. For example, many employers found that the clerical costs of installing and running Taylorite-like schemes were very high (Littler 1982).

Moreover, limits to the direct control methods of Taylor and Ford are set by increasing cooperation costs. If the linkages of workers to the work organisation are largely instrumental and entail very little commitment, then the purchase price of day-to-day worker compliance is inexorably increased during the upturn in the economic cycle when labour markets are tight. More broadly, Taylorite forms of work organisation are acceptable to employers only within certain types of product market. As I suggested in the introduction, if price ceases to be the predominant factor in exchange and non-price factors, such as

reliability, quality and design, assume a larger significance, then this
places a heavier emphasis on worker cooperation and worker commitment. In Taylorite/Fordist organisations workers are neither trained to
show, nor rewarded for, their initiative. For example, here is an
account by one American worker:

> I am – or was – an American auto worker. I built GM cars for 16 years. Then,
> in March (1980), I was laid off indefinitely. . . . It was not the worker who
> determines the quality of a car, but the executives in Detroit and the plant
> supervisors. The worker who performs a certain task 320 times a day, 5 days a
> week, knows more about the specifics of this particular job than anyone else.
> Yet, in 16 years, I have never been consulted on how to improve a job
> qualitatively or quantitatively. There are suggestion programs but their main
> concern is always 'how to save the company's money'. The auto worker can
> only build as good a car as he is instructed or permitted to build. We on the
> line take our cue from those in the head office. If they don't really care about
> quality, they can't expect us to either (Douglas 1980: A.5).

In this environment workers regard any demand for initiative or commitment as simply a bargaining counter in the struggles with supervisors and employers. The effects of this are clearly demonstrated in a
careful study comparing assembly-line production of air conditioners
in the USA and Japan. The average production defects of the American
conditioners were 63.5 defects per 100 units compared to 0.95 in the
Japanese machines. The failure rate of products from the highest
quality Japanese producers were between 500 and 1000 less than those
of the lowest quality producers in the United States.

One important factor in these dramatic differences in manufacturing
efficiency lay in the fact that most of the Japanese air-conditioner
companies' new assembly-line workers were trained *in all jobs on the
line* for about six months. In contrast, the American workers received
only several hours or days of instruction and usually just for a single
task – a classic Taylorite pattern associated with high turnover rates
(Garvin 1983).

(5) Job Redesign in the 1970s and the 1980s
The influence of Taylorism and Fordism in job and technology design
has often been implicit. Indeed, the most striking thing about most
British factories is that job design is *nobody's* responsibility. Certainly
the typical line manager does not spend his day thinking about job
design. So how do jobs get 'designed'? The common managerial view is
outlined by L.E. Davis:

> . . . there is still a strong commitment to the proposition that meeting the
> requirements of the technology (process, equipment) will yield superior job
> performance, measured by organisationally relevant criteria, and a deep-

seated conviction that the same performance will not be achieved if technological requirements are not given exclusive consideration.

(Davis and Taylor 1972: 300–1).

In other words, a widespread technocratic ideology means that jobs and tasks and peoples' working lives are treated as the residual factor of the relationship between machines and products.[5]

During the late 1960s and early 1970s, the apparent problems of technocracy and Taylorite strategies (organisational rigidity and inflexibility, the expansion of organisational complexity to handle fragmented work, the underutilisation of worker initiative, and numerous indicators of worker dissatisfaction) led to the emergence of a job redesign movement, largely based on industrial pyschology, and a more broadly based Quality of Working Life (QWL) movement. The latter is conveniently symbolised by the *Work in America* report (1973) and *On the Quality of Working Life* report (Wilson 1973) in Britain. Such reports, and other writers, put forward principles of 'good' job design which are the precise opposite of Taylorian principles. Five principles have typically been put forward:

(a) Principle of closure – the scope of the job should include all the tasks necessary to complete a product or process. Theoretically, the predicted result is that work acquires an intrinsic meaning and people can feel a sense of achievement.

(b) Incorporation of control and monitoring tasks. Jobs should be designed so that an army of inspectors is not required. The individual worker, or the work team, assumes responsibility for quality and reliability.

(c) Task variety, i.e. an increase in the range of tasks. This implies a principle of comprehensiveness, which means that workers should understand the general principles of a range of tasks so that job rotation is possible.

(d) Self-regulation of the speed of work and some choice over work methods and work sequence.

(e) A job structure that permits some social interaction and perhaps cooperation among workers.[6]

Through the 1970s these principles were the gospel of a few avant-garde consultants, and though there were isolated examples of new work systems, job design generally remained tied to traditional Taylorian principles. Despite this, through the latter half of the 1970s and the early 1980s the pressure of, mainly Japanese, competition has forced many Western corporations to re-examine their philosophy of job design and control from a solid, 'down to earth' perspective – that of profits. However, the recent trends in job design cannot be all grouped together. As several authors have pointed out (Kelly 1982; Savall 1981), there have, in general, been three types – reorganisation of Fordist assembly lines, group technology and job enrichment. In this paper I will say something about the first two forms of job redesign.[7]

The reorganisation of assembly lines has been concentrated in consumer industries, especially electrical appliances. Such changes have been associated with increased product variations in more competitive markets. Generally, depending on the type of product and the price structure, a large corporation needs at least two years to get back its investment of setting up a new mass production line. But, partly because of Japanese competition, the pace of change has quickened such that a comfortable cruise along a two-year profit path has turned into a bumpy ride. It needs to be remembered that Fordist techniques are product-specific involving specialised machinery and narrow skills which are not readily transferable. The result has been that mass production facilities have become excessively inflexible and a cost burden, as it becomes harder to consolidate the mass production of a standard product. Thus the product market pressure has been to create more flexible work forms able to accommodate more rapid product changes without creating an entirely new line (Sabel 1982: 199; Kelly 1982: 88). Most of the redesign changes in assembly lines have still resulted in production processes with one-man work stations; often more cooperation between workers is possible, but is not usually essential to the flow of production. However, some experiments in redesigning assembly lines have explicitly recognised the value of cooperative team work and these experiments can all be loosely categorised under the heading of 'group technology'.

Group technology represents a realisation by some employers of the value of work groups as a basis for work organisation. Such groups have been tried in mass production industries such as cars in Sweden and Germany. For example Volkswagen started experimenting with such groups at its new Salzgitter engine plant in 1975. Normally car engines are built on a conventional fixed speed assembly line with task cycles of about one or two minutes. Instead, Volkswagen began a small-scale experiment with four groups of seven workers (two teams on each shift). Within the groups four men worked on assembly, two did testing and one man was in charge of materials. The entire group was decoupled from the machine-paced line but had to meet a quota of seven engines per team per day. The workers received special training so that they could do all of the team jobs and were free to rotate job assignments as they wished. Each group had a team leader (*Gruppensprecher*) who was responsible for liaison with management, and foremen were eliminated (Jenkins 1978).

The results of the Volkswagen experiment highlighted two over-lapping problems of such work groups, which have been repeated in different situations and economies. First, semi-autonomous work-groups run up against the existing power-balance between labour and capital. Employers see such job redesign as an opportunity to undercut the union in the workplace, whilst the unions tend to be opposed to informally elected workgroup leaders as potential usurpers of union influence. This conflict of interests occurred at the Salzgitter plant with the eventual outcome that the team leaders were converted into shop stewards and foremen were brought back to oversee the groups as Volkswagen wanted to prevent the erosion of management power.

Apart from the issue of autonomous groups as a threat to the existing structures of shopfloor power, there was the question of how the specially trained team workers fitted into the skill and wage hierarchy. The enlarged jobs caused a union/management dispute over wage levels. The unions demanded that the workers should be paid at a skilled rate which Volkswagen resisted. In effect, this recombination of tasks across Taylorian boundaries disrupted the Babbage principles of labour cheapening, which involves stripping a skilled job to an essential core and paying less for all ancillary and servicing tasks performed by unskilled workers. Volkswagen concluded that they did not want masses of re-skilled workers on the basis that they had no jobs for them – they did not fit into the normal structure.

In 1978 the experiment was ended. Volkswagen management con-sidered the system too costly and that it was not possible to fill the factory with the 'dreams of another world' (Jenkins 1978: 20). In general, mass production industries have proved to be a hostile milieu for group technology. In batch production the story has been more complex.

It is still the case that the vast majority (up to 80%) of engineering components are produced in batches of less than 1000. This is sig-nificant because traditional batch production costs from ten to thirty times more than mass production of an item. This is because of the need continually to reset the machines and the considerable delays in the movement of components between machines. Most items spend long periods collecting dust on the factory floor queuing for the next process.

In looking at batch production in the early 1970s, Turner noted that it is complex, because succeeding batches require different machining operations in different sequences. This entails a large amount of variety and great uncertainties. Associated with this complex pattern is a lack of complete knowledge of the production system by management such that instead of a production planning programme there is a monitoring of work-in-progress by an army of progress-chasers and harassed foremen (Turner 1970).

In the early 1960s one solution to these problems was the evolution of so-called 'group technology'. This originally was a technical term referring to a new lay-out of production based on grouping together all the machines necessary to complete a particular type of component. This in turn was based on classification of all components, standard-isation as far as possible and grouping the components into 'families'. It improved machine utilisation and it speeded up the throughput of work by simplifying the flow of work.

But in creating a cellular work structure, engineering employers also created new work groups. At first this received no explicit attention, but as skilled machinists' dissatisfaction with their loss of discretion over the sequence of work increased (the machinists could no longer choose the easiest job first, or the safest job when they were tired, or the most lucrative job in terms of bonus) and as employers recognised the potential of job flexibility, the notion of semi-autonomous work groups was given increasing emphasis. This potential was based on machine 'stretch-out', i.e. setting up more machines than workers, and re-training so that workers could move from lathe to drilling machine to grinder. But beyond this stretch-out some companies have given the new work groups some discretion over work methods and job assign-ments secure in the knowledge that worker discretion is severely restricted by the control built into the system (Green 1978: 18).

Thus, group technology in batch producing industries has created a tendency for the development of flexible work groups based on generalised, skilled machinists with a lack of rigid job boundaries. There is a return, reminiscent of the traditional internal contract, of work allocation to the group, not the individual (Littler 1982). In so far as charge-hands and foremen are eliminated, this reduces control and coordination costs to the employer. Such groups also increase worker adaptability and enable the team to cope with the absences of any of its members. But whatever the managerial advantages of group tech-nology, after a limited spread to about 10% of batch engineering firms in the early and mid-1970s, the process of diffusion came to a halt. This was because the information burden of setting up a reliable group technology production system was too great – there were too many variables and too much unpredictability. Now, with the spread of flexible machining centres and cheaper shopfloor mini-computers, the pattern of change will probably accelerate.

In general, the introduction of flexible work groups has occurred in very different industrial sectors and in firms varying in size and technology. The extension of small-scale experiments has often been opposed by both unions and management and the diffusion of such groups is still very limited (Savall 1981: 69–71 and 98–101).

In recent years one variant of autonomous shopfloor groups has become popular, namely Quality Control (QC) circles. Essentially these are small groups of workers (about 5–20) usually led by a foreman or senior worker who meet regularly to study and solve all types of production problems. In addition, such groups are intended to stimulate motivation and involvement on the shopfloor. Unlike earlier human relations ideas, QC circles involve systematic training of shopfloor workers and access to technical assistance to solve problems.

The original idea of QC circles was American: the basis being the notion of improved worker motivation through employee participation in the decision-making process. The process was transplanted to Japan in the 1950s, where it was adopted and reworked by several management theorists, particularly Kaoru Ishikawa. The ideas gained popularity in Japan in the 1960s and early 1970s and were re-cycled to the West in the later 1970s surrounded by the aura of Japanese productivity and economic success. By 1982, at least 750 organisations in the USA had made use of QC circles and well over 100 firms in Britain had experimented with them, including Rolls Royce and Wedgewood (Bradley and Hill 1983: 292). Such ideas have never been totally absent from British shopfloors. The idea of 'briefing groups' designed to bring workers, supervisors and senior managers together to discuss 'common problems' is perhaps more familiar in the British context, but is clearly allied to the QC concept (Hull 1978: 35).

Given that QC circles are *not* the same thing as work groups, what effects have they had, or are likely to have, on job design? The main effect is to bridge the mental/manual divide inherited from Taylorism. QC circles tend to break with the traditional practices and assumptions implicit in most Western managerial control systems. Firstly, there is the assumption of high commitment to the work organisation such that workers will devote time and effort, even outside of work hours, to the analysis of work-related problems. Associated with this, QC circles involve workers (at least in theory) in a genuine study process, requiring company resources and training. Moreover, study groups are, after management vetting, provided with the means to institute new work practices in order to overcome the problems of productivity and quality.

All of this contrasts sharply with the conventional Taylorite assumption that workers know how to increase productivity or ensure quality but are holding back for no justifiable reason. It is assumed that worker indifference or even sabotage are the normal problems that management has to face and overcome. Indeed Taylor's starting-point was the pervasiveness of what he called 'soldiering'; i.e. a deliberate collective slow-down (Taylor 1903: 30). Similarly, conventional factory suggestions schemes maintain the mental/manual divide by assuming that any useful suggestions will be analysed and implemented by management personnel.

One interesting example of the introduction of QC circles in the West is that of Fords. The Ford Corporation, frightened of Japanese competition, decided in 1980 to implement the system in all its twenty-five manufacturing and assembly plants in West Europe involving all 140,000 shopfloor workers. The overall programme in 1980/81 was called 'After Japan'. Ford's stated objectives were to improve the quality of its products, reduce scrap and encourage worker involvement. The unstated objectives were (probably) to increase labour productivity, change manning levels and traditional work practices (*Financial Times*, 9 May 1980; *Guardian*, 11 June 1980).

Ford followed the Japanese pattern of QC circles with some interesting differences. Each of its QC groups consisted of 8–15 people including a supervisor plus a representative from the quality control department. The reason for the inclusion of the latter is that the Taylorian inheritance has meant that production problems and quality control are the responsibility of staff departments divorced from the shopfloor, whereas in Japan the production worker and his foreman is much more responsible for checking the quality of his own work before it moves on down the line.

Another difference from the Japanese situation, is that in Japan the labour force is all-Japanese, young and relatively well-educated. At Fords the circles often consist of a mixture of West Indians, Asians, Southern Europeans as well as English workers. The first thing that the circles demonstrated as forums of communication was that the traditional managerial methods of communication – posters and job instructions – often meant different things to different ethnic groups!

The attempted rushed adoption of Japanese QC circles by Fords led to the opposition of the main union – the Transport and General Workers Union. Rank and file union leaders complained that all changes in working practices should be discussed and mutually agreed with the union, and that the proposals cut across existing union structures (*Financial Times*, 9 March and 25 April 1981). The outcome is that so far QC circles have not been introduced in British Ford plants, but have spread across the rest of the European plants. Other British firms, such as Wedgewood, have had more success in introducing QC circles but the overall impact of this form of 'Japanisation' has yet to be determined.[8]

Conclusions

In this chapter I have attempted to outline the significance of Taylorism on job design and argue that its influence needs to be analysed and demonstrated. We have seen that its influence, though considerable, did not follow a simple pattern in British industrial history. Taylorism was essentially based on job fragmentation, though it was often modified in its implementation and, as I have argued, a mixture of labour strategies was possible (Littler 1982).

Fordism was a distinct labour management strategy in that it was systemic requiring the re-organisation of the entire factory and involved non-Taylorite control techniques. But it also took over the basic job design dynamics of Taylorism. The internationalisation of technology and the mechanism of the multinational corporation assisted the spread of both Taylorism and Fordism, especially in the mass production industries.

Taylorism and Fordism as forms of work organisation are constrained by certain economic and technical limits and carry co-ordination and control costs. In particular Taylorism and Fordism are set within a certain pattern of product markets and inter-capitalist competition. In the late 1960s and early 1970s it began to look as though the accumulation of labour problems plus the shift in product markets, necessitating greater flexibility and with an emphasis on quality and reliability, were creating a crisis for Fordism. Bosquet's 'The Prison Factory' (1972) represented the vivid picturing of this crisis.

However in retrospect Bosquet's work represents the high peak of a naive, radical optimism about job redesign prior to the New Depression of the later 1970s and early 1980s. Manufacturing industries responded by sucking in more and more immigrants and marginal labour and by seeking low wage zones in the Pacific Basin etc. Re-organised assembly lines and group technology remained limited experiments. Now, the accumulated millions of the unemployed in the West frighten workers, work groups and trade unions into the acceptance of changes in work practices.

Nevertheless, labour market pressures will not revolve the economic wheel back to the 1930s and the labour intensifications of Bedaux. Ford of Europe along with many other industrial corporations still needs to elicit 'the 100% effort' and worker initiative if it is to eliminate layers of the managerial bureaucracy and achieve both flexibility and high quality – all of which is required to face up to Japanese competition and the new market conditions. Ford's 'After Japan' programme is a convenient symbol of the continued pressures for change.

Notes

1. This paper has benefited from work jointly done with Graeme Salaman, whom I would like to thank for help and support.
2. This is particularly true of the French literature. It was very noticeable at the recent 'Colloque International Sur Le Taylorisme' held in Paris, 2–4 May 1983. See for example B. Coriat, 'Taylorisme et nouvelles technologies', mimeo.
3. For an explication of Babbage's Principle, see Littler, 1982, p. 18.
4. These figures are only guesstimates – there are no precise figures. One indication is provided by Wild (1974). In a survey of 84 companies using mass production, he found that only 46% of manual workers were actually engaged on mass-production work.
5. This, of course, raises the question of the relationship between machines and human skills. Because of shortage of space it is not possible to deal with this question here. The work of Rosenbrock is illuminating in this area; e.g. see Rosenbrock, 1981.
6. Apart from the *Work in America* report and the *On the Quality of Working Life* report (written by N.A.B. Wilson), see Davis, 1957 and 1966; Walton, 1974; and Hackman and Oldham, 1975.
7. For a discussion of job enrichment see Kelly, 1982, chapter 7.
8. See *Employment Gazette*, 91, 3, May 1983 on QC Circles, pp. 102–4. In September 1982 a British 'National Society of Quality Circles' was set up to bring together organisations that operate QC circles. This parallels the American organisation – the 'International Association of Quality Circles' which now has 5000 corporate members. For an interesting study of Japanese firms operating in Britain and their management methods, see White and Trevor (1983).

References

Abernathy, W.J. (1978), *The Productivity Dilemma*, Basic Books.
Bedaux Archives (1926–39), Microfilms 1–27.
Bosquet, M. (1972), 'The prison factory', *New Left Review*, **73**, 23–34.
Bradley, K. and Hill, S. (1983), 'After Japan: the quality circle transplant and productive efficiency', *British Journal of Industrial Relations*, **XXI**, 3, November. 291–311.
Bright, J.R. (1958), 'Automation and Management', Harvard University, mimeo.
Copley, F.B. (1915), 'Frederick W. Taylor: revolutionist', *The Outlook*, **111**, September.
Davis, L.E. (1957), 'Toward a theory of job design', reprinted in Davis and Taylor (1972), 215–217.
Davis, L.E. (1966), 'The design of jobs', reprinted in Davis and Taylor (1972), 299–327.
Davis, L.E. and Taylor, J.C. (eds.) (1972), *Design of Jobs*, Penguin.
Douglas, M. (1980), 'Auto workers can only do as well as Head Office permits', *Albuquerque Journal*, 24 July.
Flink, J.J. (1975), *The Car Culture*, MIT Press.
Ford, H. (1922), *My Life and Work*, Doubleday Page.
Fridenson, P. (1978), 'The coming of the assembly line to Europe', in Krohn, Layton and Weingart (eds.) *The Dynamics of Science and Technology*, D. Reidel.
Gallagher, C.C. (1980), 'The history of batch production and functional factory layout', *CME*, April, 73–76.
Garvin, D. (1983), 'Quality on the line', *Harvard Business Review*, September/October.
Gospel, H. and Littler, C.R. (1983), *Managerial Strategies and Industrial Relations*, Heinemann.
Green, K. (1978), 'Group technology in small batch engineering'. Paper presented at Nuffield Deskilling Conference, mimeo.
Hackman, J.R. and Oldham, G.R. (1975), 'Development of the job diagnostic survey', *Journal of Applied Psychology*, **60**, 2, 159–170.
Hull, D. (1978), *The Shop Steward's Guide to Work Organization*, Spokesman.
Jenkins, D. (1978), 'The West German humanization of work programme: a preliminary assessment', WRU Occasional Paper no. 8.

Kamata, Satoshi (1982), *Japan in the Passing Lane*, Pantheon.

Kelly, J.E. (1982), *Scientific Management, Job Redesign and Work Performance*, Academic Press.

Levine, S.B. and Kawada, H. (1980), *Human Resources in Japanese Industrial Development*, Princeton University Press.

Lewchuk, W. (1983), 'Fordism and British motor car employers, 1896–1932', in Gospel and Littler (1983), 82–110.

Linhart, R. (1981), *The Assembly Line*, John Calder.

Littler, C.R. (1978), 'Understanding Taylorism', *British Journal of Sociology*, 29, 185–202.

Littler, C.R. (1982), *The Development of the Labour Process in Capitalist Societies*, Heinemann.

Lund, R.T. (1978), 'Numerically controlled machine goods and group technology: a study of US experience', MIT, mimeo.

Meyer, S. (1981), *The Five-Dollar Day: Labor Management and Social Control in the Ford Motor Co., 1908–21*, State University of New York Press.

Porter, H.F. (1917), 'Four big lessons from Ford's factory', *System*, **31**, June.

Rose, M. (1975), *Industrial Behaviour: Theoretical Developments since Taylor*, Allen Lane.

Rosenbrock, H.H. (1981), 'Engineers and the work that people do', *IEEE Control Systems Magazine*, **1**, 3, September.

Russell, J. (1978), 'The coming of the line: the Ford Highland Park plant, 1910–14', *Radical America*, **12**, 29–45.

Sabel, C.F. (1982), *Work and Politics*, Cambridge University Press.

Savall, H. (1981), *Work and People*, Clarendon Press.

Taylor, F.W. (1903), 'Shop management', reprinted in Taylor (1964).

Taylor, F.W. (1964), *Scientific Management*, Harper & Row.

Turner, B. (1970), 'The organization of production – scheduling in complex batch production situations', in G. Heald (ed.), *Approaches to the Study of Organizational Behaviour*, Tavistock, 87–99.

Walton, R.E. (1974), 'Innovative restructuring of work', *The Worker and the Job: Coping with Change*, (ed.) by J. Rosow, Prentice Hall.

White, M. and Trevor, M. (1983), *Under Japanese Management*, Heinemann.

Wild, R. (1974), 'Mass production in engineering', *International Journal of Production Research*, **12**, 5, 533–545.

Wilson, N.A.B. (1973), 'On the Quality of Working Life', Manpower Papers no. 7, HMSO.

Work in America (1973), Report of a Special Task Force to the Secretary of Health, Education and Welfare, MIT Press.

3 Management's Redesign of Work: Labour Process, Labour Markets and Product Markets

John Kelly

Introduction

Since the publication of Braverman's *Labour and Monopoly Capital* in 1974, theoretical and empirical studies of the labour process have centred almost exclusively on the dynamics, scope, pace and significance of deskilling. Much of this work has progressively dismantled the theoretical structure built up by Braverman as it has come to grips with the ambiguities and problems lurking throughout his text. One of these problems was the apparent existence of a countervailing trend to deskilling, variously described as job enrichment, autonomous work groups, or simply job redesign. If deskilling was an integral and inexorable feature of the capitalist mode of production why were some firms able to reverse the detailed division of labour and recombine fragmented jobs into larger units? Was such redesign of work merely a 'cosmetic exercise' (whatever that might mean) as Braverman suggested? Was it perhaps just a temporary interlude in the onward march of deskilling, distinctive only because of its glaring and short-lived contrast with the normal fate of most jobs? Or did it represent a superficial and pragmatic accommodation by employers to a passing crisis of legitimacy?

Judged by its scale, by the numbers of jobs' 'enriched' in the advanced capitalist countries in the post-war period, job redesign is not a particularly significant movement, as compared with say the spread of assembly-lines and work study in the 1920s and 1930s. Theoretically, job redesign is far more significant because it constitutes a critical, test case for the exploration of a number of theories of the division of labour, both Marxist and non-Marxist. It can in particular be used to construct the rudiments of a theory of managerial practices in the division of labour which transcends the 'productionism' of Braverman, and that challenges his bleak, undifferentiated picture of capitalist control of the labour process.

This chapter sets out to ask three questions: first, given the pervasiveness of the fragmentation of work, particularly in manufacturing, and the conventional wisdom that regards such work organisation as the only path to high productivity, control and profitability, why were some firms in the post-war period able to reverse the detailed division of labour and achieve the same results? Second, what are the implications of such redesign of jobs for control within the labour process, i.e. what is the *political* significance of job redesign? And third, how successfully do the various analyses of job redesign help us understand what is happening to work organisation in the current recession? This third question is premised on the assumption that any theory which is *unable* to account for current managerial practices is *ipso facto* inadequate.

Labour Process Theory

There is a fairly wide measure of agreement on at least some of the central weaknesses in Braverman's analysis of the labour process (Kelly and Wood 1983; Littler 1982; Wood 1982). His exclusion of class struggle, or worker resistance, justified on methodological grounds, has been shown to be the source of serious theoretical and empirical weaknesses: an over-deterministic and mechanistic conception of capitalism as a law-governed politico-economic machine, and an underestimation of the actual role of class struggle in shaping the organisation, control and location of the labour process and of capital accumulation. Equally Braverman's conception of Taylorism as the 'explicit verbalisation of the capitalist mode of production' raises serious epistemological problems: how do we discover which of several management practices articulate the interests of capital? What is a 'verbalisation' of a mode of production? Empirically, it has been shown that only on the most vague and diffuse definition of Taylorism is it possible to argue for the unsurpassed and unchallenged dominance of Taylorism in the labour process. Some of the French analysts of Taylorism, e.g. Montmollin (1974), favour such broad definitions. On any more refined or discriminating definition Taylorism does not 'dominate the world of production' in the way that Braverman suggests, but coexists with a variety of non-Taylorist practices. These two points are of course linked: it is the existence of class struggle and worker resistance which provides the precondition and part of the explanation for variations in management practice.

There are two further aspects of Braverman's analysis which have been widely accepted (or at least not very explicitly challenged) but which seem both theoretically and empirically to be equally good candidates for rejection. Braverman's analysis of *changes* in the labour process, in particular his analysis of the rise of Taylorism and of the consequent process of deskilling, is located almost entirely within the labour–capital relationship, conceived in purely antagonistic, not contradictory, terms. Second, he argues it is the overriding necessity to secure *control* over the labour process, to inaugurate the *real* subordination of labour in Marx's terms, which lies at the root of the deskilling process, and which provides the key to understanding management behaviour.

As we shall see, several theorists of job redesign have built their analyses on these two assumptions, both of which can be challenged. To begin with, the capitalist mode of production is *not* characterised solely by the contradiction (or conflict) between labour and capital: it is also marked by the anarchic production of commodities for exchange by individual, competing capitals. Capitalism is defined not only by the status of labour as commodity and by the sale of labour power to capital, but by the buying and selling of all goods as commodities in markets. To account for observed changes in the division of labour we must therefore consider the possible role of competition between capitals, as well as conflict between labour and capital. To put it another way, it is not simply the *extraction* of surplus value in the labour process which is problematic for capital, but the *realisation* of that surplus through the sale of commodities in markets (see also Littler and Salaman 1982). Equally, we must consider the purchase of labour power in labour markets as potentially problematic for firms, particularly under conditions of full employment. In other words we need to consider the *full circuit* of industrial capital as the starting point for analyses of changes in the division of labour: purchase of labour power; extraction of surplus value within the labour process; realisation of surplus value within product markets. There is no sound theoretical reason for privileging one moment in this circuit – the labour–capital relation within the labour process – if our objective is to account for changes (or variations) in the division of labour. Marx (1970) emphasised 'the abode of production', rather than purchase and sale of commodities, because he was searching for the origin of surplus value. A different objective has no need to share the same emphasis.

But *how* should we conceptualise the relationship between changes in the division of labour and the full circuit of capital? One approach is to consider the different moments in the circuit as equivalent to different 'factors', each of which may exert some influence, more or less independently, over the organisation of work. In their important study *The Social Organization of Industrial Conflict* (1982) Edwards and Scullion adopt such an approach, repeatedly stressing that whilst product markets have some influence on forms of behaviour such as strikes, turnover and the like, the primary influence must be sought within structures of control in the labour process, i.e. within the labour–capital relation at the point of production. In an earlier study (Kelly 1982a) I argued that the origins of job redesign initiatives had to be sought in the development of product markets, and not by reference to 'labour problems' such as turnover, absenteeism, etc. These (and other) attempts to compare the weights of different moments in the circuit of capital now seem to me theoretically unsound. There is no easy or obvious way of comparing the influence of labour and product markets on managerial practices; and the different moments in the capital circuit are frequently so interdependent that it is questionable whether they can be split up analytically and then measured separately.

A more fruitful approach is to examine the circuit of capital dialectically, that is to seek out *contradictions* within the circuit as the motors of change. The full circuit consists of a series of processes, each of which is fitted together, or articulated to varying degrees: firms try to match the qualifications and attitudes of workers to their particular labour process; they endeavour to organise the labour process in such a way that it efficiently and effectively produces the desired commodities for the firm's chosen product markets. Stated in such general terms these points are obvious enough. But what happens when the moments in the circuit of capital no longer articulate as effectively as in the past? What happens when product or labour markets are rapidly transformed whilst a firm's labour process remains largely unchanged?

To answer these questions we need some way of conceptualising and assessing degrees of articulation of the different moments in the circuit of capital. The case studies in this chapter aim to provide only a tentative start on this job; their primary objective is to show that changes in the organisation of work in the post-war period cannot be accounted for by examining only the labour–capital relation in the labour process. It is the degree of *disarticulation* of the moments in the circuit of capital – purchase of labour, extraction of surplus value in the labour process, realisation of surplus value in product markets – which provides the key to understanding why some firms sought to redesign jobs in ways that apparently conflicted with Taylorist principles (cf. Laclau 1977).

Job Redesign in the Electrical Engineering Sector
One of the hallmarks of the electrical engineering sector in general, and the domestic electrical appliances branch in particular, is the widespread use of assembly lines. The classical analyses of job redesign (Kornhauser 1965; Guest 1957; Work in America 1973; Walker and Guest 1952) emerged, in part, from critiques of the negative psychological consequences of work on such lines: job dissatisfaction, boredom, stress, absenteeism, turnover, sabotage, strikes. These forms of

behaviour were all thought to be subversive of managerial efforts to raise labour productivity and to impose a variety of costs on employers – in selection, training, supervision. The assembly line, once hailed as the paragon of industrial efficiency, was now revealing its hitherto undisclosed, and substantial costs. Some employers responded by re-designing work in order to reduce its monotony, or control over workers, and reported a favourable effect on productivity and job satisfaction.

A strikingly similar analysis was developed by a number of Marxists (Friedman 1977; Gorz 1976). In these analyses, the spread of 'labour problems' or 'blue collar blues' was described instead as worker militancy, resistance or class struggle. And whilst it was true that these behaviours imposed economic costs on employers, the most significant cost was political. It was management's control over the labour process which was at stake (rather than worker motivation for job performance) and again, some firms responded by conceding elements of control to their militant and organised workforces.

The paradigmatic and sometimes dominant image in both of these accounts is the discontented, male, car-worker. Although assembly lines are used in many other sectors of manufacturing it is invariably the car industry which features in management publicity and academic promotions of job redesign. The implication then is that assembly line work is much the same whatever the product and whoever the workers: its dull and compelling logic is the source of labour problems, and therefore of one of management's responses, job redesign.

The electrical engineering sector is different in three crucial respects from this stereotypical industry. First, most of the assembly line workers (though not the ancillary and maintenance staff) are women; second, the levels of union density and union militancy are generally much lower than in the car industry. The two points are connected: women's attachment to their work is often different from that of men's, and the nature of women's trade unionism is different in turn (Coote and Campbell 1982; Mackie and Patullo 1977). Even though a growing number of women are sole 'breadwinners' or primary wage-earners in a two-income family, many continue to be centrally involved *both* in domestic work and in waged work. By contrast with men, the sphere of waged work is often not such a major source of identification and involvement. In short, women in electrical engineering in the post-war period do not fit the image of a militant, discontented workforce generating a problem of motivation, or control (though they may respond to monotonous work with absenteeism or turnover). The third point is that electrical engineering is considerably less capital intensive than vehicles. The products themselves – toasters, hairdryers, heaters and other electrical appliances – are much smaller, with fewer parts; the lines on which they are assembled often consist of no more than moving conveyor belts; and the tools used are considerably less complex than the welding and other equipment found on vehicle assembly lines. For these reasons electrical engineering flowlines are, in principle, easier to restructure.

Why then did a growing number of firms in this sector redesign jobs by reorganising their flowlines? Why did some reduce the length of their lines, from say 100 work stations to just 10 or 20? Why did some even abolish their assembly lines completely? The *numbers* of firms involved are not large: 64 case studies of flowline reorganisation were published between 1950 and 1980, and most appeared between the mid-1960s and mid-1970s (Kelly 1982a). Presumably many more cases were not publicly reported, but their exact number is unknown. In trying to explain this phenomenon we shall examine contradictions within the full circuit of capital in the electrical engineering sector.

Post-war evolution of electrical engineering
Electrical engineering had begun a considerable expansion in the 1930s in both Britain and the USA, but as a major growth area of these (and other) economies the sector 'took off' only after the Second World War as part of the post-war economic boom. The massive growth in demand for consumer durables of all kinds was matched by a corresponding growth in supply, delivered by a burgeoning number of firms (Corley 1966). The growth in the *number* of firms competing in these markets was facilitated by low barriers to entry, in turn a product of the low capital intensity of the industry. As both markets and competition grew, many firms rapidly expanded their range of products: firms that diversified in this way stood a better chance of holding up overall levels of sales because they became less vulnerable to setbacks in a particular product market. Yet this market-oriented strategy of product diversification generated a growing contradiction with the organisation of the labour process.

The long assembly line was developed by Henry Ford in the early part of this century and designed for the continuous production of just one product: the black, 'Model-T' Ford motor car. Provided the line was kept moving, it was an extremely efficient method of organising work. Indeed, at the time it produced a staggering increase in labour productivity in comparison with the old craft-dominated assembly of custom-built cars (Gartmann 1979). If we move back to the 1950s, and the assembly lines in electrical engineering we can see the emergence of two sets of problems. The first stemmed from the expansion of firms' product ranges. With a relatively small range of products it was still possible to achieve long, continuous production runs; that is, to utilise the assembly line for efficient, mass production. But as firms diversified their product ranges, they simultaneously moved away from the conditions required for efficient mass production. With a wider range of products, production runs became shorter as firms sought to respond as quickly as possible to incoming orders. Lines would be run for a few days (or perhaps weeks) on a single product and would then change over to a new product. The old parts would have to be cleared away and returned to stock, new parts obtained and fed through the line, and initial problems sorted out as workers gradually settled into their customary rhythm of work (on unpaced lines), or adjusted themselves to the line if they were mechanically paced. During the increasingly frequent periods of product change-over all workers on the line were idle; and the longer the line, the more workers, and the more time, went unused by the employer. With a stable and experienced workforce these periods of transition from one product to another could be organised quite smoothly. But many firms did not in fact have such a work force because of prevailing labour market conditions.

One of the consequences of the full employment of the post-war period was a growth in labour turnover, as workers found themselves in a seller's market. Turnover was facilitated, in electrical engineering, by the unskilled nature of the work: manual dexterity was basically all that was required for most assembly line work and training centred on the speedy application of existing skills rather than the acquisition of new ones. In many local labour markets there was far more than one employer recruiting unskilled workers for assembly-line jobs. The predominance of women in these assembly lines also meant that younger workers often stayed for relatively short periods before leaving to have children. And the expansion of such firms also contributed to relatively high rates of turnover, since quitting tends to be highly concentrated amongst new starters.

The mix of worker experience on the assembly lines increasingly exposed what came to be known as the 'balancing problem': how to divide up work on an assembly-line in such a way that each worker can function at the same pace, and the product be passed smoothly down the line. It is often difficult to divide product assembly into equal chunks for each worker on the line; in addition workers themselves vary in their abilities, experience and motivation compounding the balancing problem.

Schematically then we can say that firms' efforts to hold up (or expand) their market share through expansion of their product range generated threats to labour productivity, while efforts to hold up labour productivity with long production runs of a small product range generated a threat to their market share. The productivity problem, the securing of a high rate of labour output in the labour process was itself threatened by the operation of the labour market under full employment. In short, within the total circuit of capital in electrical engineering, there was a growing disarticulation between product market and labour process, and between labour market and labour process. It was these effects which provided the precondition for a variety of responses by firms of which job redesign was but one. Before examining these responses it must be pointed out that the operation of these effects was clearly not uniform. Electrical engineering, even electrical appliances, is not a homogeneous sector, and firms vary considerably in their product and labour markets. Consequently there is no reason to expect every firm to manifest some response to these 'problems'.

Broadly speaking there were three types of response found amongst electrical engineering firms. The first was to control the growth of product range by the deletion of old lines as new lines came on stream. Not only did this strategy reduce or control the frequency of assembly-line stoppages, it also helped control the growth of spare parts for older products. Coupled with this strategy was a parallel and supportive trend in product design, discernible from the late 1950s. If new products were to be successfully brought on stream every few years (or sometimes every year) consumers had to be prepared to discard old products in favour of new lines. One way of encouraging them to do so was by designing obsolescence into products so that they literally became useless or costly to run after a few years (Packard 1960). The same result was achieved through high productivity: by lowering purchase price (relative to maintenance and repair costs) consumers had less incentive to repair old products, and more incentive to ditch them in favour of new ones.

A second strategy was to redistribute the existing product range among plants in order to introduce some degree of product specialisation. Instead of each of, say, seven plants of a UK multi-plant firm, producing almost the whole of the firm's product range, each plant would be assigned only a portion of the range. The effect on production is the same as in the first strategy: with a smaller product range per plant, the frequency of assembly-line stoppages for product change-over is reduced. A further advantage of this strategy, which became evident in the late 1960s and 1970s, is that it facilitates rationalisation through plant closure. It is easier to assess the profitability of particular products with a high degree of plant specialisation, and easier to 'lop off' unprofitable plants/product-lines.

These two strategies both sought to 'manage' the disarticulation between product market and labour process, and to do so by controlling product range, either directly, by a reduction in its size, or indirectly, through plant specialisation in products. Job redesign emerged as a third strategy, in a first wave around 1960, and a second wave in the late 1960s-early 1970s as Coombs indicates in chapter 7 of this volume.

The reorganisation of flowlines
In a typical exercise an assembly line of, say, twenty work stations would be reduced to four lines of five stations each, or even in the extreme case, abolished altogether and replaced by individual work stations. At each new station workers would assemble a larger proportion of the product than previously (if not the whole product). Typically these changes have been introduced after careful use of work measurement. Workers have been trained for their new jobs and have normally received some increase in pay, either by regrading or through a negotiated increase in basic hourly rates. There has usually been some increase in fixed investment, either in the form of new, shorter assembly lines, or of individual work stations. In the latter cases, the payment system has invariably been changed from a group to an individual incentive, thus linking personal job performance and pay more closely than on the assembly line. In some cases, staffing levels have been reduced, though not in others.

What results have been achieved, and how can they be explained? Most firms who have reorganised flowlines have reported increases in labour productivity (physical output per person per hour) of between 10 and 20%, measured over periods of 3–18 months after the reorganisation. Longer-term follow-ups are conspicuously absent. Some of the data in these studies is questionable, or of unknown validity and reliability, but since the methodologically more rigorous studies have produced a similar set of results, it seems churlish to discount these findings.

There are two types of explanation which have been produced in order to account for the observed increases in productivity, the first of which is the classical theory of job redesign. According to this view, jobs which are redesigned to provide their incumbents with more variety, autonomy, responsibility and so on will generate higher levels of intrinsic job motivation, hence of job performance, and of job satisfaction.

There is *some* evidence to support this view, at least amongst white-collar workers, but in the blue-collar sector the picture is quite different (Kelly 1982a). Almost all cases of work redesign have involved important changes in the *context* of work, as well as its content. In two-thirds of all known cases workers have received pay rises to match the increased content of their work; in 60% of cases workers have been paid under financial incentive schemes; in just over 60% of cases, the redesign of some jobs has been associated with the elimination of others; and in the particular case of flowline reorganisation, workers shifted from flowlines to idividual work stations have been subject to more direct supervisory control. It is therefore possible to explain productivity increases engineered through the redesign of jobs in terms of classically Taylorist mechanisms: pay rises and incentives; elimination of 'surplus' labour; increased control over labour. We do not need to resort to theories of intrinsic motivation or alienation to explain why workers perform at higher levels on redesigned jobs (see Kelly 1982a).

These redesigned jobs may well have been (and sometimes were) experienced as more satisfying, at least in the short term, but job satisfaction should not be confused with job motivation; the determinants of the latter are more usefully seen as changes in pay systems, job structure and control.

How did these changes in work organisation help firms overcome contradictions within the circuit of capital? One answer, advanced by Friedman (1977) and others, is to argue that such changes constitute the adoption of a non-Taylorist strategy of work organisation, a strategy of 'responsible autonomy' aimed at harnessing the variability of labour power rather than suppressing it. One of the problems with the terms of this typology is that they can be taken too seriously and used as descriptive categories to refer to 'real' managerial practices, rather than as ideal-typical categories. In the case of flow-line reorganisation, the establishment of individual work stations in place of assembly-lines represents an articulation of Taylorist and non-Taylorist principles. Taylorist, because of the use of individual work roles, individual pay incentives and work measurement; non-Taylorist because of the auto-nomy ceded to workers. But even this answer does not come to grips with contradictions in the full circuit of capital, and the use of job redesign can be seen to have an impact on two moments in this circuit, two points of disarticulation.

By reducing the *length* of assembly lines, with a more or less constant size of workforce, firms were able, in effect, to increase the number of lines available to them. Consequently they were able to achieve a better match between the number of lines and their product range, thus attenuating the disarticulation between product market and labour process. The shorter lines or individual work stations could now be used for much longer production runs (see also Coriat 1980 for a similar argument). But firms were *also* able to influence the disarticulation between labour process and labour market. Absenteeism or turnover in firms with long assembly lines can be very disruptive of production for the reasons given already. By shortening or abolishing lines, firms reduced their vulnerability to such labour market processes. Absenteeism no longer meant long assembly lines being idle whilst supervisors hunted for replacement or utility workers: with short lines or individual work stations most workers could start their jobs at the beginning of a shift irrespective of absence levels.

By taking the full circuit of capital, and the articulation of its different moments, as our analytical starting point we have been able to offer a plausible account of the origins of job redesign which transcends the limitations of conventional labour process (or product market) theories. A similar analysis can be applied to the development of 'autonomous' or flexible work groups, particularly in capital-intensive continuous process industries, and of Herzbergian job enrichment, particularly in white-collar work. Very briefly, flexible work groups were developed as a means of managing both product and labour market contradictions relating to the labour process. In the chemicals industry world over-production by the mid-1960s precipitated a wave of rationalisation, part of which involved an attack on tight job descriptions. Although they are a relatively small proportion of total costs, labour costs were maintained at their current levels, particularly in Britain, by union demarcations and job controls which inflated the cost of labour as compared with some continental firms operating with flexible work roles and extensive inter-craft and craft-production mobility. By attempting to move away from tight job descriptions towards flexible work groups in which a set of multi-skilled workers were responsible for a set of jobs, firms sought to overcome two contradictions. Firstly, flexible work groups, at least in principle, allowed firms to negotiate for the same volume of work to be carried out by a smaller number of workers, as in productivity bargains. It thereby improved their competitive positions in product markets. Secondly, and particularly in the current recession, it has allowed firms to begin to reduce the control over labour supply and the labour process exercised by skilled workers (see also Campinos 1983 for a similar analysis).

Other firms used techniques of job enrichment based on the work of Herzberg: they redesigned routine clerical or simple administrative work to allow employees to exercise more responsibility, or to check and supervise their own work. These firms were responding to a contradiction between labour process and labour market. As Berg (1970) has observed, many US employers were progressively fragmenting and deskilling clerical work whilst simultaneously raising the entry qualifications for clerical labour. This growing contradiction was reflected in a corresponding growth of turnover and absenteeism.

One response was to adjust recruitment standards; another was to 'enrich work' by building in tasks from higher levels of the organisational hierarchy.

Job Redesign and Control

One of the issues raised by these forms of reorganisation, and theorised, for example, by Braverman (1974), Friedman (1977), Edwards (1979), Burawoy (1979) and Knights and Collinson in chapter 9 in this volume is their impact on control within the workplace. Indeed some writers, e.g. Gorz (1976) have analysed job redesign as simply a new form of managerial control over the labour process. Others e.g., Ramsay (1977, and chapter 7 of this volume), have advanced a more sophisticated variant of the same argument, suggesting that since the economic results of job redesign are often poor (a dubious observation), then its attraction for employers lies in its legitimatory functions: job redesign and allied schemes of worker participation provide a strictly limited role for workers in minor decisions, and are intended to ensnare, or incorporate them, into managerial structures of decision-making. Whether they succeed in so doing is considered, at least by Ramsay, to be an open question. Others again (Bosquet 1972; Zimbalist 1975) have conceptualised job redesign as an inherently unstable process in which minor concessions of work group autonomy increase workers' aspirations and demands and set in train an escalating process of struggle which could subvert managerial control.

The political significance of job redesign is clearly an important question, whatever one's theory of the labour process, but rather than review all that has been written on the subject I want to concentrate on three specific theoretical problems.

Managerial dominance

Some writers have sought to analyse job redesign, as well as other managerial initiatives such as worker participation by reference to managerial intentions. It is often assumed that managements will attempt to mask their 'real' intentions behind a cloud of obfuscating rhetoric. In the case of job redesign this rhetoric refers to job satisfaction, humanisation of work, even alienation, but in reality the redesign of jobs is intended to increase managerial control over the labour process and raise productivity and profitability. As an account of some managerial intentions this is uncontentious, but such accounts are often associated with the assumption that one can read off the achievements of a particular scheme from the intentions of their architects. In the case of management initiatives, this view in turn rests on the assumption that managerial dominance is an inevitable, or a necessary, feature of the capitalist mode of production. Only on this assumption is it plausible to deduce achievements directly from intentions. But is this a theoretically sound assumption? In my view it is not; the domination within capitalism of capital and its agents is an achievement that has continually to be worked at, or reproduced. There are no guarantees of managerial victory. This is partly because of class struggle and resistance; but it is also because the relationship between labour and capital is contradictory, and not just antagonistic (Burawoy 1979; Cressey and MacInnes 1980). A 'successful' job redesign scheme is one which has been modified through negotiation so that both labour and capital derive benefits as well as sharing costs. In short, achievements cannot be read off from intensions (see also Tomlinson 1982; chapter 2, 7; Urry 1981, chapter 5 for further elaboration of this point).

Essentialism

Allied to the assumption of the necessary domination of capital and its agents, is the view that job redesign has a definite, intrinsic political significance, irrespective of variations in its form or in the conditions of its implementation. It is, in essence incorporative; in other accounts, essentially destabilising, or essentially neo-Taylorism. Theoretically this assumption draws on the Hegelian distinction between essence and appearance; the 'true' meaning, or significance, of a phenomenon lies buried in its essence. I would argue, by contrast, that job redesign has *no* intrinsic, or essential, political significance whatsoever, but that its significance is a function of the strategic frameworks within which it is articulated, and the contradictions to which it is a response. A similar theoretical position was argued by Laclau (1977:99) in relation to the analysis of ideological elements, such as nationalism:

> ideological elements taken in isolation have no necessary class connotation, and . . . this connotation is only the result of the articulation of those elements in a concrete ideological discourse.

If we examine job redesign in a number of different contexts it becomes clear that its significance *does* vary accordingly.

In the early 1960s an extensive programme of experiments in job redesign was initiated under the joint auspices of the Norwegian government, the employers federation and the trade union federation (LO) (see Bolweg 1976). In the latter part of the 1960s these experiments, mainly in the creation of flexible work groups, spread to other industries and firms, but not as rapidly as had been hoped. Why were these forms of job redesign undertaken at all? We *could* answer the question by pointing to the objectives of employers. On the one hand, they wanted to increase productivity in the key export-oriented Norwegian industries; on the other hand, they wanted to secure control over the labour process in order to reduce levels of absenteeism and labour turnover. Both observations are accurate, but incomplete, for the reasons given above. The programme of job redesign was actually the product of an inter-class alliance in which labour and capital sought to pursue a variety of compatible and incompatible objectives. For the LO job redesign was *one* component of an overall strategy for democratisation of industry, itself part of the process of transition to socialism. Flexible work groups, allied to state support for an extension of trade union rights were promoted as a way of enhancing worker control over the labour process. Equally, the employers perceived such work groups as a way of 'motivating' job performance and 'involving' employees in enterprise decision-making. It was not possible to deduce in advance which of these assessments was the more accurate.

If we turn to Great Britain, job redesign had much less significance for the 'frontier of control' in the 1960s. Changes in the organisation of work were often introduced as part of a productivity agreement in which employers sought to obtain greater flexibility of workers between jobs in return for higher levels of pay. Employers were also concerned to circumvent state incomes policies which, at that time, and in the mid-1970s, prohibited wage rises above a statutory limit *unless* they were part of a productivity agreement. Finally, productivity agreements represented an attempt, in some cases, to challenge workplace trade union organisation and its associated job controls – over staffing levels, work pace, and overtime. From the workers' standpoint such agreements were often judged by their capacity to yield greater earnings: control implications were rarely perceived to be of great significance (Daniel 1970; Roberts and Wood 1982).

In the USA job redesign has been pioneered by *some* consultants as a way of undermining, or avoiding trade unions. By offering 'enriched' work, promotion prospects and so on it has been hoped (often successfully) to eradicate the sorts of discontent that were thought to fuel union recognition campaigns. One recent site for job redesign initiatives has been the new, capital-intensive, green-field sites in the southern states. There are several well-known cases in the literature in which firms relocating to the South have carefully selected and recruited 'suitable' types of workers, often with little or no previous industrial experience, to carry out work in semi-autonomous or flexible groups in new plants. Union organisation is usually absent from these plants, and from the surrounding area. There are also quite different types of job redesign, to be found in some of the northern states, and in Canada, where unionised firms have established joint labour-management quality of working life (QWL) committees. In such cases managers have sought to extend their control over the labour process and resist independent employee representation (see Kelly 1982a).

There is therefore no essence to job redesign, no intrinsic political significance that can be read off from the intentions of employers or managers, the needs or interests of capital or whatever (cf. Cutler *et al.* 1978).

Control

A third problem which has bedevilled thinking about job redesign (and indeed the labour process as a whole) is the concept of control. To say that the concept has proved difficult to pin down is an understatement, but one particular problem has been a tendency to conceive of control in unidimensional and zero-sum terms. Therefore if it could be shown that job redesign increased managerial control over the labour process, two conclusions followed. Worker control would correspondingly diminish since control is zero-sum; and such a scheme would not be in workers' interests because their interests and those of capital are antagonistic and non-overlapping (see also Littler and Salaman 1982).

Let us return to the form of job redesign described in the electrical engineering sector and consider its implications for control. On the one hand, workers individually had more control over their work pace since they were no longer obliged to work at the pace set on the whole line. They also had more control over time, for the same reasons: breaks could be taken to suit their own individual requirements and without the permission of supervisors. On the other hand, again as individuals, workers were more visible to management; it is far easier to allocate responsibility for low output or poor quality when workers function at individual work stations than when they are collectively operating an assembly line. Beyond that, production is less vulnerable to disruption by absenteeism or turnover (and perhaps stoppages) precisely because the organisation of work has been individualised; in that respect, management control over the labour process may have increased. How then are we to compare these various aspects of control since they appear incommensurable? And if we cannot compare them how can we reach any general assessment of shifts in control? The problem is compounded when we bring other forms of job redesign into the picture. Flexible work groups depend for their performance effectiveness on workers' willingness to be mobile between jobs, and in that respect such groups provide workers with an additional sanction, or basis for control, in the form of withdrawal of mobility. The operation of such groups also illustrates the point made by Littler and Salaman (1982) that management control cannot be seen merely as a coercive imposition on workers; it frequently rests on more or less active consent by workers (cf. Burawoy 1979; but also see Knights and Collinson, chapter 9 in this volume; for a slight variation on this thesis).

The political significance of job redesign has therefore proved extremely difficult to assess in general terms because of these theoretical problems: the assumption of managerial, or employer, domination; the assumption of an essential meaning common to all forms of job redesign; and the assumption of control as a zero-sum concept. The effect of abandoning these assumptions is to make us realise that the significance of job redesign is much more open-ended and contingent, and that in any case it may not usefully be captured within the framework *only* of control: other implications – staffing levels, work intensity, wages – also need to be considered (see also Ramsay, chapter 4 of this volume).

Job Redesign in the Recession

If redesign of jobs is analysed as a managerial response to worker resistance, an attempt to secure legitimacy and reassert control, the most obvious prediction of its fate in the recession would be a dramatic diminution. On this analysis mass unemployment, state action and authoritarian styles of management have 'solved' the 'problem of control', at least temporarily; job redesign, like so many workers, is redundant. This view is paralleled in managerial literature, where writers such as Hackman (1978) have argued that 'the problem of motivation' has been removed by the recession; workers are simply glad to have jobs and willing to make considerable sacrifices to keep them.

The analysis of job redesign as a response to contradictions, or disarticulations within the total circuit of industrial capital, leads to quite different predictions. On this view, product market competition has intensified in the recession, and should provide an even greater *incentive* for the use of job redesign as one way of resolving product market-labour process contradictions. Many firms who previously had an incentive to redesign jobs were prevented from doing so by trade union power, particularly when they tried to remove ancillary jobs and break down production-craft and inter-craft job barriers. One further consequence of the recession is that with the weakening of trade union power, some firms now have a greater *opportunity* to redesign jobs. This combination of incentive and opportunity would lead us to expect an increased use of job redesign in the recession, and not a decline. What evidence then is available, and what does it show?

To begin with it is undoubtedly the case that management periodicals and conferences which ten years ago were full of case studies of 'job enrichment' and 'motivation' today contain almost no discussions whatever of these subjects. Some people have concluded that the disappearance of rhetoric or discourse marks the disappearance of practice, but this is a profound error. Management literature is notoriously subject to fads; the latest is quality circles, next year it will be something else. Indeed one of the functions of these periodicals is to report on new ideas and developments and, by implication, to drop discussion of older ideas. Job redesign is not the first practice to have disappeared from management periodicals, and certainly won't be the last, and we need to examine managerial practice directly, and not indirectly through a distorting lens.

One of the most striking features of the current recession, at least in Britain, has been an upsurge in productivity bargaining. This form of bargaining took off in the early 1960s, accelerated from the mid-1960s as a way round state incomes policies, fell into abeyance from 1970 or so, but then began to pick up in the late 1970s, again as a way round incomes policy. During the last few years, however, there does seem to have been an increase in collective pay agreements that embody changes in work practices (see Pay and Benefits Bulletin 1980, 1981, 1982; Wenban-Smith 1982; Incomes Data Services 1979a, 1979b, 1981; Financial Times 1983). Often these changes take the form of flexibility agreements, or work groups, in which a set of discrete work roles is combined into a new individual or group job. A number of firms have concluded agreements in which production workers, for instance, have taken on simple maintenance tasks formerly the preserve of craft workers, and in that sense have had their own jobs 'enriched'. In other cases, flexible groups of production workers have been created. Yet another type of change involves flexibility between different craft workers. The companies that have reached these agreements include Clarks, Tannoy, Electricity Board, BL, BSC, BP, British Ship-builders, Electrolux, Perkins Engines.

It might be objected that many of these changes in jobs have been tried unsuccessfully before, notably during the spate of 'paper' productivity agreements in the 1960s, so why should they be any more successful today? And in any case what is the justification for describing such changes as 'job redesign' when they have often formed part of a coercive rationalisation of firms with little sign of concern for 'work humanisation' or 'quality of working life?'

The major difference between today and the 1960s is the much greater level of unemployment and its effect on union bargaining power. Aggregate data on productivity increases in the 1960s show only the most sluggish upward trends. By contrast productivity in manufacturing industry has risen dramatically in the recession (see table below). Some of this increase is due to the fall in employment being faster than the fall in output; some is due to simple intensification of labour; and/or of new capital investment; some is due to the selective diminution of low productivity firms (Jones 1983). In addition we also need to consider changes in product design and work flow. But it is unlikely that these factors account for all of the observed increase in labour productivity, and that changes in work organisation have played little or no part. Both popular and academic discussions of British industrial productivity have, for many years, noted striking differences in work organisation between Britain and the continent, and it seems plausible therefore that established divisions of labour should now come under attack (see Pratten 1976; Chemicals Economic Development Council 1973; Iron and Steel Sector Working Party 1980; and Williams, Williams and Thomas 1983 for dissenting views).

Output per head, manufacturing industry, excluding oil, gas, mining

1975	1979	1980	1981	1982	1983*
100	109.4	105.2	109.1	114.7	119.3

* 1st quarter
Source: CSO Monthly Digest of Statistics, Table 7.2, July 1983.

The argument that current changes in work organisation have little in common with earlier exercises in job enrichment, or work humanisation rests on an exaggerated assessment of the significance and impact of earlier practices. Firms who introduced schemes of job redesign in the 1960s amidst a fanfare of publicity, and with accompanying changes in organisational structure and managerial philosophy were the exception, not the rule. Many exercises in job redesign were articulated within conventional bargaining arrangements and/or existing company structures, although some did have wider ramifications. Indeed this variety of forms and contexts underlines the point made earlier that the significance of job redesign is to be sought in strategic frameworks and contexts of implementation.

In any case the depth and scale of the current employers' offensive is often exaggerated. The examples usually cited of 'the new management' – BL, BSC, BR – are all state capitalist industrial monopolies which have come under considerable pressure from a particularly reactionary government. Employers further removed from the orbit of Thatcherite influence have been rather more ambivalent in their dealings with unions (see Rose and Jones, chapter 5 in this volume). Many have welcomed the new repressive labour legislation, and the government's tough stance in public sector pay bargaining, but they themselves have often sought to negotiate new working practices, rather than to impose them (see IDS reports, op. cit.). Unions are of course negotiating very often from a position of extreme weakness, a fact which places a large questionmark beside the meaning of the term negotiating. But union weakness should not be exaggerated either. Union density has fallen only a few percentage points in four years; union finances are surprisingly sound; and trade unions and collective bargaining are deeply entrenched in the system of industrial relations in this country, a fact attributable in part to managerial sponsorship and collusion, e.g. in closed shop agreements (Brown and Sisson 1983).

Detailed empirical evidence on management strategy in work re-organisation confirms these points. As Rose and Jones underline in chapter 5, the complexity and variety of managerial strategy cast serious doubt on the idea of a simple, mechanical relation between the growth of unemployment and a Thatcherite managerial offensive against the shopfloor and its trade unionism. In other words managerial 'strategy' in the recession is best understood as a complex mixture of coercion and organised consent, and not simply as coercion a la Michael Edwardes (BL). Nor should this be surprising: Thatcherism itself, at the political level, has always involved such a combination (Jacques and Hall 1983).

Coombs later argues, on the basis of Kondratieff long-wave theory, that the new technologies now diffusing in the 'downswing' of the recession require more flexibility in the labour process, and are thus *conducive* to forms of work organisation such as flexible work groups. This argument is also contrary to the simplistic view that job redesign associated with 'job enrichment' was simply a product of economic boom and worker militancy. Empirically, the position is not so clear. Verdier (1983) for instance described a case in which new technology was introduced after job redesign had 'failed' because of trade union resistance.

It *is* true that job redesign in the 1980s is part of a much wider and deeper process of retructuring of the economy far beyond the scale of the 1960s. There are major changes taking place in the structure and location of both British and international production, and the division of labour (Massey and Meegan 1981; Hoogvelt 1982). And this wider context – of capitalist crisis and restructuring – raises an important political question about the potential role of job redesign in socialist strategies, a point which I can address only briefly in concluding.

Conclusions

In this chapter I have tried to show how we can move beyond the Braverman focus on the labour process in examining managerial practices. I argued that it was necessary to examine the full circuit of industrial capital – purchase of labour power in labour markets, exploitation and extraction of surplus value in the labour process, realisation of surplus value in product markets, and not simply the labour process. And that the key to understanding changes in work organisation (or job redesign) lay in the analysis of contradictions, or disarticulation, between the different moments in the circuit. Various forms of job redesign were analysed within this framework, in a way that would not have been possible from within the domain of the labour process alone.

It was also argued that Marxist and radical analyses of job redesign had been plagued by a set of untenable theoretical assumptions: the necessary dominance of capital and its agents, the idea that job redesign possesses an intrinsic, or essential, political significance, and the notion of control in the labour process as a unidimensional, zero-sum concept. The rejection of these assumptions has several consequences, one of which is to open up some political space around the issue of work organisation, by rescuing it from the realm of an inherently capitalist anti-working class practice. The Scandinavian trade unions and labour movement, and to a lesser degree the French and Italian union federations (CGT, CFDT, CGIL) have tried to articulate forms of job redesign within political and economic strategies designed to organise the transition to socialism (see Kelly 1982b). Some Marxists, of course, regard the notion of transitional strategy and tactics, such as radical forms of the alternative economic strategy, as no more than new forms of class collaboration and reformism. But a growing body of Marxist work in the 1970s has moved beyond this mode of political thinking to take strategy seriously (Cutler *et al.* 1978; Hirst 1983; Tomlinson 1982). Within this Gramscian Marxism there is, in principle, space for political organisation and struggle around a vast range of issues. And one of the major contributions of feminist thinking has been to insist that personal experience – in the family, in sexual relations, at work – be considered a central part of any socialist project. The analysis of job redesign presented in this chapter is consistent with, and supportive of, this mode of political thinking.

References

Berg, I. (1970), *The Great Training Robbery*, Penguin.
Bolweg, J. (1976), *Job Design and Industrial Democracy*, Martinus Nijhoff.
Bosquet, M. (1972), 'The prison factory', *New Left Review*, 73, 23–34.
Braverman, H. (1974), *Labour and Monopoly Capital*, Monthly Review Press.
Burawoy, M. (1979), *Manufacturing Consent*, University of Chicago Press.
Campinos, M. M. (1983), *Le Taylorisme dans les B.T.P.*, Communication au Colloque International sur le Taylorisme, Paris.

Chemicals Economic Development Council (1973), *Chemicals Manpower in Europe*, HMSO.

Coote, A. and Campbell, B. (1982), *Sweet Freedom*, Picador.

Coriat, B. (1980), 'The restructuring of the assembly line: a new economy of time and control', *Capital and Class*, 11, 34–43.

Corley, T. (1966), *Domestic Electrical Appliances*, Cape.

Cressey, P. and MacInnes, J. (1980), 'Voting for Ford', *Capital and Class*, 11, 5–33.

Cutler, A. *et al.* (1978), *Marx' Capital and Capitalism Today*, Vol. 2, Routledge and Kegan Paul.

Daniel (1970), *Beyond the Wage-Work Bargain*, London: PEP, 1970.

Edwards, P.K. and Scullion, H. (1982), *The Social Organization of Industrial Conflict*, Blackwell.

Edwards, R.C. (1979), *Contested Terrain*, Heinemann.

Financial Times (1983), 'Enter the jack-of-all-trades', 17 August.

Friedman, A. (1977), *Industry and Labour*, Macmillan.

Gartmann, D. (1979), 'Origins of the assembly line and capitalist control of work at Ford', in A. Zimbalist (ed.), *Case Studies on the Labour Process*, Monthly Review Press.

Gorz, A. (1976), *The Division of Labour*, Harvester.

Guest, R.H. (1957), 'Job enlargement – revolution in job design', *Personnel Administration*, 20(2), 9–16.

Hackman, J.R. (1978), 'The design of work in the 1980s', *Organizational Dynamics*, 7(1), 2–17.

Hirst, P. (1983), 'The division of labour, incomes policy and industrial democracy', in A. Giddens and G. Mackenzie (eds.), *Social Theory and the Division of Labour*, Macmillan.

Hoogvelt, A. (1982), *The Third World in Global Development*, Macmillan.

Incomes Data Services (1979a), *Productivity Schemes*, Study 186, IDS.

Incomes Data Services (1979b), *Changes in Work Organisation*, Study 203, IDS.

Incomes Data Services (1981), *Productivity Improvements*, Study 245, IDS.

Iron and Steel Sector Working Party (1980), *A Hard Look at Steel*, Parts 1, 2, 3. NEDO.

Jacques, M. and Hall, S. (eds.) (1983), *The Politics of Thatcherism*, Lawrence and Wishart.

Jones, D.T. (1983), 'Productivity and the Thatcher experiment', *Socialist Economic Review 1983*, Merlin.

Kelly, J.E. (1982a), *Scientific Management Job Redesign and Work Performance*, Academic Press.

Kelly, J.E. (1982b), 'Useful work and useless toil', *Marxism Today*, August.

Kelly, J.E. and Wood, S.J. (1983), *Taylorism and the recession*, Paper to the Colloque International sur le Taylorisme, Paris.

Kornhauser, A. (1965), *The Mental Health of the Industrial Worker*, Wiley.

Laclau, E. (1977), *Politics and Ideology in Marxist Theory*, NLB/Verso.

Littler, C. (1982), *The Development of the Capitalist Labour Process*, Heinemann.

Littler, C. and Salaman, G. (1982), 'Bravermania and beyond: recent theories of the labour process', *Sociology*, 16(2), 251–269.

Mackie, L. and Patullo, P. (1977), *Women and Work*, Tavistock.

Marx, K. (1970), *Capital*, Vol. 1 (1967), Progress Publishers.

Massey, D. and Meegan, R. (1981), *The Anatomy of Job Loss*, Methuen.

Montmollin, M. (1974), 'Taylorisme et anti-Taylorisme', *Sociologie du Travail*, 16, 374–382.

Packard, V. (1960), *The Wastemakers*, Penguin.

Pay and Benefits Bulletin December issues, 1980, 1981, 1982.

Pratten, C. (1976), *Labour Productivity Differentials Within International Companies*, Occasional Paper 50, Department of Applied Economics, Cambridge.

Ramsay, H. (1977), 'Cycles of control: worker participation in sociological and historical perspective', *Sociology*, **11**(3), 481–506.

Roberts, C. and Wood, S. (1982), 'Job redesign and collective bargaining', in J.E. Kelly and C.W. Clegg (eds.), *Autonomy and Control at the Workplace*, Croom Helm.

Tomlinson, J. (1982), *The Unequal Struggle: British Socialism and the Capitalist Enterprise*, Allen and Unwin.

Urry, J. (1981), *The Anatomy of Capitalist Societies*, Macmillan.

Verdier, E. (1983), *Dix ans d' "enrichissement du travail" dans une compagnie d'assurances: marges de manoeuvres ou choix strategiques?*, Communication au Colloque International sur le Taylorisme, Paris.

Walker, C.R. and Guest, R.H. (1952), *Man on the Assembly Line*, Harvard University Press.

Wenban-Smith, G. (1982), 'Factors influencing recent productivity growth-report on a survey of companies', *National Institute Economic Review*, **101**, *August*.

Williams, K. Williams, J. and Thomas, D. (1983), *Why Are the British So Bad at Manufacturing?*

Wood, S. (1982), *The Degradation of Work?*, Hutchinson.

Work in America (1973), MIT.

Zimbalist, A. (1975), 'The limits of work humanisation', *Review of Radical Political Economics*, **7**(2), 50–59.

4 What Is Participation For?
A critical evaluation of 'labour process' analyses of job reform

Harvie Ramsay

One facet of the upsurge in interest in worker participation in the developed capitalist societies which dates from the second half of the 1960s has been a concern with redesigning jobs themselves. To a greater or lesser extent in different countries, reform at this level has been encouraged by the official voices of government, employers and unions. A mighty literature has grown up reporting on experiments, most of it having a tenor of approval, enthusiasm and optimism common to all sectors of the discussion of participative innovations. The enhancement of job satisfaction, productivity and quality of output are proclaimed, with their attendant benefits for both employee and employer. France appointed a Minister for Job Enrichment to promote moves in this area; in the United States the Department of Health, Education and Welfare established a 'task force' of academics to report on the area, and in 1973 Senator Edward Kennedy promoted a 'Worker Alienation and Technical Assistance Bill'. In Britain the Department of Employment's Work Research Unit exists to stimulate and investigate developments in job reform. The first impression is of a monolith, rosy-hued in the light of a humanised, post-capitalist dawn.

Despite the numerical dominance of the voices of this orthodoxy on job reform in its various guises (job rotation, job enlargement, job enrichment, semi-autonomous group working, quality control circles, etc.), its uncritical and almost atheoretical cast renders it a straw target for the critic. It takes no account of competing interests, and so of competing definitions of success, and rarely explores the possibility, let alone the facts, of failure. Its preoccupation with integration and the elimination of conflict renders talk of 'democratic' work organisation transparently rhetorical, drawing on the aura of legitimacy surrounding references to democracy with little supportive substance in experiments that seem chiefly about engineering consent. The manipulative style of much of the literature and the practices it describes has been effectively enough criticised by pluralist commentators who accurately detect the superficiality of its break from human relations paternalism.[1] These critics are less ready to examine the claims that job redesign achieves its managerial aims, however, and this will concern us below.

Some proponents of job reforms find themselves frustrated by the mystique that veils the proposals in robes of 'human' benefits and quality of working life. They perceive a danger that this might put off hard-headed business executives concerned with less diaphanous yields. One such frustrated practitioner complains: 'It is not widely understood that we are proposing an alternative way to manage that we believe will ultimately result in a more favourable profit and loss account.' (Whitsett 1971: 23).

That sentiment would undoubtedly be echoed by the approach to the analysis of job reform with which this paper is most concerned – those writing in the 'labour process' tradition. This approach has been inspired by the development of certain concepts from Marx, particularly through the work of Braverman (1974). The perspective has gained considerable ground in academic business studies circles, as the conference from which this collection is drawn testifies. Clearly its stress on the exploitative nature of the relationship between labour and capital lends a very different edge to any agreement with Whitsett's observation. But while a critical alternative which seeks to dissect the fantasies of job reform can only be welcome, a closer examination of writings in this school of thought reveals major disagreements and perhaps some more fundamental flaws. It is to this examination that I shall turn first.

Braverman, the Labour Process and Job Reform
Braverman is concerned to analyse an 'historical evolution' (1974: 17), whereby the development of social forms results from a meshing of capitalist priorities with the technology the system generates. For Braverman the core of this evolution lies in the methods used at the point of production to pump surplus value out of the worker; that is, the labour process. The key to the generation of profit lies in how successfully the labourer can be applied to fixed capital, and the history he writes is one of the refinements of management techniques for this purpose. The strength of Braverman's analysis lies in its efforts to reintroduce the political economy of class to studies of the workplace, when such a perspective seemed to have retreated to analyses of the state and of social inequality, abandoning the office and factory to the limp empiricism of industrial sociology. This it achieves by reasserting the centrality of production to class analysis, and of class to the system of production. There results an attentive consideration of how battles over the valorisation of capital are fought out around the desks and machines where work takes place.

Broadly, the 'labour process' approach, if we can momentarily suspend problems in identifying a single beast fitting this description, draws on the concepts of 'formal', and 'real' subordination of labour. Formal subordination is a result of the dominance of the capitalist labour market and the private control of capital. It entails the concept that workers have no choice but to sell their labour power or starve, which enmeshes them in the generation of surplus and so subjugation to the system of valorisation. However, in many jobs workers nonetheless retain a large measure of autonomy in how their work is carried out. The pressures of competition between capitals, of crises and (in the view of some) an inevitable decline in the long-run profit rate, of labour's resistance to 'rationality', and of changing technologies, all compel capital to develop its strategy towards direct control of the worker. Autonomy is replaced by direction, discipline and other methods to dictate not only that labour does produce for capital but *how*, through what work methods.

The expression of this encroaching enslavement of man to machine, following Braverman, is taken to be Taylorism. This entails the application not of specific techniques proposed by Taylor – important though work study and piecework might be, for instance – but rather of the principles underlying his approach. These principles are delineated as the fragmentation of tasks that, kept together in their previous form, required extensive learning (deskilling); the separation of the planning of work from carrying it out (social division of labour, of head and hand); and the direct monitoring and control of each stage of the labour process. The leverage to sustain this is an incentive system which rewards obedience. 'Control' in this account arises from the subjection of labour to machine and human discipline at the point of production, and it is this which makes possible an enhanced rate of exploitation. The 'labour process' view of participation, or of any management policies which purport to improve or ameliorate the condition of the worker, derives from this conception of control. Thus these devices are deception, seeking to lure the worker further into collaborating in his/her own exploitation.

For Braverman the policies that seemed at odds with Taylor were merely a surface gloss. They are 'faddish' (1974: 35), offering:

> a studied pretence of work 'participation', a gracious liberality in allowing the worker to . . . move from one fractional job to another, and have the illusion of making decisions by choosing among fixed and limited alternatives designed by a management which deliberately leaves insignificant matters open to choice (1974: 39).

Elsewhere 'human relations' and 'industrial pyschology'

practitioners are described as 'the maintenance crew for the human machinery' subjected to Taylorism (1974: 87).

The neo-Fordist Variant

The specious piety of those who proclaim the supposed common interests of management and employees, agglutinated by management realisation of employee needs and willingness to fulfil them easily provokes the kind of revulsion Braverman and other critics have expressed. The analysis Braverman supplies affords a clear and material basis for an alternative comprehension. It embodied certain shortcomings which ensured that it would not be the final word, however.

The problem with Braverman's approach which has attracted the greatest attention is its failure to account for the development of these approaches and their grip on articulated business ideology. Why should either ideological adaptations, or the need to maintain the 'human machinery' (these are, it should be noted, rather different functions), arise in particular periods? One answer, true to Braverman's focus on the labour process and its concomitant notion of control, but quite different in its assessment of the significance of the new management techniques, is that which sees them as appropriate to a particular stage of capitalist development of the productive forces. Just as Braverman saw 'monopoly capitalism' as a stage beyond 'machinofacture', and the stage at which labour becomes really, not just formally, subordinated to capital by Taylorism, so certain revisionists in the camp see Taylorism too as only one stage in this process. Taylorism finds its clearest expression (or for some its first successor) in the fragmented and deskilled form of work on the assembly line ('Fordism'). But it is now superseded by 'neo-Fordism', a form of organisation appropriate to maximising labour intensity under more automated systems of production.

This development of Braverman is rarely located more concretely as a feature of certain industries, but it implicitly applies to the most modern – the process industries seen as the haven of de-alienated work by such as Blauner (1964). As such it re-reads this supposed 'humanisation', purportedly made possible by the development of the forces of production under capitalism, into 'labour process' terms.

The formulation of this alternative seems to have arisen initially in French debates. The term 'neo-Fordism' first became familiar to English-speaking readers through Palloix's (1976) work, but he in turn draws on Aglietta who provides the clearest statement of this analysis:

> there is a change in the general principles of work organization whenever there is a change in the modalities of capitalist management of the labour process. Automation brings with it the possibility of such a major trans-

> formation because it replaces the rigid integration of the mechanical principle
> with an integration that is both more flexible and more far-reaching. . . . The
> workers are no longer subjected to a constraint of personal obedience, but
> rather to the collective constraint of the production process. . . .
> Job enrichment, leading to the formation of semi-autonomous groups, is . . .
> the mode of work organization corresponding to the general principle
> formulated above. . . . (Aglietta 1979: 128–9)[2]

The new human relations, with its stress on job redesign, thus
becomes an expression of a new order, as Taylorism becomes out-
moded. The 'enriched' jobs are not, of course, genuinely granting
responsibility to workers. The real decisions are programmed into the
automated work system. The enhanced freedom of movement, self-
regulation of work pace, opportunity for interaction with others and so
on are real, but their apparent significance as represented by management theorists and governments proselytising about 'quality of
working life' is illusory. Control has not been eased; jobs may require
more learning for some operators, but this 'skill' does not include
autonomy in choice of method of work and related decisions as did
craftwork. Management's conspiracy proceeds ineffably to the
realisation of its objective at the worker's expense.

The Voluntarist Variant

The determinist variants offered by Braverman on the one hand, and
the 'neo-Fordist' view on the other, do not exhaust the repertoire of
analyses from a labour process perspective. A further group of writers
have been critical of the fatalism of progressive real subordination of
labour and success for management in the development of its techniques. Worker resistance in their view remains an ever-present
potential. The history of the labour process is one of struggle, not of the
automatic advance of capital.[3] These writers, who can be labelled
'voluntarists', argue that the origins of job enrichment are less
conspirational on management's part than a determinist view implies,
and that control is not pre-programmed but is contestable. Managerial
tactics may backfire and open up a 'space for struggle' for workers,
providing them unintentionally with a degree of autonomy from which
to resist management encroachment. The view of management intent is
little changed (though less security and certainty is implied), but its
likelihood of unimpeded achievement is compromised.

This alternative approach is clearly attractive in a number of ways.
Management are evidently not omniscient nor omnipotent, and the
outcomes for new strategies they adopt (or, in some cases, adapt from
worker demands) are a matter for empirical determination. Nor is the
notion that pre-Taylor or pre-Fordism or pre-neo-Fordism workers

exerted controls which they lose under the new disguised assault of capital easily defended against accusations of romanticism. It is grotesquely sweeping in its judgement, neglecting differences between industries, contradictory changes between different grades and locations, the effect of gender considerations, and so forth. It remains important to avoid the opposite presumption to Braverman's as well, though. Not all workers at all times resist successfully or to the same degree; nor is the resistance of one group necessarily 'progressive' – it may, for instance, work to the disadvantage of others.[4] Contradictions, after all, cut both ways; they do not just undermine the effectiveness of managerial strategies.

The voluntarist strain of the labour process debate brings a further different perspective on the nature and implications of job enrichment. From Friedman's (1977) analysis of 'responsible autonomy' to Bosquet's (1977) optimistic assessment of job enrichment as unintentionally provoking worker interest, and so uncorking the bottle of pressure for democratic control of work, a variety of arguments have supported this *within* the context of a focus on changes at the job level (that is, the level at which labour process views tend to concentrate analysis). Marglin's (1979) analysis of job enrichment as 'catching flies with honey' nonetheless closes with an appeal to the vulnerability of a management forced to attempt to regain control by these means, however despicably cunning the traps they weave may be, and hence implies that advantage may be found from them by workers. Zimbalist (1979), like Friedman, distinguishes worker-initiated 'enlargement', 'rotation' and the like from management-regulated proposals, seeing these as having far more potential. But in general he too is fascinated by the possibility of an unplanned unleashing of worker interest and militancy being instigated even by management-sponsored job enrichment programmes.

Finally, even the considerably more developed analyses of job redesign advanced by Kelly (chapter 3 in this volume), or of other developments in enterprise-level industrial relations by Cressey, MacInnes and Norris (1982), neither of which focus so narrowly on the job itself, also entertain possibilities of advances for labour. The political significance of their analytical conclusions is evident, and I shall return to it at the end of this paper. Firstly, however, I shall turn to a scrutiny of problems in the 'labour process' approach, which to a considerable degree recur in various mutations among all the variants described. This will lead to a consideration of the pivotal concept of control.

Participation, Control and the Labour Process

The contribution of labour process analyses to the question posed in the title of this paper might most easily be called into question if we were to examine the introduction and outcomes of representative forms of worker participation. But the possibility exists that job reforms are not reducible to just another participative innovation, having instead a distinctive genesis and nature. In any case, it is to the analysis of job redesign that labour process approaches are best equipped to contribute. Hence this paper will focus on changes at this level, to evaluate the perspective on its strongest ground.

One way into an assessment of a labour process approach is to reconsider the concept 'labour process' itself. In general terms, the labour process describes the application of labour to the means of production (materials and whatever technological devices are available) to produce use values, though under capitalism it takes a more specific form: applying labour power to capital in order to make possible valorisation through the market place, and so the production of exchange values. There is no a priori reason to delimit the 'application' of labour power to the point of production itself – it may be extended to encompass all social activity which facilitates production, which in the logic of Marx's analysis involves all aspects of the organisation and the social and cultural milieu within which it exists. The state's activity, for instance, may be seen as a necessary condition of production, and in this sense as involved in the social relations which constitute a particular labour process.[5] Yet analysts in the contemporary 'labour process' tradition use the concept to focus attention specifically on the point of immediate production as we have seen. While this has the apparent strength noted earlier of returning class analysis to the workplace, it is also the source of major weaknesses.

A number of examples may serve to highlight the problems, all of which stem from the supposition that it is through the direct control and intensity of utilisation of labour power at the point where products are made that capitalism reproduces and extends itself, and so that this is the locus of all struggles against capital. The difficulty can be expressed as a narrow conception of production, or as a narrow representation of the moments through which valorisation is achieved. Thus the neglect of the family and domestic labour leads to a definition of housework as non-productive, and ignores the contribution the associated sexual division of labour in the home and outside it makes to the achievement of surplus and its appropriation by the employer (Beechey 1977, 1978, 1982). In the 'workplace' (the very term can now be seen to be problematical), the use of information technology may enable the employer to rationalise production without necessarily intensifying labour effort (Murray 1983; Child, chapter 6 in this volume). Or in the wider corporate structure, multinational corporations may achieve stability of production by dual-sourcing, by exploiting cheap labour markets, and may enhance profits by manipulations in the circulation of commodities, e.g. by transfer pricing, tax avoidance, currency speculation and the like. None of these activities *necessarily* entails intensification of labour (Littler and Salaman 1982).

Moreover, if the contradiction between capital and labour is acknowledged, it becomes apparent that conflict becomes a 'normal' state of affairs, and it is its absence which has to be achieved rather than its presence provoked. This makes concerted management efforts to minimise or eliminate manifest conflict potentially a major factor in levels and stability of production. The use of job enrichment along with high wages and 'good' conditions of work is a strategy often employed to this end, commonly involving attempts to exclude trade unions from the company altogether – an approach which seems to operate with some success in IBM or Texas Instruments, for instance. Better still, lower resistance to change and general job flexibility may be achieved (Coriat 1979; Kelly, chapter 3 in this volume; Littler, chapter 2 in this volume). Here the use of purportedly 'participative' techniques may enhance profitability by integration, again rather than intensification of labour.

It will be observed that the issue of worker participation has resurfaced, in the context of a suggestion that it may yield advantages to capital of a different form to those upon which labour process theories concentrate our attention. For most critics on the left, participation is seen as a device to increase the control of capital under the guise of advancing the worker's influence. But the precise way in which such 'control' may be achieved, and the degree to which participation achieves it at all for capital, has been left poorly conceptualised. It is to these questions we must turn next.

The obvious motivation employers may have for introducing participation, in particular at job level, is to increase worker commitment and effort seeking the intensification of labour described in most labour process analyses. This intention is the one discovered by Lupton, Tanner and Schnelle (1979) in their European survey of job redesign practice:

> The reasons which prompted a concern to redesign manufacturing systems in radical ways have rarely included an explicit and single-minded commitment to a set of humane values. Rather they have been a piecemeal response to events in labour markets and product markets with economic ends in mind. (p. 53)

This strategy may be re-read in a way less tied to labour process analysis narrowly conceived, however. Lupton *et al.* find labour flexi-

bility and attracting a high quality workforce are important factors
mentioned by companies, and such changes may be seen as logical for
firms producing for markets requiring rapid product changeover. This
forces a widening of the explanatory framework to consider the 'full
circuit of capital' (Kelly, chapter 3; cf. Littler, chapter 2).[7] Littler
copes with such a widening of scope by defining layers in the labour
process, moving from the point of production to a concomitant structure of control in the employing organisation, in turn set within a
societal 'employment relationship' (1982: 42–3). These layers have
separate if interacting dynamics in Littler's model. This opens up the
possibility of strategies for employer control at one level leading to
greater worker autonomy at another, a theme which is taken up by
Kelly (chapter 3 in this volume; Wood and Kelly 1982) as a basis for
important optimistic conclusions on the opportunities of an advance for
labour being attained through such managerial strategies. This in turn
involves the resurrection of a concept conceived in the demonic
domains of pluralist industrial psychology, namely 'positive-sum
control', on which I will have more to say in a moment.

The extension of or extrusion from the labour process approach in
the latter contributions remains for the most part rooted in 'production'
effects still rather restrictively conceived. Yet Lupton and his
colleagues' survey also found as stated aims 'to avoid revolutionary
protest, or response to trades-union pressure' (1979: 53). If we raise our
purview beyond immediately visible impulses, it is suggested that these
options, of stemming local or social disruption or challenges to management authority, may prove far more important than the above accounts
would permit us to think. I have argued for just such a social engine of
management innovation on the participation front, with schemes being
introduced during periods of pressure on management's legitimacy
from below and tending to fade away once that pressure was removed
(Ramsay 1977, 1983a, 1983b). Participation was a concession on
management terms, both conciliatory and an effort to contain disruptive pressures, and if possible to gain ground for management by
persuading employees into an 'enterprise consciousness'. In the words
of a British Institute of Management publication in 1968, 'radical relief'
was needed 'to avoid an explosion'.

Because participation was found to be promoted and then neglected
under successive phases of the capital-labour struggle, I coined the
phrase 'cycles of control' to describe the consequent historical pattern.
The term 'control' was never very closely interrogated in the original
formulation, but it implied that management initiatives headed off or
restrained the demand for more substantial changes in authority
relations. Indeed for some writers certain innovations have been seen as

deliberate designs for this end," though my own interpretation was less conspiratorial. However, it was also argued that, at the level of the enterprise, participation was only marginally if at all successful in achieving employee integration and support, contrary to mythology on the subject." It was suggested that if participation did have anything more than a brief impact it either took the form of *de facto* bargaining, or else its influence was a cumulative one at the societal level, i.e. it created the appearance of a responsive, reformable enterprise structure, so legitimating the system, notwithstanding local disappointments. Indeed, had participation enjoyed the success commonly attributed to it, it is hard to see why once employers had discovered it they should ever lose interest in it thereafter. Thus the nature of control embodied in this analysis stresses ideological gains rather than directly profitable or productive ones.

The above analysis focused chiefly on consultative and other representative forms of participation, along with profit-sharing, and as noted earlier it remains open to question whether 'participative' changes in job organisation are part of the same phenomenon at all, or whether they are subject to different influences better described by labour process theories, and so to the historical pattern described therein. There may indeed be some justification for applying the 'cycles' analysis more cautiously here, notwithstanding the partial relevance implied by Lupton and his colleagues' finding noted earlier. Nonetheless, I shall argue below that there are other good reasons for considering job reforms as part and parcel of wider participative trends in key respects for three reasons: firstly, the apparent coincidence of its initiation; secondly, the extent to which its 'success', too, is mythical; and thirdly, the emphasis in particular periods on it being 'reform' or 'humanisation' instead of just 'redesign' (i.e. the need to distinguish changing jobs from the way the change is depicted and advertised).

Whether this be vindicated or not, though, it would be difficult to accept the claim that both capital and labour can 'gain' control through job reforms or any other means without bastardising the very concept of control. Control is a relational concept, not a substance which lies outside a relationship ready to be seized in variable handfuls. To talk of a 'positive-sum' in which both sides can 'gain' is to engage in analytical legerdemain, slipping into a functionalist usage which conceives control as being shared between actors over an external environment. In an effort to evade this trap, it is necessary for promoters of the idea to distinguish different 'levels' at which control can operate – separating control over work from control over the organisation and appropriation of surplus being the basic notion entailed by such approaches. [10] But it is open to question whether control at different levels, if it were possible to talk in such terms, would be commensurate at all; if the separation can be made, the comparability is also lost, and it becomes meaningless to try to 'sum' the two. Moreover the resulting distinction appears to recreate a separation which other recent commentators have successfully attacked as untenable – that between 'formal' and 'real' subordination of labour, which approximates very well to control at organisational level over surplus versus control at the level of the job.[11] That distinction was argued to create polarised, equally problematical readings of determination – those which saw 'real' control as fundamental, celebrating all job control gains as victories over capital; and those which saw 'formal' control as basic so that gaining or being ceded local autonomy was a deception within the structure of exploitation. The politics of the former is that of encroachment and political gradualism – and its revival is therefore not unexpected in a climate where many writers seek to justify an Alternative Economic Strategy.

It seems to this author that to separate job control from social relations of surplus creation is precisely to fragment the 'circuit of capital', and to detach work itself (a technical process) as one arena of struggle from organisational (social) control. This involves another way of putting our earlier comments on the concept of 'labour process' itself. Production is simultaneously a technical and social process in which 'technical' matters are constrained and indeed defined by social relations of which they are part and parcel, and vice versa. It is this structural perspective, viewing control as a nexus of capitalist social relations, and stressing the internality of one 'face' of these relations with all others, which follows from the rejection of the two poles of mechanical argument above. Yet this in turn seems to warn of the likely futility of 'nibbling' strategies which ignore the interdependence of the different facets in order to justify piecemeal changes.[12]

Let us consider, for a moment, an increase in autonomy which would seem to benefit management and worker. Take the 'black box' or 'spy in the cab' resisted by transport drivers and employers alike. Without this instrument drivers could decide how far and fast to drive unhindered by observation. The employer could turn a blind eye to obvious law-breaking on continuous driving, speed and so forth and gain lower overall costs and often faster delivery. Yet it would be meaningless to analyse the driver's autonomy separately from the wage and consumer goods system which compels such efforts, and shapes the desire for the 'autonomy' which enables that driver to 'choose' to take risks. In short, the bourgeois concept of freedom has to be invoked to maintain the image of a 'gain' from this autonomy. Surely we do not have to resurrect old arguments about the value of such 'freedom' for labour under capitalism?

The same argument applies where a degree of choice of action in an incompletely refined production process (i.e. almost all existing jobs in some degree) allows a worker to take chances to keep production going – so creating the kind of 'accidents' described in one penetrating analysis of safety at work (Nichols 1975). Again control cannot be analysed layer by layer without losing any useful meaning, and once this device is lost notions of 'positive sums' dissolve before our eyes.

Does Job Enrichment 'Succeed'?

This is not to say that a priori job enrichment must serve management, even if they fully comprehend its implications. Presumption to this effect is vulgar Marxism. The judgement must be an empirical one, allowing for the presence of contradictions, and so of management's inability to predetermine outcomes; but this applies equally to more 'optimistic' views, which ignore structural limits and constraints on the potential for change. It would take a romantic to imagine workers would be motivated and empowered by job enrichment to storm the citadels of investment planning, for example; in that degree, at least, the predisposition of this approach is to be sceptical of the trans-formative capacities of job reforms.

The companion question to that asked in the title must therefore be 'What, in practice, does job enrichment do?' It is to the credit of the anti-fatalist school that they insist on asking this question, instead of lapsing into determinist functionalism. It may be that they have not answered it carefully enough, however. Just because management are stimulated by a promise of bountiful productivity, for instance, does not mean that this is the end result of their efforts.

One problem in distinguishing an impulse created by a crisis in competition and productivity from a need to repair legitimation is that the two are likely to go hand in hand. They follow a pattern that seems to conform historically to some version of the 'long wave' charted by Cronin (1979, 1980; see also Coombs, chapter 7 in this volume) to explain upsurges in striker militancy. One such upsurge erupted inter-nationally during the 1960s and 1970s (Dubois 1978). One aspect of this period was thus a proliferation of labour demands for democratic rights at work, which coincided with and threatened to exacerbate a growing pressure on corporate profitability.[13] The management and state response in the various advanced capitalist nations was startlingly similar, including the introduction of a range of participation schemes (Ramsay 1983b).

It would be possible to argue that job redesign should be regarded as distinct from other 'participative' innovations at this time, if it were found to be employed to resolve productivity problems only. But there is a powerful plausibility to a reading of such experiments as part and parcel of the more general vogue for participation. It fits as part of an employer's repertoire of changes 'soft on power', alongside profit-sharing or strictly advisory consultative bodies, for instance (Clegg *et al.* 1978). Hence the fabled Swedish programmes, heavily publicised with glossy summaries of successful experiments, are most cogently explained as a counterpoint to union and employee demands for greater bargaining rights and ability to regulate the working environment (Martin 1976). The same case can be argued for other countries, where the major phenomena of job reform appear to be the braggadocio of official research units and 'tripartite' bodies set up to promote 'quality of working life', alongside the public relations activities of companies and consultants.[14]

It may yet be that this outer, most visible skin of the corpus of job redesign conceals a more substantial change. Although there seems to be no systematic evidence, a glance at the reports of experiments suggests a concentration in 'frontier' sectors, such as those employing process technology, or in electronics, or parts of the finance and other white-collar sectors being swept by information technology. Even so, technology may not be the key variable – all of these sectors being at the forefront of the internationalisation of capital and involving many of the largest enterprises in existence, to mention possible alternative causal connections.

It is also possible to gain contradictory impressions of whether job enrichment is most likely to be introduced where labour is organised and troublesome, or weak and unable to resist changes intensifying labour. The latter is suggested by Braverman (1974: 36), who points to the frequency of reforms in the jobs of non-unionised white-collar employees. Similarly it has been argued that women workers are particularly vulnerable to management on this score.[15] On the other hand, the use of enrichment to coax 'troublesome' workers is suggested by the Tavistock proposals for the Durham mines (Trist *et al.* 1963), or the adaptations to the 'gang' system in what became British Leyland factories in Coventry (Melman 1958; cf. Friedman 1977). In the Swedish context, Nycander (1978) suggests that job reforms have been attempted only where the workforce is challenging management control, and is unheard of in textile factories with predominantly female, non-militant labour. Once again the pattern is confused – and if it were clear, it is not apparent in any case which possibility would vindicate which analysis.

The most serious potential flaw in all labour process analyses, however, brings us back to the question of outcome. The image of 'success' has been donated by accounts whose reliability cannot be accepted by a serious critical assessment. Despite the volume of hallelujahs, there are several cooler evaluations of the orthodox evidence which expose the paucity of its claims. Their presumption of worker motivation, for a start, relies on a remarkably long connecting chain from increased variety or responsibility to increased interest, and so to greater satisfaction, whence comes an attitude of enhanced loyalty to the employer and willingness to exert effort, and so finally greater productivity, lower absenteeism and labour turnover as the behavioural output. The chain has numerous potential weak links.[16] Any of the pessimistic labour process views which imagine employees to be deceived into accepting job redesign at face value thanks to management manipulation merely add a further link to this corroded leash. The alternative labour process option views job enrichment as a public relations cover-up of changes which the worker *experiences* as intensified labour. This view is implied by the much-repeated quotation from Nichols and Beynon: 'I never feel "enriched" – I just feel knackered' (1977: 16), or by the six American car workers who reported disliking the Saab group-working system, particularly complaining about the pace of work and the rigours of group discipline.[17] Given the problems of sustaining such control in the face of dissaffection,[18] the prospects of success seem jaded.

It comes as no surprise, therefore, to find that the reports of increased productivity themselves are derived from a body of material of which 'little pretends to be scholarly, and that which does is notoriously poor' (Swartz 1981: 63). Blackler and Brown reach similar conclusions, citing a survey which finds that almost all job redesign studies suffer from 'severe methodological deficiencies',[19] a claim which their own investigations tend to support. Wall and Lischerson, meanwhile, find that an examination of the supposed relationship between participation and satisfaction leads them to be impressed 'by the *lack* of evidence in support of this thesis' (1977: 14).

Some of the most telling critiques of the orthodoxy have come from writers scrutinising certain experiments in detail. Carey, for instance, re-analyses the results of the Norwegian experiments with semi-autonomous work groups, and concludes that 'success' in conventional terms is achieved only when a group bonus system exists to provide the incentive.[20] Even Daniel, a firm advocate of job enrichment regards it as workable only if conflicts are dealt with through negotiation over rewards for increased responsibility and effort.[21] And Kelly in a number of studies, notably of classic Tavistock experiments, concludes that the role of pay incentives is severely underplayed by the researchers in their conclusions (Kelly, 1978, 1982).

These findings at the very least moderate the degree to which job redesign itself can be seen as the source of management miracles, and thereby open up the topic to voluntarist or generally sceptical arguments. Kelly nonetheless argues that intensification of labour, including job loss where worker organisation is poor, is a major intention and to some extent outcome of the new arrangements (Kelly 1980). Similarly Coriat (1979) provides extensive evidence of reduced down-time and greater productivity at Renault, very much in neo-Fordist style, though without much reference to workers' experience and perceptions of the changes. It would be foolish to ignore these findings, and so deny that management *may* markedly advance the rate of exploitation by directly inducing effort through job redesign. But it would be equally foolish to treat this as the typical, permanent result without good cause – and that cause is not yet provided.

In order to reinforce the argument emerging so far, I shall now present two company case studies. Both seem to augur well for some labour process interpretation in that they involve 'frontier' process technology, and both were initiated at a time of competitive presssure and squeezed profit margins. However, both also coincide with the breakdown of traditionally paternalist strategies towards labour and with challenges from below. As such they seem to afford a promising terrain for assessing the perspectives discussed above against the career of job enrichment.

ICI

ICI has received a good deal of publicity for its attempt to introduce job enrichment from the late 1960s. Although experiments took place before negotiation of the Weekly Staff Agreement (WSA), these were isolated, and the only available accounts are those by the consultants, Paul and Robertson (1970). Nor did they enjoy demonstrable success among manual staff even on these writers' admission.[22] A series of subsequent innovations, tied up with WSA's ambitious version of productivity bargaining, seem thereby to suit the labour process argument well as far as management purpose is concerned. Moreover, at least one report heralds the agreement as creating a new working relationship with immense organisational benefits (Roeber 1975). Another based on one plant (Gloucester) is euphoric about satisfaction spin-offs but more sanguine about the cost to management of any productivity gains (Daniel 1970, 1973; Daniel and McIntosh 1972). Roeber, too, claims considerably enhanced efficiency and satisfaction at Gloucester, and at Hillhouse, asserting in the latter case that workers were enthusiastic despite union hostility. He uses this last claim as a platform to reject an alternative study, by Roberts and Wedderburn (1974) conducted on behalf of the TUC, which draws on shop stewards' criticisms of the scheme. He argues this is discredited by the gap between workers and their representatives, who ritually resist changes that threaten the *raison d'être* of their own support and thereby (a significant observation this) obstruct the potential gains. Roeber voices, then promptly buries, a 'small niggling worry' that management 'manipulation' might be the chief process at work (1975: 267).

If we turn back to the study of Gloucester from which Daniel drew his enthusiasm, some significant doubts start to emerge. The authors, Cotgrove, Dunham and Vanplew, report that the changes in work experience remained marginal – 'basically the work remained monotonous. . . . Consequently, for most, work had little meaning.' (1971: 103). At most boredom was reduced, rather than positive interest being generated: there was only an 'enlargement', not an 'enrichment' of tasks (1971: 134–5). The comparison with Nichols and Beynon[23] is mutually reinforcing. For Cotgrove *et al.* technology is the constraining factor (not, it should be noted, the facilitating factor) on significant change (1971: 136). Moreover, there were signs that any experienced leavening of monotony tended to wear off as time went on and novelty dissipated. Significant gains for management in reduced manning and stability of production were reported, but how far these were attributable to job redesign and how far to a particularly successful productivity bargaining strategy and attendant wage adjustments is questionable (see also Knights and Collinson, chapter 9 in this volume). And this, it should be stressed, is a much-cited example of success.

These problems with enthusiastic accounts make it reasonable to turn to an alternative source, Roberts and Wedderburn's study (1974). This readily confirms an impression gained from Roeber, but one which he dismisses as anachronistic (i.e. unpalatable to his evolutionary assumptions), namely that Gloucester is atypical for its acquiescence in the changes. In the North-East of England, particularly at the huge Wilton site, resistance was obdurate, while other sites also offered evidence of reluctance and determination to resist management blandishments.

Roberts and Wedderburn report that their overwhelming impression from interviews with stewards and members was that job enrichment was regarded with suspicion, but seen as a minor aspect of the WSA. Wilton stewards dismissed it as a nonsense, relying on gross management exaggeration of the increased responsibility involved (Roberts and Wedderburn 1974: 45). At Doncaster, the proposals for flexibility-as-enrichment apparently failed to prevent the discussion activating worker sensitivity to the market value of demarcation, so that stewards claimed flexibility had actually decreased (1974: 42). Enrichment was seen as purely 'horizontal' (greater work loads) not 'vertical' (assuming management authority), and so viewed as work intensification. The emphasis on job enrichment as a real change came almost entirely from management spokespersons – implying to this writer that ideology and public presentation were the key forces at work.

In the decade and more since WSA, it is difficult to find much sign of the job enrichment strategy being pursued, a fact which tends to confirm its marginality. Moreover, job enrichment was only one of a number of participative strategies which management invoked: they also revamped their consultation system, inaugurated briefing groups, and in the mid-1970s re-jigged the profit-sharing scheme. It seems to make sense once more to see the management concern with job enrichment not as an isolated feature, but as an integral part of a considered strategy of presenting the company as 'participative'. Indeed, on profit-sharing ICI was quite open in stating that such schemes could not be expected to motivate directly, but rather created a general ethos of a distinctive, 'human' employer. In this ICI were probably far more successful than the vast majority of firms, thanks not least to their exceptional persistence.

Nonetheless, even this general approach dissolved in the face of recession. In 1980 a cut of 4000 jobs through rationalisation of the fibres division was announced, followed in 1981 by a merger of plastics and petrochemicals also expensive in jobs losses. In neither case was the much-vaunted consultation machinery used to signal changes (*Financial Times*, 6 March 1981). It seems unlikely that job enrichment retains much viability in the face of sweeping changes from on high (see again Knights and Collinson in this volume).

In short, then, job enrichment at ICI does not fit well with the 'labour process' focus, although the potential for resistance at least is indicated in some of the reports. It fits more readily into a wider analysis of participative and negotiating strategies, within which it has played a relatively marginal role.

'Epoch'

The second company case study has also been the subject of a good deal of public analysis, but to disguise the identity I shall not identify the studies other than my own which are drawn on below.

The company concerned had, like ICI, launched a series of de-manning exercises in the early 1960s. This had damaged a paternalistic reputation among employees, and in a period of innovation elsewhere in the industry this company, too, sought to give its productivity programme a better packaging. At the company level, the result was a statement of philosophy which sought to present the company in stereotypical neo-human relations terms, with much rhetoric concerning the 'joint optimisation' of technical/profitability goals and individual employee development. This, again as in ICI, became the basis of joint working parties between stewards and management at plant level, with a number of job reform experiments as its supposed embodiment. The Epoch efforts involved a particularly prominent management consultancy, so providing a test-bed for an important and influential approach to job redesign.

Two of these experiments have received particular attention. The first, at 'Gooplant' is represented by laudatory analyses in print from at least two managers and one (derivative) account from a consultant. Claims of significant success in raising output and reducing absenteeism are made, supposedly arising from spontaneous operator enthusiasm. Reading between the lines of the most detailed management account, we find that the experiment offered responsible autonomy to workers because the plant was a unique one on which standardised management controls had failed to get a grip. It may be suggested, then, that the decision to delegate was an effort to see if those at the job level, appropriately persuaded and induced, could handle the vagaries. (This raises a general question of whether job autonomy is a feature of automated technology *per se*, or of transitions to new technology during which control systems have not been stabilised and variations made predictable. I shall comment further on this.)

The account thus far seems to fit reasonably well with 'labour process' views. A query is raised, though, by noting that the figures quoted on absenteeism actually show a marked, steady rise for three years after the introduction of the new arrangements (although the text seems to argue the opposite). The misgivings are confirmed in a subsequent study of the Philosophy which checked this experiment out a few years on. The authors found that responsible autonomy, far from 'working', had led to 'fantastic trouble', with each shift going its own way in organising production. Quality of production was 'atrocious', and the main feature was instability. The response was to re-standardise operations over five years (Taylorism?). That the consultant's eulogy referred to above was published at the time of definitive decay of the experiment speaks volumes for the quality of such reports, and caused anger amongst management fighting to regain lost ground.

The other plant, 'Southbank', offered still more ideal circumstances for testing job redesign claims. It was newly constructed, supposedly designed to principles which envisaged job enrichment as an inbuilt feature. The published managerial account claims that the plant was launched on the basis of participation from the ground floor up and, notwithstanding some modifications of work practices in the first couple of years, produced notable results vindicating the Philosophy. The academic re-evaluation of the Philosophy referred to in the previous example is far less critical in this instance. The authors conclude that innovations were far less spectacular than has been claimed, and that the Philosophy actually had only a marginal impact on the plant's design and working. Nonetheless, they accept the claims of union and employee involvement in the establishment of the new system, and that some features of job enrichment survived, although the radical decision not to appoint chargehands or foremen was rescinded due to 'technical problems'.

My own research at this plant suggests the above critique has not been far-reaching enough by a long way, as the observations below indicate. Firstly, my first interviews with shop stewards, and that with the local union official, revealed no knowledge of their supposed participation in plant design, nor of the existence of a book celebrating the establishment and design of the plant. The notion that the plant had been specially designed provoked primarily incredulity, and on several occasions (by managers and operators) I was told I had 'come to the wrong place' if I wanted to see real innovations at work. Management admitted that the Philosophy had been abandoned in all but name, for being too concerned with human factors and too little with technical ones.

A number of areas of conflict had arisen which had motivated the retreat. At the dock, where tankers were offloaded, I was told that problems of dealing with an hierarchical shipside organisation called for an authority figure to deal with captains. However, supervision was also reintroduced at the other end of the process, on the rail gantry, the reason given being that an insecurely fastened hatch caused a fire some miles away in shipment. Both changes suggest the problems of autonomy for management control (and also incidentally show that semi-autonomous groups were tried on the 'periphery', in relatively unautomated parts of the process). The lack of commitment and persistence on management's part – reinforced by a fire in the plant itself which also impelled the re-stressing of 'technical' controls – is also noteworthy.

A further key area of dispute concerned manning and flexibility, and this also shows the importance of pay in the interaction once more. Firstly, the original proposal was that operators would have to become proficient in seven tasks to reach the top salary grade. This, it was complained, became dangerous as some jobs were learned then forgotten in the scramble to qualify for the cash, and eventually flexibility was reduced to four tasks. A few years later the term 'flexibility' itself became a focus of dispute. The union read it as meaning operators could move between tasks on a planned or emergency basis, but rejected management interpretations that emphasised the right of a shift manager to redirect labour within a shift to cover areas of particular pressure arising from production variance or employee absence. This would have reduced plant manning. At the time of my study the dispute had been referred to arbitration.

This flexibility issue re-emerged in the area of the rail gantry with reference to job enrichment. Despite the reintroduction of supervisory regulations, operators could decide on allocation of jobs among them-selves, changing within a shift if they wished (though they rarely did), and also undertook certain checking and clerical duties. Management hoped that in return the employees would be cooperative and flexible. They expressed frustration at the ungratefulness, as they saw it, of the men concerned. Freedom was not used in the 'right way', the operators letting the area of the gantry become filthy once they were issued with gloves, for instance. Initial overmanning had been intended to cover the introduction of new feed-lines, but proposals to add a third were met with demands for a *pro rata* increase in manning. Such manage-ment complaints, mirrored by operator cynicism concerning manage-ment intent, led to claims that people had let the Philosophy down, being unwilling to work as a team.

Once again, a closer look reveals the thinness of the 'labour process' explanatory focus. Nor does simple resort to voluntarist critiques seem adequate. Management adhesion to the principles and the implied strategy of work reform once again emerges as remarkably tenuous. Job enrichment throughout the company appears as an addendum to pro-ductivity bargaining. Moreover, the exercise appears to be far more one in regaining legitimacy after the industrial relations blunders of the early 1960s than of conspiratorial tactics aimed at labour intensifi-cation. Of course the latter was hoped for – but in an idealist fashion, and so poorly worked out. In this case the ideological exercise was probably less successful than in ICI, because there were far fewer and less well fitted strings to the participation bow. Either way, the Philo-sophy seems to have had a fairly minor impact on labour-management relations, and by the mid-1970s was no longer given credence in the company.

The Fate of Job Enrichment
The eventual outcome of both these case studies saw the job enrichment innovations fading from the scene. If this observation can be generalised, it implies that at the least such experiments are not as successful as the omnipotency image of management implicit in the labour process view suggests. After all, if job enrichment were so successful why should management ever revert to other approaches?

Further, if the decline in interest in job enrichment fits that of participation more generally, then the argument is bolstered that it must be analysed as part of those changes and their links to legitimacy crises.

At the moment, only impressionistic comments are possible. It is certainly my own feeling that job enrichment *has* faded from view in Britain along with participation more generally since the recession began to bite hard in 1979. This seems to be supported by an international scan. Already in 1978 one writer, previously a notable enthusiast and a believer in the inevitable progress of 'job power', had reached the conclusion that failure was predominant (cf. Jenkins 1974 with Jenkins 1978). The unions in Sweden, Denmark, the Netherlands, France and elsewhere had grown suspicious and scornful, while very few companies had actually made job reform or any participative form an integral part of their corporate policy, despite their public claims.

Other sources confirm the trend. Marglin (1979) comments that US work reforms 'quickly wilted' once tight labour markets removed the pressure for them. In Sweden the unions became disillusioned with the stagnation of experiments and withdrew from the joint management-union body monitoring innovations (Brannen and Caswill 1978). The SAF also expressed itself dissatisfied with their experience (*ibid*). In Norway, too, the early forecasts by academics of a Patemanesque 'take-off' of interest in participation proved to be a victim of management's ability to obstruct any change which threatened to become too radical and so to question their authority instead of protecting it.[24] Thus a 'stagnation phase' set in there also (Bolweg 1976). In France, interest in job enrichment was also found to have faded with the easing of pressure on management (Berg, Freedman and Freedman 1978).[25]

The depth of management's commitment to job enrichment does not seem very great from available evidence. Apart from that offered in the case studies, two very different investigations, by Nichols and Beynon and by Berg *et al.*, confirm this suspicion. The former quoted the manager who doesn't doubt the Herzberg theory at all, only 'its applicability to industrial situations' (1977: 41). The latter remark on 'the downright indifference among managers' reflected in 'the cyclical quality of managers' interest in reform' (1978: 255). If this indicates the view of job enrichment as a strategy maintained for its appeasement value, whatever the initial hopes, then it explains the syndrome of which Whitsett complains, whereby 'the programs of behavioural scientists are often thought of as luxuries' which are 'cut out first in times where money is tight' (1971: 23). Moreover, even Braverman refers to job enrichment as a response to rebellion (1974: 35), and

Kelly, too, stresses the 'ideological' role of job redesign philosophy through its denial of fundamental economic conflict (1982: 49).

On the other hand, if these impressions prove misleading, and many managements are permanently attached to job enrichment, then some version of the labour process analysis could remain the main resource for explaining the trend. Then again, if labour has successfully invaded the political economy of the schemes, the voluntarist explanation gains ground. Despite the evidence cited above, which supports the approach suggested here, a good deal more considered and impartial investigation is required for a confident conclusion. The claims made elsewhere in this volume about the functionality of redesigned, enlarged jobs in certain industries, have a plausible ring. It may, however, be possible to make these accounts consistent with that suggested here to a degree, if we distinguish redesigning jobs *per se* from exercises which are represented as 'democratic', 'participative' or concerned with 'quality of working life'. It does seem that exercises in redesign which could be sold as participative are far less likely to be so packaged in the current climate. This tentative suggestion offers some prospect for identifying the value of modified labour process analysis.[26]

Another possibility also seems worthy of consideration. Instead of assuming that a major technological transition ushers in a new era, for some of enhanced autonomy for the worker, would it not be reasonable to posit autonomy and the problematic nature of labour control for management as a particular phenomenon of the transitional period in any industry itself? In the early stages routinisation and monitoring of tasks is still in development, and information technology tends to appear in a somewhat higgledy-piggledy fashion. This 'organic' situation may persist for some time, particularly as the new technology continues to be elaborated and refined; but one would not expect this to be necessarily a permanent state of affairs. If this conjecture is sound, then greater room to manoeuvre on the job, which may or may not be tagged 'enrichment', cannot be presumed for the long run, although in the short run they might have the potential to go 'against the stream' of the general trend towards participation schemes.

Conclusion

There seems to be good reason to proceed with at least considerable caution in re-reading job enrichment through any of the 'labour process' perspectives reviewed in this chapter. The more plausible, less sweeping arguments arising from that general approach may afford some basis for developing our comprehension of the processes at work, but so too, it is suggested, may the alternative approach indicated earlier and deriving from the 'cycles' analysis of participation schemes.

There remains one final question important enough to deserve further attention, and that concerns the political implications of those voluntarist analyses that speak of positive-sum control, space for struggle and progress through job redesign. Such arguments rest on the view that employers who concede autonomy, whether through technical necessity or as appeasement, are at one and the same time seeking gain and exhibiting the vulnerability of their control. Job enrichment, it is further suggested, has no intrinsic quality that favours labour or capital – it is a tool which may, potentially, be turned against its wielder.

My response to this is implicit in earlier comments, but requires spelling out beyond the specific critique of positive-sum control notions. It is correct to argue that no analysis of any social process under capitalism can proceed by a priori, determinist fatalism, for this ignores the possibility of contradictions and so unintended outcomes. Nor, incidentally, can it employ the equally abstracted, a priori reasoning that characterises many of the voluntarist counterparts of this view.[27] Much of the assessment must be empirical, and if it can be shown that large numbers of workers have made major strides through job enrichment the task of theory is to account for this, not to deny that bees can fly merely because in theory they should not. My own observations would suggest that an empirical survey reveals precious little in the way of advances, or even opportunities for advance, for labour.

In any case, an empirical approach should not become empiricist; it does not mean that a structural analysis, not readily reducible to a sum of observations of social actions, has no place. And a structural analysis surely could not allow us to imagine that a management device such as job reform in no way bears the marks and so constraints of its social production, even if its result is contested. Such a claim could be possible only if the actual changes introduced are abstracted from the entire context in which they are conceived, designed and applied. Certainly we would no longer think of regarding a piece of machinery as socially neutral in itself – it is to be hoped that the vulgar materialism which detaches the nature of things from the relations within which they are produced has been sufficiently discredited to be dispensed with. Yet such a rejection can only apply *a fortiori* to claims concerning phenomenon like job enrichment.

Job enrichment is, after all, designed by management to serve the needs of capital. Management may not be omnipotent, but they do have extensive resources; they may not be omniscient, but nor are they stupid, and moreover they have the capacity to learn from mistakes in a far more deliberate, collective way than the labour movement.[28] Part of the attraction of job reform, as distinct from some other forms of participation, is that it is 'soft on power', affording little or nothing in the way of concessions on business decision-making and carrying little danger of getting out of hand. Management can thus retain their capacity as gatekeeper to close down an arrangement which gets out of hand – as the case studies and some of the other examples cited earlier illustrate (cf. Zimbalist 1979: xxi). There are other constraints on the impact of changing job structures within the context of existing work-place organisation and worker consciousness, which make it somewhat unlikely that the idealistic notion of a snowballing set of worker demands would necessarily occur, or that more militant and socialist views would follow;[20] sectionalism seems far more likely, for instance, and probably with management encouragement. An evaluation of such real-world constraints leads to an assessment of the likelihood of major employee advances through job reform which lies short of utterly impossible, but somewhere between there and highly improbable.

If such considerations take us still further beyond the 'nitty-gritty' focus of labour process, then provided that we do not forget the importance of the activity of work itself this cannot be a bad thing. For it seems that the effort of the approach to restore attention to class power and class struggle has ironically tended to diminish the scope and strength of class analysis. Moreover, in consequence the subsequent debate has reproduced once more all the variants of Marxist thinking, displaying reformism, determinism, economism, voluntarism, idealism, all furbished as if newly discovered. In short, there has been no magical resolution of the old arguments under the labour process spell; incantation continues to prevail over recantation.

Notes

1. See, for example, Strauss, 1968; Fox, 1974; Anthony, 1977.
2. Similar observations, though less rigorously developed, are offered by Ernest Mandel around this period too – see his 1975, p. 583.
3. See, for example, Elger, 1979; Friedman, 1977; Cressey and MacInnes, 1980. Montgomery's analysis (1979) of worker resistance to scientific management strategies in the United States in the first three decades of the twentieth century affords a similar message.
4. See, for example, the case studies examined by Hyman and Elger, 1981.
5. This argument concerning the problems of base/superstructure arguments, and arguing for the internality of all relations of production within the capitalist mode, is developed in Corrigan, Ramsay and Sayer, 1978, 1980.
6. Murray also discusses the use of other means of decentralising production – such as the use of outwork or sub-contracts – which increase the flexibility and reduce the cost of production without necessarily intensifying labour.
7. This point is an elaboration of that made by Coriat, 1979. It appears to resurrect the circumstances described in more orthodox industrial sociological studies as 'craft

administration' (Stinchcombe 1959) or 'organic systems of management' (Burns and Stalker 1961).

8. See, for example, Halévy, 1922, p. 152; Child, 1969, p. 48, both on Whitleyism.

9. The general pattern of results of participation schemes are discussed at length in Ramsay, 1980, 1982.

10. A number of recent efforts to argue for potential benefits from job 'enrichment' adopt this form: Wood and Kelly, 1982; Kelly (chapter 3 in this volume); P. Edwards, 1983; Rose and Jones (chapter 5 in this volume) all afford examples.

11. Cressey and MacInnes, 1980. Ironically, most revivals of the separation in its new form remark approvingly on this critique, for reasons explained below.

12. It should be noted that a similar analysis of control, by Cressey *et al.* 1982, is taken by them to imply that 'space' for struggle exists, not severe limits. This conclusion seems quite at odds with the logic of the rest of their argument.

13. See, for example, Hill, 1979; Glyn and Harrison, 1980; and cf. the report by the Department of Industry reported in *British Business* in September 1981 (*Financial Times*, 7 September 1981).

14. Ramsay, 1983a, provides evidence to this effect on, *inter alia*, Japan, the USA and the Netherlands.

15. Cf. Swartz, 1981, p. 67. Brown, 1976, observes that many of the classic human relations studies involved female employees. An impressionistic scan of the Strathclyde area also affords more than one example of job enrichment for largely female workforces known to the author.

16. See, for example, Hulin, 1971. The work of Baldamus, 1961, indicates the potential advantages of rhythmic work over more varied tasks as well as their costs.

17. *Financial Times*, 28 January 1975 and 30 July 1976. Cf. also Hunnius, 1979, p. 512.

18. Nichols and Beynon, 1977, illustrate management's problem in gaining acquiescence even from employees who seemed politically fairly conservative.

19. Blackler and Brown, 1975, referring to a review of research by Cummings and Salipante (1975).

20. Carey, 1979. Carey's comments provoked a fierce exchange on the subject with Emery, one of his chief targets.

21. Daniel, 1970, 1973; Daniel and McIntosh, 1972, and his contributions to a debate with Goldthorpe (Daniel 1969, 1971).

22. The researchers seek a variety of excuses for the failure of experiments among manual staff to produce supportive evidence, such as a 'swamping' of results by rows over holidays and threats of plant closure (1980–81), or a lack of evidence on work quality (1970: 77, 78).

23. Now revealed as a study of ICI by M. Hales, 1980 (q.v.).

24. Based on personal discussions with researchers involved in the Norwegian project. 'Patemanesque' refers to the influential work of Pateman, 1970.

25. Cf. de Mann (1978) on the Netherlands, describing the way academics sought to play the game of respectability and status-enhancement with government and employers, to the fury of the unions.

26. Nevertheless, arguments that the rise and fall of attention to different techniques in the management literature is merely 'faddish' tend to underrate the importance of ideological practices, seeing them as somehow less 'real' than other practices.

27. As in the many publications by Hirst, Hindess and numerous collaborators; for a review and critique see Corrigan and Sayer, 1978.

28. This does not mean memories do not fade, and that imperfect strategies are unrepeated – as the 'cycles' analysis discussed earlier itself confirms.

29. That this militancy does not necessarily follow is well illustrated in what is a far more favourable context on the face of it – worker cooperatives. Wajcman, 1983, shows how defeat is likely and can sap belief in alternatives; Greenberg, 1981, finds a growth of 'possessive individualism', tending away from socialist views.

References

Aglietta, M. (1979), *A Theory of Capitalist Regulation*, London: New Left Books.
Anthony, P.D. (1977), *The Ideology of Work*, London: Tavistock.
Baldamus, W. (1961), *Efficiency and Effort*, London: Tavistock.
Beechey, V. (1977), 'Some notes on female wage labour in capitalist production', *Capital and Class*, 3, Autumn, 45–66.
Beechey, V. (1978), 'Women and production: a critical analysis of some sociological theories of women's work', in A. Kuhn and A.M. Wolpe, *Feminism and Materialism: Women and Modes of Production*, London: Routledge and Kegan Paul, 155–197.
Beechey, V. (1982), 'The sexual division of labour and the labour process: a critical assessment of Braverman', in S. Wood (ed.), *The Degradation of Work*, London: Hutchinson, 54–73.
Berg, I. Freedman, M. and Freedman, M. (1978), *Managers and Work Reform: A Limited Engagement*, New York: Free Press.
Blackler, F.H.M. and Brown, C. (1975), 'The impending crisis in job redesign', *Journal of Occupational Psychology*, 48, 187–193.
Blauner, R. (1964), *Alienation and Freedom: The Factory Worker and His Industry*, Chicago: University of Chicago Press.
Bolweg, J.F. (1976), *Job Design and Industrial Democracy*, The Hague: Martinus Nijhoff.
Bosquet, M. (1977), 'The meaning of "job enrichment"', in his *Capitalism in Crisis and Everyday Life*, Hassocks: Harvester Press.
Brannen, P. and Caswill, C. (1978), 'Changes in law and values', in D. Gregory (ed.), *Work Organization: Swedish Experience and British Context*, London: SSRC, 245–254.
Braverman, H. (1974), *Labor and Monopoly Capital: The Degradation of Work in the Twentieth Century*, New York: Monthly Review Press.
Brown, R. (1976), 'Women as employees: some comments on research in industrial sociology', in D.L. Barker and S. Allen (eds.), *Dependence and Exploitation in Work and Marriage*, London: Longman.
Burns, T. and Stalker, G.M. (1961), *The Management of Innovation*, London: Tavistock.
Carey, A. (1979), 'The Norwegian experiments in democracy at work: a critique and a contribution to reflexive sociology', *Australia and New Zealand Journal of Sociology*, 15(1), March, 13–23.
Child, J. (1969), *British Management Thought*, London: George Allen and Unwin.
Clegg, C.W., Nicholson, N., Ursell, G., Blyton, P.R. and Wall, T.D. (1978), 'Managers' attitudes towards industrial democracy', *Industrial Relations Journal*, 9(3), 4–17.
Coriat, B. (1980), 'The restructuring of the assembly line: a new "economy of time and control"'. Originally published in *Sociologie du Travail*, 1, 1979. Reprinted in translation in *Capital and Class*, 11, Summer, 34–43.
Corrigan, P.R.D., Ramsay, H. and Sayer, D. (1978), *Socialist Construction and Marxist Theory*, London: Macmillan.
Corrigan, P.R.D., Ramsay, H. and Sayer, D. (1980), 'The state as a relation of production', in Corrigan (ed.), *Capitalism, State Formation and Marxist Theory*, London: Quartet, (a substantially rewritten version of 1977).
Corrigan, P.R.D. and Sayer D. (1978), 'Hindess and Hirst: a critical review', *Socialist Register*, 194–214.
Cotgrove, S., Dunham, J. and Vanplew, C. (1971), 'The nylon spinners: a case study in productivity bargaining and job enrichment', London: George Allen and Unwin.
Cressey, P. and MacInnes, J. (1980), 'Voting for Ford: industrial democracy, and the control of labour', *Capital and Class*, 11, Summer, 5–33.
Cressey, P., MacInnes, J. and Norris, G. (1982), 'The modern enterprise, shop-floor organisation and the structure of control', in D. Dunkerley and G. Salaman (eds.), *The International Year Book of Organization Studies 1981*, London: Routledge and Kegan Paul 271–302.

Cronin, J.E. (1979), *Industrial Conflict in Modern Britain*, London: Croom Helm.

Cronin, J.E. (1980), 'Stages, cycles and insurgency: the economics of unrest', in T.K. Hopkins and I. Wallerstein (eds.), *Process of the World System*, London: Sage, 101–118.

Cummings, T.G. and Salipante, P. (1975), 'The development of research-based strategies for improving the quality of work life', Paper to NATO Conference on Personal Goals and Work Design in Blackler and Brown, *op cit.*

Daniel, W.W. (1969), 'Industrial behaviour and orientation to work – a critique', *Journal of Management Studies*, **6**(3), October, 266–275.

Daniel, W.W. (1970), 'Beyond the wage-work bargain', London: PEP.

Daniel, W.W. (1971), 'Productivity bargaining and orientation to work – a rejoinder to Goldthorpe', *Journal of Management Studies*, **8**(3), October, 329–335.

Daniel, W.W. (1973), 'Understanding employee behaviour in its context: illustrations from productivity bargaining', in J. Child (ed.), *Man and Organisation*, London: Allen and Unwin, 39–62.

Daniel, W.W. and McIntosh, M. (1972), *The Right to Manage*, London: PEP.

de Man, H. (1978), 'Social science in the game of Dutch labour relations: the case of the COP experiments in organisational democracy'. Paper to European Institute for Advanced Studies in Management Conference on 'Power and Influence in Organisations', Brussels, May (mimeo).

Dubois, P. (1978), 'New forms of industrial conflict', in C. Crouch and A. Pizzorno (eds.), *The Resurgence of Class Conflict in Western Europe since 1968, Vol. II, Comparative Analyses*, London: Macmillan, 1–34.

Edwards, P.K. (1983), 'Control, compliance and conflict: analysing variation in the capitalist labour process', University of Warwick (mimeo), February.

Elger, A. (1979), 'Valorization and deskilling: a critique of Braverman', *Capital and Class*, 7, Spring, 58–99.

Fox, A. (1974), *Man Mismanagement*, London: Hutchinson.

Friedman, A. (1977), *Industry and Labour: Class Struggle at Work and Monopoly Capitalism*, London: Macmillan.

Glynn, A. and Harrison, J. (1980), *The British Economic Disaster*, London: Pluto.

Greenberg, E.S. (1981), 'Industrial self-management and political attitudes', *American Political Science Review*, 75, 29–42.

Hales, M. (1980), 'Living thinkwork: where do labour processes come from?', London: CSE Books.

Halévy, E. (1922), 'The present state of the social question in England', in *The Era of Tyrannies*, London: Allen Lane.

Hill, T.P. (1979), *Profits and Rates of Return*, Paris: OECD.

Hulin, C.L. (1971), 'Individual differences and job enrichment – the case against general treatments', in J. Maher (ed.), *New Perspectives in Job Enrichment*, Van Norstrand Reinhold, 159–192.

Hunnius, G. (1979), 'The politics of work humanization and power-sharing', *Economic Analysis and Workers' Management*, 13(4).

Hyman, R. and Elger, A. (1981), 'Job controls, the employers' offensive, and alternative strategies', *Capital and Class*, 15, Autumn, 115–149.

Jenkins, D. (1974), *Job Power*, London: Heinemann.

Jenkins, D. (1978), 'Forces and failures in European industrial democracy', *Manchester Business School Review*, 3(1), Autumn, 11–18.

Kelly, J.E. (1978), 'A reappraisal of sociotechnical systems theory', *Human Relations*, **31**(12), 1069–1099.

Kelly, J.E. (1980), 'The costs of job redesign: a preliminary analysis', *Industrial Relations Journal*, **11**(3), July/August, 22–34.

Kelly, J.E. (1982), *Scientific Management, Job Redesign and Work Performance*, London: Academic Press.

Littler, C.R. (1982), *The Development of the Labour Process in Capitalist Societies*, London: Heinemann.

Littler, C.R. and Salaman, G. (1982), 'Bravermania and beyond: recent theories of the labour process', in *Sociology*, **16(2)**, May, 251–269.

Lupton, T., Tanner, I. and Schnelle, T. (1979), 'Manufacturing system design in Europe', in C.L. Cooper and E. Mumford (eds.), *The Quality of Working Life in Western and Eastern Europe*, London: Associated Business Press, 44–75.

Mandel, E. (1975), *Late Capitalism*, London: New Left Books.

Marglin, S.A. (1979), 'Catching flies with honey: an inquiry into management initiatives to humanize work', in *Economic Analysis and Workers' Management*, **XIII(4)**, 473–485.

Martin, A. (1976), 'From joint consultation to joint decision-making: the redistribution of workplace power in Sweden', *Current Sweden*, **111**, April.

Melman, S. (1958), *Decision-Making and Productivity*, Oxford: Blackwell.

Montgomery, D. (1979), *Workers' Control in America*, Cambridge: CUP.

Murray, F. (1983), 'The decentralisation of production – the decline of the mass-collective worker?', in *Capital and Class*, **19**, Spring, 74–99.

Nichols, T. (1975), 'The sociology of accidents and the social production of industry injury', in G. Esland *et al.* (eds.), *People and Work*, Edinburgh: Holmes MacDougall, 217–229.

Nichols, T. and Beynon, H. (1977), *Living with Capitalism*, London: Routledge and Kegan Paul.

Nycander, S. (1978), 'The importance of the industrial relations setting in Sweden', in Gregory (ed.), op. cit. 19–27.

Palloix, C. 'The labour process: from Fordism to neo-Fordism', in Conference of Socialist Economists Pamphlet No. 1, *The Labour Process and Class Strategies*, London: Stage 1.

Pateman, C. (1970), *Participation and Democratic Theory*, Cambridge: CUP.

Paul, W.J. and Robertson, K.B. (with F. Herzberg) (1970), *Job Enrichment and Employee Motivation*, London: Gower.

Ramsay, H. (1977), 'Cycles of control: worker participation in sociological and historical perspective', *Sociology*, **11(3)**, September, 481–506.

Ramsay, H. (1980), 'Phantom participation: patterns of power and conflict', in *Industrial Relations Journal*, **11(3)**, July/August.

Ramsay, H. (1982), 'Participation for whom? a critical review of worker participation in theory and practice', Ph.D thesis, University of Durham, April.

Ramsay, H. (1983a), 'Evolution or cycle? Worker participation in the 1970s and 1980s', in C. Crouch and F. Heller (eds.), *International Yearbook of Organizational Democracy. Vol. I. Organizational Democracy and Political Processes*, London: Wiley, 203–225.

Ramsay, H. (1983b), 'An international participation cycle: variations on a recurring theme', in S. Clegg, G. Dow and P. Boreham (eds.), *The State, Class and the Recession*, London: Croom Helm, 257–317.

Roberts, C. and Wedderburn, D. (1974), 'ICI and the unions: the place of job enrichment in the weekly staff agreement', Report to the TUC Social Sciences Working Party, mimeo, Imperial College, Industrial Sociology Unit.

Roeber, J. (1975), *Social Change at Work*, London: Duckworth.

Stinchcombe, A.L. (1959), 'Bureaucratic and craft administration of production: a comparative study', *Administrative Science Quarterly*, September, 168–187.

Strauss, G. (1968), 'Human relations – 1968 style', *Industrial Relations*, **7**, 262–276 (reprinted in D.F. McFarland, 1971, 107–127).

Swartz, D. (1981), 'New forms of worker participation: a critique of quality of working life', *Studies in Political Economy*, **5**, Spring, 55–78.

Trist, E., Higgin, G.W., Murray, H. and Pollock A.B. (1963), *Organizational Choice*, London: Tavistock.

Wajcman, J. (1983), *Women in Control*, Milton Keynes: Open University Press.

Wall, T.D. and Lischerson, J.A. (1977), *Worker Participation: A critique of the literature and some fresh evidence*, Maidenhead: McGraw-Hill.

Whitsett, D.A. (1971), 'Job enrichment, human resources and profitability', in J. Maher (ed.), *New Perspectives in Job Enrichment*, New York: Van Norstrand Reinhold, 21–34.

Wood, S. and Kelly, J. (1982), 'Taylorism, responsible autonomy and management strategy', in S. Wood (ed.), *The Degradation of Work*, London: Hutchinson, 74–89.

Zimbalist, A. (1979), 'Introduction', in Zimbalist (ed.), *Case Studies on the Labor Process*, New York: Monthly Review Press.

5 Managerial Strategy and Trade Union Responses in Work Reorganisation Schemes at Establishment Level

Michael Rose and Bryan Jones

Introduction

Is industrial capital in the process of redrawing the 'frontier of control' with labour that existed for most of the post-war period? At first sight there appears little doubt that the combination of depression and an economic and political programme that has removed protection from 'market forces' has enabled employers and managers to roll back both formal and informal trade union influence. It is often said that the current industrial restructuring of Britain constitutes an economic and social experiment for the advocates of neo-liberalism.

The thesis that we present here is that the impact of these changes on company and plant level relations between managements and work-groups also constitutes a critical test for theories of managerial control of work organisation and industrial relations processes, certainly within a British context, perhaps more widely.

Marxist and Marxist-inspired theories of work organisation and industrial relations, as well as various strands of organisation theory, emphasise that control of work group behaviour, in the performance of jobs and over the expression of grievances, stems directly from high level managerial 'strategies'. The present political and economic conjuncture surely supplies organisational controllers with unique opportunities to develop and apply such strategies. The time is thus highly opportune to test the adequacy and relative merits of the various concepts of managerial strategies of control. In particular we might expect the well-publicised dismantling of many shopfloor union checks on the prescription of work loads and content of work practices to make possible, and be achieved through, more forthright strategies for re-organised work and re-arranged bargaining structures which will maximise management 'control'.

Our study of relevant changes in six industrial establishments over the past two years suggests two severe problems with prevailing theories. (Some technical details are provided about the six cases in the

Appendix.) Firstly, that current usages of the terms 'strategy' and 'control' are somewhat misleading guides both to actual management conduct and to the causes of particular outcomes in work organisation and industrial relations. Secondly, that the character of managerial control methods that are developing out of the current industrial flux are likely to be uneven and, in the longer term, limited in their emasculation of plant-level influence.

The doubtful conceptual adequacy of prevailing theory is examined in the second section of this paper. In brief our claim there is that the pursuit of managerial policies in the organisation and re-organisation of work has to be more clearly distinguished from policies that might be aimed at industrial relations. Marxist-inspired theories tend to ignore one of these two spheres, or merge them together in order to claim that changes in each are attributable to coordinated strategy seeking to push back an undifferentiated 'frontier of control' to managements' general advantage.

In no sense do we deny that managements have sought and achieved objectives such as changed manning levels and intensified workloads at labour's expense since the 1979/80 watershed. However, in our view many of the changes that have occurred and are still occurring in the spheres of both work and labour-management representative institutions weaken rather than confirm many notions of the force of generalised and coherent strategies of control.

In their oversight of these factors there are parallels between some Marxist approaches and organisation theory perspectives whether of a structural-determinants or of a 'strategic choice' type. Many attribute to managerial action a high level of coherence and fixity of purpose; this may follow from the assumption that an innovation as important as a work reorganisation scheme (WRS) can be understood *only* in the light of the concept of deliberate strategy. In a few cases, the term 'strategy' seems to be adopted without sufficient consideration of its logical implications, much as it is used in journalism and popular discourse. Yet coordinated and consistent campaign plans may often *not* be explicitly formulated at senior levels in British companies. *Or* if they are worked out (and such plans are, of course, made in some companies), perhaps at lower managerial levels, then their pursuit across several areas of enterprise activity as well as work processes (e.g. in changes to bargaining and consultative arrangements) may limit the extent to which they can be said to have pushed back a one-dimensional 'frontier of control' which figured as a prime objective of an original strategic plan.[1]

Our case-study evidence in the third section of the paper indicates not only that the relevant managerial policy and practice lacks the detailed 'strategic' character so often attributed to it, but that such is the unevenness of current changes to work organisation and plant bargaining arrangements, in some respects circumstances are improving the prospects for *continuing* influence of unions and work groups in *new* areas of local management decisions. The two overriding reasons advanced for these linked hypotheses are firstly that the controls over the workforce that are currently being sought are often essentially interim tactics rather than a central objective of management's current policies; and secondly that the process of implementation of WRS policy objectives is, or becomes, more open-ended than textbook management suggests because of the administrative and social structure of the firm.

The most relevant features of this structure for this discussion are: the administrative divisions of the company and its management groups; the prevailing and desired functional organisation of work roles and task structures; the philosophy or ideology professed; and the history and character of the workforce's representative institutions – including, in our cases, the varying tactics pursued by union representatives in multi-union establishments.

Our account must begin, however, with a brief assessment and classification of the major changes affecting labour-management relationships in Britain over the past three or four years.

(1) Five Aspects of Control

We shall be arguing in the course of this paper that the concept of employer or management *strategy* is fraught with problems. We have a similar, if less acute, unease about the term *control*, particularly as it appears in such expressions as the 'frontier of control' – although the latter expression formed part of the title of a research project whose results we shall refer to in our discussion (Rose and Jones 1983). But for the moment, we shall continue to use both of these terms, and begin with what will probably seem an uncontroversial claim; namely, that it is widely believed that there is currently occurring an offensive by British employers to shift back the frontier of control from a position it had reached following the advance of labour in the 1960s and 1970s (Hyman and Elger 1981).

Most of the facts utilised in such arguments are well-known and not in any sort of dispute; for example, figures for plant-closures and redundancies, strike-rates and defeats of the labour side in strikes, the programme of restrictive legislation, and so on. There appears to be an equally obvious and economical way to interpret these facts: i.e. that they demonstrate clearly that employers have been enjoying an increase in their power at the expense of labour. It seems warranted to go on to make the additional claim that one result of employers' gains in market power is a regained effective control of employees, and that this is both an aim and a result of an unfolding offensive by employers as a whole, which will have a counterpart in employer and manager strategies at plant level.

But an assertion such as this latter one is rather more complicated and far less readily justifiable than it seems. To show why, we shall shortly examine the notion of strategy and then present our research evidence. But first, we want to point out that when the 'Employers' Offensive' is evoked at least five major aspects of control by employers seem to be involved, although this is not always well recognised by contributors to the debate. Once again, abundant evidence of employer action under most of these could be cited but we shall merely call attention to well-attested trends. The key areas we wish to distinguish are the following: work operations, employment practices, superordinate-subordinate relations, employee representation, and what we term 'interpretative frameworks'.

(a) Operations and work patterns

The wide range of industrial changes in the past few years, as firms contract or diversify product ranges and at least some new industries replace older ones, makes it advisable to assess work organisation aspects in the context of firms' field of 'operations'. A focus on production processes, work routines *per se*, or a particular definition of the labour process may miss the wider context of change.

Rationalisation has meant switches away from conventionally manned work processes to new, less labour intensive or entirely re-designed processes on 'Greenfield' sites. Here and elsewhere through redundancy exercises and the merging of previously 'demarcated' skilled and semi-skilled operations 'flexibility' in task repertoires may, in many instances, have 'intensified' work loads (Lane 1982; Massey and Meegan 1982; Kelly, chapter 3 in this volume; Ramsay, chapter 4 in this volume).

But these changes, along with frequently over-estimated automation by microelectronic technology, are more varied in terms of their effect on job control and administrative coordination than a straightforward reference to 'intensification' of labour would suggest. Where, for example, electricians are trained in electronics to make up for a shortage of technicians, or when administrative hierarchies are flattened to cut costs and speed communication by eliminating middle management grades, then the consequent pattern of 'flexible' working can have different control applications than simply adding a few maintenance tasks to operative jobs or vice versa. For these reasons we identified and concentrated on 'Work Reorganisation Schemes' and not just labour reductions as a key feature of current management initiatives.

(b) Employment practices
Most publicity here has gone to 'innovation' in employment practice utilised by Japanese firms operating in Britain (White and Trevor 1983) though few cases are known of British companies who are embarking on wholesale imitation of 'post-Confucian' arrangements. Much more ample evidence is to hand of more piecemeal moves involving new grading schemes, the provision of new or novel fringe benefits, extended training, etc. Where such changes are occurring they can be viewed as signs of a trend towards a more particularistic relationship between companies and individual employees, which in some cases may be interpreted as growing 'familiarism' but in others has been acquiring a potentially authoritarian character with the introduction of computer systems capable of logging individual performance as well as filing comprehensive personal data.[2]

(c) Superordinate-subordinate relations
Management periodicals and other material intended for management consumption have talked excitedly of the prospect that 'prerogatives' are being reclaimed on a wide scale (cf. Fazey 1983; The Economist 1982). The popular press regularly headlines the defeat of 'disorderly' actions such as strike-threats or union opposition to disciplinary decisions. In workplaces, managers or supervisors who might have reached informal accommodations with worker representatives at an earlier date now insist upon applying formal rules about procedures. Many employees no doubt feel that in their general dealings with superiors they must take care not to appear wilfully non-compliant or 'insubordinate'. Along with these changes go signs of more 'positive' alterations in the relations of managers and managed, or at least of aspirations towards them, as when employer spokesmen evoke the partnership between labour and management which they can success-fully glimpse behind the veil of the wages-contract.

(d) Employee representation
One can argue that many employers have taken their cue from the government and adopted a step-by-step approach to union-based employee representation, merely aiding its gradual erosion by enforcing agreements about provision of facilities or access strictly to the letter whilst subscriptions lapse and efficient shop stewards become hard to find amongst the rank-and-file. But there is no shortage of

speculation that much tougher anti-union legislation can be expected, together with further restriction of shopfloor union activity; the example of anti-union moves amongst American employers is often cited in this regard (Davis 1982). It is even tempting to argue that the interest many managers have maintained in 'participation' is proof that they recognise the importance of unions for worker involvement in plant affairs, which they would prefer to achieve through alternative institutions, the two most commonly quoted ones being QWL programmes and Quality Circle devices. Thus, just as corporatism at the level of the state has receded with government hostility to tripartite bargaining, so the 'microcorporatism' of establishment-level industrial relations is in retreat and might seem to be headed for eventual abandonment.

(e) Interpretative frameworks

Whilst government figures evoke a 'new spirit in British industry' many signs can be found of a parallel effort by business and industrial spokesmen seemingly intended to modify substantially the mental sets with which employees operate. Common themes are the severity of external economic competition, the gravity of the industrial crisis, the inevitability of 'structural unemployment', the need for unity in the face of the danger, and the irresponsibility or worse of persons who disagree with an analysis along such lines (echoing what has been labelled in Whitehall circles as the 'TINA approach' – 'There is No Alternative').

If the 'employers' offensive' is to be taken in a rigorous sense then we should expect to find, in a 'typical' case, a planned and successful effort to reassert managerial control in each of the foregoing five areas. British Leyland is often taken as such a case – and one which also seems to demonstrate clearly the close harmony of employer and government intentions. Some of the better known features of the BL case – confrontation with unions, exemplary dismissal of shopfloor militants, direct propaganda campaigns, massive redundancies, robotisation of jobs, introduction of a directive style of management, projection of a unitarist management ideology, and other anachronistically authoritarian actions – seem to indicate unambiguously that strategies that could be termed 'directive-militarist' in character are a continuation of current political circumstances.

Yet a crucial question is to what extent can BL be taken as the paradigm case, not so much on the grounds that it is the best-known one, which is incontestable, but on the grounds that it is a model which has been or will be followed on such a wide scale that it can be taken as typical? We return to such questions later. But first, we need to say something more about the difficulties with the 'strategy' concept to which we have already referred.

(2) Concepts of Strategy and Control

The term control is used in the literature on industrial relations and work organisation in various ways: as a synonym for the capacity to exercise power, as an administrative network of rules and conventions, as a technical system for the regulation of work effort and task fulfilment, and in a more general and looser sense as institutionalised checks on the variability of actions and behaviour of individuals and agents.[3]

A thorough analysis of the implications of these different uses is beyond the available time and space we have here. In the near future we hope to present another review of the relevant literature on this topic. Our immediate concern is with the relation between management re-organisations of the work process and their attempts to change relationships with plant level unions through local bargaining arrangements. To make clear the differences between our own approach and some of the theoretical assumptions currently available it seems necessary to point out the absence (or understatement) in prevailing perspectives of a satisfactory conception of the social structure of the firm: *within* which the pursuit and implementation of various types of control over behaviour and processes takes place and as a *result of changes in which* different forms of controls may be secondary rather than primary consequences. A brief review of some representative theories suggests that such omissions may be behind a tendency to inflate the role of management strategy as the source and vehicle for changes in organisational controls and a related inability to specify satisfactorily the determinants of such strategy.

Strategies, and the controls which are presumed to follow automatically from their execution by management, are either taken as expressions of functional imperatives which traverse the economy and the industry or, conversely, as an internally generated process by management which is adduced to explain why these imperatives can be denied or overridden. In the next section we try to demonstrate (with evidence from our case studies) how management approaches to the change of work processes and industrial relations lack the characteristics of a detailed plan of campaign implied by the term 'strategy'.

The weaknesses in existing theories arise largely because different forms of a 'problem of control' are posited as a manifold feature of industrial organisation and management actions are then read backwards from these instances and interpreted as strategies to resolve them. In this way other processes and conditions which might have given rise to the control aspects come to be overlooked. Of particular concern to our current analysis is the manner in which these misleading characterisation of a management strategy of control lead to a conflation of analytically and possibly empirically distinct areas of management activity such as the organisation of work within the operations sphere and the conduct of industrial relations in the area of employee representation.

Within the field of 'organisation theory' the taxonomic approach of the early Aston school and of Joan Woodward was distinctive for associating managerial adoption of distinct control systems directly with such structuring parameters as production technology and market environment. Similarly labour process perspectives such as Braverman deduce the central Tayloristic organisational strategies for the control of administrative and production work from underlying functional imperatives of surplus value extraction and competitive capital accumulation. This kind of emphasis upon determination by universal structuring conditions exposes these explanations to criticism for failing adequately to allow for variation in the predicted organisational outcomes. Thus Braverman is criticised for his cursory dismissal of non-Taylorist managerial techniques and the strategic centrality of organised work resistance.[1] Likewise the Aston and Woodward approaches were found wanting because of the various exceptions to the administrative systems predicted as following from technologies and scale of operations (Child 1972; 1973).

On the basis of implicit or explicit reference to the economic sovereignty of the 'giant' modern corporation both organisation theorists and writers inspired by Marxist assumptions have instead emphasised the scope for a range of choice in the adaption to, or manipulation of, the external economic and internal technical environments. For Child managerial coalitions could align a preferred product market with internal modes of work organisation allowing different 'trade-offs' between efficiency and indulgency preferences (Child 1973).

Later versions of segmented labour market theory, notably the work of Richard Edwards, suggest a similar level of scope for differing organisational strategies which increasingly swap rigid forms of work control for employee conformity to corporate norms of responsibility. Schemes which can be chosen as alternatives or supplements to historical precursors such as Taylorism were largely made possible by the corporations' relative autonomy from market pressures up until the mid-1970s (Edwards 1979).

However whilst these perspectives tend to elevate managerial strategy into a relatively unconstrained initiator of potentially variable organisational schemes (including, within the organisation theory perspectives, the manipulation of the technological constraints by adjustments of 'socio-technical' job redesign), the corporate sovereignty over the 'environmental' pressures which makes organisational controls creations of top level strategic management appears much less assured when faced with *either* massive internal challenges from the workforce (Britain in the mid-1970s?) and collapse of product markets (Britain and America in the 1980s).

We would argue that the vulnerability of internal systems to such pressures demonstrates not just the limitations of postulating securely based strategic choice of controls but the inadvisability of characterising the observed arrangements as strategic creations in the first place. But first consider apparently more comprehensive accounts of the bases of managerial control strategies.

Marxist accounts of managerial strategy in British industry *have* attempted to identify the broader economic pressures that might be responsible for the coordination of industrial relations and production policy within the enterprise. But, once again, strategy and control are presented as a mutually conditioning pair which leads to the economic constraints and the social structure of the enterprise being reduced to this single polarity.

Andy Friedman provides a dual characterisation of managerial strategy into the 'direct control' policies of Tayloristic work-organisation and rule by managerial prerogative (essentially the same as Braverman's version) and the granting of 'responsible autonomy' to 'central' groups of workers in the execution and administration of their immediate work routines. Trade union influence, or the technical expertise of different groups of workers, constitutes *internal* constraints encouraging 'top managers' to cede responsible autonomy at different periods. The *external* pressures constraining managers to adopt one policy or the other are taken from Friedman's case study of the Coventry motor car industry. Short-term pressures of demand and competition are increasingly overlaid by the more fundamental constraints of the industry's product cycle. *Within* the enterprise the institutionalisation of bargaining into 'procedure' provides another tool for tying down emergent work-group controls to minor and temporarily acceptable levels of devolved responsibility (Friedman 1977: 78–9, 99–102, 109–11).

Our objections to this *kind* of analysis (for it shares some elements with segmented labour market theories and with 'radical' industrial relations perspectives) are not that management do not gain from some of these arrangements, nor that they do not perceive such gains. The problem, as we see it, is that the various forms and levels of controls are not explained on their own terms. Instead, various features of British enterprise organisation, work group autonomy and bargaining relationships are mistaken for subsidiary elements of the overriding strategy of control.

In this way different aspects of what we have termed the sphere of employee representation (collective bargaining, consultative and participatory arrangements) comes to be presented in an instrumentalist fashion: as institutions which can be developed and discarded as and when the dictates of a control strategy require. In this way writers as diverse as Richard Hyman and Alan Flanders characterise different aspects of employee representation as instruments for securing compliance and control in the sphere of work organisation.[5] Again it should be stressed that it is not being claimed that participation schemes, or agreements on procedure will not, and have not been used to support policy objectives in another sphere. What *is* highly problematic is the teleological element in such accounts. The pattern of developments in one or several firms may not have arisen as expressions of a strategy (in the usual sense of a planned and coordinated plan of detailed objectives and implementation) but as only contingently related decisions arising from different short-term or localised pressures.

Similarly the bifurcated characterisation of strategies into responsible autonomy versus direct control, or participation versus repression risks (without a more detailed differentiation) becoming trivial as events over long periods of time have to be compressed into one of two categories of explanation. If the tide is always either on the ebb or the flow then the proposition may be accurate but not of much more utility.

To link control over work organisation and process with strategic managements' use of spheres such as industrial relations can be doubly reductionist. It ignores the problematic character of *vertical* integration between management activities. But there is a variety of evidence to suggest that at least some corporate-level executives in Britain place a low salience on policies for the regulation of their labour affairs (Winkler 1974; Marsh 1982; Loveridge 1981). As a result, the element of strategy for the individual plant is extremely limited as Loveridge's analysis of the federal firm has especially shown. Consider secondly the *horizontal* dimension of managerial policy-making: between different functions and administrative specialisations at plant or divisional level. These aspects suggest a complexity that may seriously handicap the feasibility of any 'strategic' pursuit of coordinating control objectives through the various departments and dimensions of management activity that might be concerned. The apparent failure of even the supposedly tougher-minded American manufacturing managements to execute strategic coordination of productivity exercises indicates the complexity of planning and execution required of their frequently less professionalised British counterparts (cf. Judson 1982).

Finally it is necessary to recognise that control in the organisation of work processes (and the limitation of union influence in related labour relations questions) may conceivably be only subsidiary (though linked) aspects of management strategies which are more likely to be aimed at goals of financial control, sales and marketing. Similarly in several of the case studies, to which we now turn, firms' 'strategy' for the recession was primarily seen as a switch to new products and more reliable methods of producing and delivering these rather than a concern to subordinate labour and routinise the work process further.

(3) The Implementation of Work Re-organisation Schemes

In order to see whether management strategy can be comprehensive enough, in the current depression, to take systematic advantage of weaknesses in the powers of unions at company and plant level we need to ask in what ways work re-organisation schemes and industrial relations policies might be effective enough to establish new levels of control. Several of the theories reviewed above might lead us to expect a common strategy aimed at reducing unions' and workers' say in the planning, direction and execution of work tasks. Management efforts towards these re-organisations would be pursued through a dismantling of union 'suzerainty' over administrative controls and the overthrow, or at least the by-passing, of forums for negotiation or consultation on changes.

The evidence both from our case study firms and the reports of others strongly suggests that all of this scenario is incorrect both as a generalisation and in terms of detailed effects where the closest approximations to such a strategy are pursued. A full-blooded confrontational IR strategy may be the weapon chosen for such harsh (or even punitive) measures as the closure of particular plants. But where the objective is a more 'efficient' or productive arrangement of production or administrative work processes our evidence suggests that the more complex the changes planned then the more likely it is that managers will seek to share some elements of decision-making, at least for some groups of workers. Conversely the dynamic of detailed strategy implementation may alter the pace or character of the changes in ways that are incompatible with the existence of a detailed and comprehensive type of control-oriented strategy.

Since there was some evidence to suggest that plans for changes to methods and responsibilities of working are pursued independently of the formal industrial relations process (Jones 1982; Francis *et al.* 1982) our enquiries with particular firms distinguished between Work Re-organisation Schemes and any adjacent Industrial Relations Strategies. The criticisms made of the current usage of the concept of the 'labour process' are too detailed to repeat here.[6] But our preference for the term work organisation was made in the light of these and also because it did not bias our examination towards manual jobs in production work. It also avoided our involvement in debates that were largely irrelevant to our purposes but which continue to beset the study of work in clerical, administrative and ancillary functions from a labour process perspective.

However it would be extremely short-sighted to assume as some industrial sociologists have (though the labour process approach claims not to) that changes in work tasks can be studied without reference to other institutions and processes in the establishment or enterprise. A WRS may therefore involve change in all of the areas referred to above: operations, employment practices, employee representation, super-ordinate-subordinate relationships, and interpretative frameworks. For reasons of economy we restrict the analysis to the operations and employee representation spheres because the former overlaps most closely with the focus of comparable labour process perspectives and the latter because of its salience for the debates over managerial strategies.

One further set of distinctions has been made in order to compare the content of WRSs. Throughout the following discussion the changes referred to concern four dimensions of 'work': (i) *task execution* (whether this be manual or mental) for the individual worker; (ii) *work planning* for a work-group or department (e.g. of materials, sequences of jobs, etc.); (iii) *work-direction* decisions as to whether any particular worker will perform this or that task at a particular time (the more discretion a work role possesses, the less will direction be made by a superior); and (iv) *functional organisation* – do work roles combine a number of functions necessary for an establishment's operations, or are requirements such as maintenance and distribution kept administratively separate from adjacent functions such as production? (This last consideration is worth bearing in mind when evaluating the significance of schemes which claim to 'enlarge' jobs since it impinges on the overall administration of the firm or establishment and not simply task structures that remain isolated within a department.)

These distinctions relate to both the 'vertical' (authority/decision-making) and 'horizontal' (range of task expertise) features of contemporary work organisation. Applied to the six firms which we studied in some depth (out of a broader pool of some sixteen firms of which preliminary enquiries were made) they provide a further refutation of the progressive de-skilling/expansion-of-Taylorism theme in the labour process literature and require that special attention be given to the notion of 'responsible autonomy' as a WRS strategy.

All our firms were promoting 'flexibility' between occupations in functionally distinct areas of their operations. The motives were normally the obvious ones of reducing total labour costs. They were often predictably concerned with exploiting the weakening of trade union resistance that had previously relied upon occupational demarcation lines. However (a point which will be expanded in a moment), the industrial relations process by which these initiatives were pressed varied significantly in their character; and, secondly, the outcomes in terms of vertical and horizontal features of the re-fashioned work process often contradicted any simple principle of managerial control.

Perhaps the clearest example of this latter point was in a drinks manufacturer where delivery drivers not only took over some of the responsibilities for route scheduling from the sales department but also played a leading role in the design of the new system. The management 'control' was confined to greater certainty that customers' orders would be met and some decrease in associated unit labour costs. However a point not lost on the union side was that the drivers' advance on the planning, direction and functional-divisions dimensions referred to above considerably enhanced the level of dependence of the company upon the drivers.

In these kinds of schemes it is often difficult to ascribe a definite shift along a notional frontier of control between management and workers because a WRS which seems to penalise one group of workers may enhance the work of another group – at least in terms of the dimensions outlined above. In a private steel company for example the mechanical crafts convener was bitter about the WRS which had given some maintenance tasks to production workers but the latter had clearly added to their task repertoire and gained an element of work planning. A similar extension occurred within a single-union work group in the consumer electronics firm studied. Partly under the influence of 'human relations' work designers (and partly a cost-conscious Tayloristic work-study engineer!) separate test checks were removed from a separate (male) inspection post and distributed amongst women assemblers on a re-designed assembly line.

An even clearer example of a rise in the vertical axis of a work role occurred in a confectionary plant where investment in advanced microelectronic process equipment was accompanied by an upgrading of some operatives (albeit at the cost of massive redundancies) to process control posts. An entire tier of first-line supervisors who previously 'controlled' the scheduling of materials and packaging and direction of workers on sub-divided tasks was removed and the new 'operatives' made responsible for their own planning of operations on their line and discretion over an extended range of tasks.

These examples may prompt two types of response in our audience. Either they are a naive vindication/reiteration of Blauner's prospectus for non-alienated and self-directing work groups; or that they confirm the advantages to management control of carefully planned 'responsible autonomy'. The first of these responses is easily dismissed (see also Ramsay, chapter 4 above). Delegated controls remain limited to certain levels and functions of the establishments operations. Workers in the enhanced jobs just described still come up against various administrative and technical constraints in the exercise of their newly gained discretion. Several of these and other quotable examples also illustrated that the changes that managements had sanctioned had little explicit concern for work-humanisation. But the existence of these managerial considerations does not, on our evidence, confirm the changes as examples of responsible autonomy strategies.

The reasons for this rejection are twofold. First the process of formulation and implementation of a WRS tends to lack the provision for detailed specification of outcomes, coordination between managerial levels and functions, and overall coherence necessary to characterise it as a strategy for control. Secondly the more comprehensive a 'strategy' does become, then the greater the probability of the involvement of workers and unions (contrary to the employers' offensive picture) and the more equivocal the role of the industrial relations institutions of the establishment or enterprise in influencing the final character of changes in the WRS into outcomes that unambiguously enhance the outright control of production management.

These two considerations – the problematic degree of 'strategic' policy formulation and implementation, and the further uncertainties added by the more ambitious inclusion of employee representation in the plans – are illustrated through a comparison of the changes planned and achieved at the consumer-electronics firm just mentioned and at another case the body-plant of a car manufacturer.

The body-plant exemplifies the lack of coherence and detail in WRS strategies. Changes there were pursued largely on the initiative of the production manager. There was no divisional, let alone corporate, policy on the form of organising work on a new body-press line. Division contented itself with laying down financial limits and 'Japan-phobia' meant that changes had to meet severe manpower reduction targets. But the eventual scheme for the re-organisation of tasks between maintenance, setting and production tasks differed markedly from the arrangements at similar plants in the division. The scheme finally adopted reduced job categories from ten to three and expanded the skills and responsibilities of craft mechanical workers while effectively reducing these for the semi-skilled production workers.

The outcome was largely a result of the technical objectives of the production manager who conducted bilateral negotiations with all the unions concerned before agreeing the final scheme with the AUEW convener. The industrial relations department played hardly any role in these changes and indeed was generally judged to have had its influence severely eclipsed since the general rationalisation phase had begun.

In this case then the detail changes in the WRS enhanced the 'job control' of one section of the workforce largely through a traditional sequence of horse trading and consultation between the production manager and shopfloor leaders over manning levels and task responsibilities without a detailed provision for such changes in a company level strategy and largely without formal and specific industrial relations policy-making. The fact that WRS changes for other groups of workers were pushed through with much less consultation and with a distinct shift of their work planning and direction opportunities to middle managers emphasises the eclecticism of 'strategy' in this establishment.

By contrast, the promotion of change at the consumer-electronics plant was comprehensive in outline (up to a point) and apparently consistent in the approach to all sections of the workforce. Corporate management had re-organised operations into a divisional 'product group' arrangement with all responsibility for production and industrial relations devolved to the management of the groups. In 1978/79 (interestingly *before* the onset of new 'economic realism' in the UK) a new product and production plan had been initiated by a senior manager for the group in order to catch up with Japanese rivals. Although the 'strategy' had been deliberately designed to give priority in change to the design and production engineering management, the group's champion had insisted on moving industrial relations down from corporate level and on developing a more participative personnel and IR style of management to negotiate the changes with the unions. As a consequence not just individual IR managers but also personnel and IR issues in general were given prominence in various aspects of the changes.

However what this case illustrates is that the broader the scope of operations planning becomes, then the more open-ended its final outcomes in terms of the 'control' features of the WRS. The lengthy and detailed consultation proceedings had been welcomed and (they claimed) turned to some advantage by the union representatives of the production workers (see above).

Detailed changes to manning and work routines had turned these union representatives into management's first line of consultation to the discomfort of the shop managers and supervisors who felt their roles to be diminished relative to that of the shop stewards. The deliberate injection of personnel management considerations into the detailed design of the new production line and its operation had also confused expectations about the final form this took. Some sort of compromise seemed to have been necessary in the layout of the line and the work planning in order to introduce an element of group working to particular sections. This innovation was not 'strategic' since it was viewed differently by each of the management participants: personnel, works-engineers, and shop managers, but it clearly represented something that would not have occurred without the participative/humanisation concerns of the personnel managers.

A final complication at this plant concerned the craft engineering workers whose stewards continued to hold out against 'flexibility' changes to the existing craft demarcations. At the time of our most recent visit to this plant, management's continued adherence to a consultative and fully negotiated approach to each change had prevented any overriding of the engineering stewards' opposition.

The rather different management policies and WRS outcomes in these two cases suggests that what may be defined as 'responsible autonomy' in the sphere of working practices may arise for reasons other than the existence of an overall strategy. Responsibility *can* form part of a more considered style of implementing general aims and embracing both the industrial relations and operations spheres of management. But then it is unlikely to achieve the control over the final form of work organisation that would be consistent with a strategy that knew in advance the range of control required for both WR and IR spheres.

Let us note several points from the earlier discussion of management handling of employee representation. In each plant, management continued to recognise established union bargaining partners, in most cases was perhaps more open-handed in its information provision, and had in some cases adopted an explicit policy of greater 'involvement' via consultation for at least some unions. On the other hand, in multiunion plants some parts of management policy hit at inter-union solidarity, whether intentionally or not; and there existed in three cases a policy of reducing the number of recognised bargaining units. As we have seen, however, each case was affected by specific local contingencies or circumstances, and the broad picture that emerges is one of plant particularism with considerable flexibility and even extemporisation in the management approach. A factor that affected the latter was union response, which itself varied greatly from one establishment to another, and from one union to the next.

This complexity must be reduced here to certain trends. First, we can make the general point that lack of a 'strategic' approach to the change situation was even more apparent amongst unions than in the case of employers. At national level, craft unions are more likely to have policies of a relatively definite kind for work re-organisation than are general worker unions. At the local level, such differences are less apparent. For instance, it was a convener from a general union who was one driving force behind the new delivery system in the brewery. Even in the car-body plant, the claim was made that general union stewards has evolved 'strategies' (the senior shop steward's word) involving 'alternative packages' of measures that constituted a 'positive' response. But these were acknowledged to be 'not always worked out carefully beforehand', and it was clear that they formed not so much an element in any plan that could really be termed strategic as rather hastily composed *ad hoc* responses to management proposals. The senior steward's claim that a wealth of knowledge existed amongst shop stewards about how the plant could be operated was no doubt justifiable; but the group lacked both the opportunity to see beyond immediate threats and changes and the back-up services necessary for transforming this knowledge into a credible counter-plan. They did not consider that their union could supply this expertise from its own central facilities, and were probably correct.

But the convener of a union representing craft workers, who felt much the same thing about his union headquarters, had in this same plant been behind a series of agreements which resulted in both a security for his members, at the expense of some flexibility on non-skilled job elements, but also new opportunities for skill acquisition. Similar opportunities had been rejected by the general worker union. In the steel firm, however, it was the production workers' union which was seen from the craft union perspective as pursuing a longer-term policy of appeasement to management on the demands of the latter for flexibility in working practices, in order to make gains including a rise in skill level and involvement. There was some justice in this view, but it seems an exaggeration to describe the kinds of accommodation apparently being practised as a strategy, since they contained a high degree of opportunism. (It is worth noting that steel is an industry where the production workers' union is able to keep track without too much difficulty of technical and organisational trends directly relevant to the longer-term prospects of their members in individual plants.)

As noted, some kind of longer-term policy about work re-organisation was more likely to exist at national level in unions with a major craft constituency. But the action which such unions pursued locally could vary sharply from one case to another. We cited the case of the steel firm, where the convener of the union representing most craft workers claimed with great bitterness that his union was incapable of resisting a management drive to eradicate demarcations, whilst production workers and other craft groups saw advantages in the management aims. This convener acknowledged that some former work practices had been sold out, and appeared to consider that such monetisation made the best of a situation where, as he put it, 'the law of the jungle applies'. His one hope was that the market would one day improve sufficiently for his men to claw back the advantages they had bargained away.

In the consumer-electronics company, the convener of the same union was also faced with a move to greater flexibility, in particular over maintenance work on new equipment involving a second craft union – one noted incidentally, both for the quality of its central information and advice service and for having evolved clear policies on work re-organisation. But the first convener insisted that the possible conflicts of interest that arose did not worry him unduly, even though each union had been bidding against the other to have the new tasks recognised as entirely its own preserve. A longer-standing strategy of joint action with other sites' unionists had been undermined by the switch to plant bargaining mentioned in the discussion of the WRS above.

The importance of company and plant specificity for union approaches is illustrated here by the craft union preferring to fall back on a localised version of the previous oppositional stance towards management policies. On the other hand, the general workers (uninformed, as noted, by an official policy) were quicker to seize what they regarded as opportunities to increase their security and expand some work tasks.

There is no need to cite more material. What emerges from these examples is what might seem almost a random character in the propensity of unions at plant level either to resist management initiatives, to acquiesce in them, or to bargain concessions for innovations in the form of non-money advantages such as higher security, grading, or job quality. We recognise that in a study of broader scope we might identify some clearer pattern. However, we also think it is worth considering the possibility that how unions will respond at local level to work re-organisation will, in British manufacturing industry, not follow any simple pattern. Our reasons for saying so will not be laid out here, since we are concerned with union responses not in themselves but as an influence on management strategies.

However, we recall the general trend towards shopfloor power and either company, plant or workplace bargaining structures in the 1960s and early 1970s. This may have given rise to a substantial degree of 'plant particularism' in bargaining institutions, job control structures, union jurisdiction, inter-union relations, and so on. Industrial relations actors thus came to operate within an infrastructure of practices and legacy of past actions which in each case took on highly specific forms.

What seems clear already is that managements are still prepared, indeed often deem it necessary, to elicit cooperation from union representatives with differing degrees of consultation and participation in the implementation of change. Even though in many cases the 'shock of the new' is limiting many local representatives to largely predictable types of response.

Conclusion

We have brought a limited but suggestive amount of evidence to bear upon a selected set of 'strategy' issues that arise in workplaces. We recognise there exist many others. We hope to deal properly at some later date, for example, with the relationship between WRS and IR policies, on the one hand, and those set by top executives in other 'strategic' areas at plant and divisional level. But we feel that our findings are sufficiently representative[7] to allow us to make several provisional conclusions about relevant theory and the pattern of changes currently taking place. We deal first with the 'control' and 'strategy' concepts.

(a) Strategy

Considerable care needs to be taken when using the term strategy to describe changes achieved by managements in spheres of WRS and IRS. Employers have greater power in labour markets, and they may seek various tighter management controls in all areas as a result. Much prevailing commentary suggests either that they will necessarily do so – and will do so successfully – or that whatever they do demonstrates the existence of a managerial strategy. This seems a teleological approach, mistaking effects for purposive process. Our claims and evidence suggests that much management policy making and execution (at least in the sphere of WRS) is piecemeal, un-coordinated and empiricist. Grander strategies may well exist amongst firms with a more integrated management policy process. But even the execution of this is crucially dependent upon the powers and influence of key figures in the management structure which predates change.[8]

Detailed planning and implementation of a strategic character is also problematic in British firms (although it is no doubt attempted) because the means and conditions of 'strategic' goal achievement can simultaneously shade over into becoming demanding objectives themselves. This consideration contrasts with some views of managerial control strategies in the literature. Contrary to British managements having or choosing to execute WRSs simultaneously through unilaterally favourable changes to style, method, or institutions of collective bargaining, there is a distinct possibility that they may have to make concessions in that IR sphere or be prepared to open up a 'second front'. Nevertheless the separate dynamics of this exercise may preclude the prediction or accomplishment of detailed aspects of the WRS.

(b) Control
Proponents of strategy-as-control would, no doubt, respond to these propositions by claiming that they only confirm the sophistication of control strategies which can increasingly cede minor responsibilities and privileges to workers and trade union representatives in order to gain a higher level of global control. Our view is that to consistently maintain such an argument it is necessary to clarify or re-define the meanings and dimensions of control more accurately.

It may be that it is the dimensions of control rather than the frontiers that are changing. Over-generalising slightly from our examples it seems that job-control of the craft sort (shopfloor bargaining to maintain demarcations and limit manning and work-pace changes within those definitions) may be being superseded by: (i) enhanced task responsibilities for many work roles (operations sphere) at the minimal expense (for managers) of immediate supervisory controls, accompanied by (ii) a displacement of bargaining into areas of decision-making (over a wider employment policy, re-equipment, the redesign of operating functions) where not only have union representatives not previously been invited to cooperate, but craft bargaining perspectives have made them fear to tread.

(c) Employers' offensive
These observations are thoroughly consistent with the findings of a Bradford team (Wilson *et al*.: 1982) that the positive influence of British unions on key management decision areas such as plant location or equipment purchasing has up to the present been very low.[9] Nevertheless they suggest that if trade unions can, during this part of the economic cycle, get themselves invited into the ante-rooms of management power it might, under some circumstances, prove extremely difficult to keep a tight rein on their presence and demands during an upturn. It depends to a significant extent on what capacity British unions can develop not only to make such demands but to do so

persuasively. The approach of Italian unions as reported by writers such as Barisi (1983) is highly instructive in this regard, and a complementary part of our own research concerned with the capacity of British trade unions to marshall technical and other expertise[10] may help to define the issues better.

For the present we merely note that British managers, as yet, show no inclination to follow some government figures as far down the anti-union road as the latter might wish. A ready explanation for this is that it demonstrates a preference for manipulation and co-optation. Equally, however, it raises a further question (that this paper can only pose) which is just why it may be that many British managers seem to *need* to work through trade union representatives to the extent that they still do.

Finally, it may be worth pointing out that there is a danger of viewing the activities of British employers as a whole through the blue mist of the Edwardes Factor; if the term 'employers' offensive' must be used then it should be recalled that we are not talking about something identical to what has been claimed to be occurring in the United States. British employers have far greater power *vis-à-vis* labour than they possessed five years ago. But this evident shift in the overall balance of power between capital and labour does not translate automatically into movements in frontiers of control within workplaces that can be accurately specified and predicted in every case, or even in most cases. And where commentary aspires to stimulate a newly galvanised resistance within the labour movement exaggeration or mis-interpretation of employers' gains may well not have such an effect. On the contrary, it may contribute to demoralisation and demobilisation, and thus in a failure to seize and make the best use possible of those opportunities that do exist. An independent outside observer, we believe, would be rather impressed with the overall survival capacity of British unions at plant level during a catastrophic period.

Notes

1. Similar issues are raised in the recently published collection of papers on corporate strategy and industrial relations edited by Thurley and Wood (1983). Unfortunately this volume has appeared too late to be dealt with systematically in this chapter.
2. We encountered such a case in one of our case establishments.
3. For a review and assessment of the prospects of control as a rule governed system for industrial relations see Purcell and Earl 1977. The broader relationships between industrial relations' controls and power in the workplace are the subject of Herding's 1972 comparison of USA and West German evidence, and of course Goodrich 1975. Control characteristics as a general administrative focus of the total organisation is evaluated by Child (1972). The Marxist usage of control as power in

the social relations of production is defined by Friedman in his introduction to *Industry and Labour* cited below. Stephen Hill (1981) provides an overview and rationale for treating control as one of the central issues for industrial sociology and industrial relations.

4. Cf. amongst many others, T. Elger, 'Braverman, capital accumulation and deskilling', Wood and Kelly, 'Taylorism, responsible autonomy and management strategy', both in S. Wood (ed.) 1982; Friedman (1977); Edwards (1979).

5. For Hyman, industrial relations institutions are defined by their instrumentality for management work process objectives as: 'the processes of control over work relations' (Hyman 1975: 12) while 'workers can exert their own control only at the expense of the employer' (p. 27). Though formulated partly as a rejection of the liberal-pluralist perspective of Flanders for whom 'managements . . . can only regain control by sharing it' (Flanders 1975: 172) (through recognised and 'orderly' local bargaining arrangements) the two writers share a view that the principle of IR institutions and their practical purpose is, or could be, to resolve control issues in the work process.

6. Awareness of the fundamental conceptual deceptiveness of the labour-process theory is, at the moment, confined to a few relatively neglected but crucial criticisms. See, for example, Cutler, 1978, Loveridge, 1981.

7. For a discussion of the representativeness of our six cases see Rose and Jones, 1983. We make no claims that our sample possesses any statistical validity. On the other hand, we have no reason to believe our cases are as a whole unrepresentative of general trends in British manufacturing industry.

8. In this respect it is interesting that Hebden, a senior manager with Massey Ferguson, interpreted the personnel role in strategy (a) as a problem of setting the tightest possible quantitative criteria as the most effective way of ensuring strategic coordination, rather than qualitative involvement; and (b) saw the whole area as so subject to conflicting pressures that a single individual manager with a fixed and clearly-defined brief had to be appointed.

Francis, Snell, Willman and Winch (1982) may have uncovered a similar problem of strategic coordination when they found that many critical investment and implementation decisions for new production technology in engineering were effectively the results of efforts by an individual manager acting as an 'innovation champion'.

9. Wilson and his colleagues (1982) found hardly any serious involvement of unions in 'strategic' management decisions in the mixture of organisations that they studied. Our own case studies also confirm that union involvement takes place only at low levels in the company. However, our evidence that the implementation process still involves several key refinements of overall requirements (where such strategic processes do exist) suggests that operational decision, and union involvement in these, could be more influential (at least over the character of re-organised work processes) than an analysis of the initiation of schemes would indicate. Wilson *et al.* admit that the influence of unions in the implementation phase (which they did not study) may be greater than in the formulation stage (p. 339).

10. This part of our enquiry was concerned in particular with the ability of trade union national centres, especially their research departments, to provide 'expert' back-up for unionists at plant or company level who are drawing up, for example, counter plans to those of management in WRSs.

References

Barisi, G. (1983), 'La négociation syndicale sur la politique industrielle', *Etudes en Sociologie du Travail*, Paris: Université de Paris, **VII**, GST, 101–126.

Child, J. (1972), 'Organisation structure, environment and performance: the role of strategic choice', *Sociology*, **6(1)**, 1–22.

Child, J. 'Organisation: a choice for man', in J. Child (ed.), *Man and Organisation*, London.
Cuthbert, N.H. and Hawkins, K.H. (1973), *Company Industrial Relations, The Management of Industrial Relations in the 1970s*, London.
Cutler, A. (1978), 'The romance of labour', *Economy and Society*, 7, 1, February, 74–95.
Dunkerley, D. and Salaman, G. (eds.) (1981), *The International Yearbook of Organisational Studies*, London.
Economist (1982), 'Breaking British unions' grip', 282, 7223, February, 13–14.
Edwards, R.C. (1979), *The Contested Terrain*, London.
Elger, T. (1982), 'Braverman, capital accumulation and deskilling', in S. Wood (ed.).
Fazey, I. Hamilton (1983), 'Managers and the shop floor: a growing confidence', *Financial Times*, 4 January.
Flanders, A. (1975), *Management and Unions: The Theory and Reform of Industrial Relations*, London.
Francis, A., Snell, M., Willman, P. and Winch, G. (1982), 'The impact of information technology at work: the case of CAD/CAD and MIS in engineering plants', *Mimeo*, Department of Economics and Social Studies, Imperial College, London.
Friedman, A.L. (1977), *Industry and Labour*, London.
Goodrich, C.L. (1975), *The Frontier of Control*, London.
Hebden, H.J. (1973), 'Controlling and evaluating personnel strategy: the approach of Massey Ferguson', in N.H. Cuthbert and K.H. Hawkins (eds.).
Herding, R. (1972), *Job Control and Union Structure*, Rotterdam.
Hill, S. (1981), *Competition and Control at Work*, London.
Hyman, R. (1975), *Industrial Relations: A Marxist Introduction*, London.
Hyman, R. and Elger, R. (1981), 'Job controls, the employers' offensive, and alternative strategies', *Capital and Class*, 15, Autumn, 115–149.
Jones, B. (1982), 'Destruction or redistribution of engineering skills? the case of numerical control', in S. Wood (ed.).
Judson, A.S. (1982), 'The awkward truth about productivity', *Harvard Business Review*, September–October.
Lane, T. (1982), 'The unions: caught on the ebb tide', *Marxism Today*, September.
Loveridge, R. (1981), 'Business strategy and community culture: policy as a structured accommodation of conflict', in D. Dunkerley and G. Salaman (eds.).
Marsh, A. (1982), *Employee Relations Policy and Decision Making*, London.
Massey, D. and Meegan, R. (1982) *The Anatomy of Job Loss*, London.
Purcell, J. and Earl, M.J. (1977), 'Control systems and industrial relations', *Industrial Relations*, 8(2), 41–54.
Ramsay, H. (1977), 'Cycles of control', *Sociology*, 11(3), 481–506.
Rose, M. and Jones, B. (1983), *Work Reorganisation and Unions: Procedural and Organisational Frontiers in British Industrial Relations*, end of Grant Report HR7504/1. Social Science Research Council, February.
Thurley, K. and Wood, S. (eds.) (1983), *Industrial Relations and Management Strategy*, London.
White, M. and Trevor, M. (1983), *Under Japanese Management: The Experience of British Workers*, London.
Wilson, D.C., Butler, R.J., Cray, D., Hickson, D.J. and Mallory, G.R. (1982), 'The limits of trade union power in organisational decision making', *British Journal of Industrial Relations*, 20(3), 322–341.
Winkler, J.T. (1974), 'The ghost at the bargaining table: directors and industrial relations', *British Journal of Industrial Relations*, 12(2), 191–212.
Wood, S. and Kelly, J. (1982), 'Taylorism, responsible autonomy and management strategy', in S. Wood (ed.).
Wood, S. (ed.) (1982), *The Degradation of Work? Skill, De-skilling and the Labour Process*, London.

Appendix: Managements' Strategies for Industrial Relations and Work Reorganisation in Six Case Studies

(1) Sample

Twelve different plants were visited. Six firms were chosen for in-depth interviewing. These six were not randomly chosen but selected according to several other methodological and substantive criteria (see Rose and Jones 1983, Section IVc). The final six firms were from different industrial branches and for convenience are referred to as below:

(i)   Beer (brewing industry);
(ii) Sweets (food);
(iii) Electro (consumer electronics);
(iv) Automotive (motor vehicle manufacture);
(v)   Offices (electronic and other office equipment);
(vi) Steel (private sector speciality steels).

(2) Beer

Marginal redundancies had first been effected without a WRS. The significant change was the WRS for the sales and distribution departments. This scheme focused on work group planning and functional reorganisation. Draymen had enlarged their task repertoire into the routing and customer liaison functions of beer deliveries that had previously been left to sales staff. There was little or no technology change but a less directive supervisory mode, higher task discretion, higher work intensity, and slightly reduced manning levels had followed. A notable feature of this WRS was that detailed design was the responsibility of drayman who had spent a preparatory period working in the sales department, with extensive negotiation and consultation down to work-group level. Management use of academic 'work humanisation' specialists had also been of importance.

(3) Electro

WRS here focused upon a re-equipment and automation of an assembly line introduced to manufacture a more sophisticated product in conscious imitation of Japanese competitors (the line equipment itself came from a Japanese supplier). As described below the WRS was one part of an integrated management strategy which included industrial relations and employment policies as well as elements of a technocratic-pluralist philosophy. Principal changes in work tasks concerned the automation of simple insertion tasks and a simultaneous enhancement of jobs on another section of the line who were given test and inspect duties as well as insertion. This 'enlargement' was at the expense of specialist testing occupations – those jobs were eliminated. Conscious attempts had been made to create a work group identity (though not an independent authority) by engineering the new line into a U-shape to facilitate contact and awareness of production problems and progress. An attempt was also being made to achieve some functional integration by bringing electrical and mechanical maintenance work into the work-shop administration. At the time of our visits, however, this development was being slowed by reluctance amongst the craft union (for the mechanics) and the electrical maintenance manager.

(4) Automotive

Three distinct schemes had developed, two of which were linked to the introduction of a new body-press line purchased for production of a new model passenger car elsewhere in the company. The other scheme involved the introduction of computer aided design into the tool drawing office and an attendant move to shift work. WRS on the line had meant demanning and increased work intensity for the semi-skilled handling jobs. Part of this same labour reduction on the press line had involved the contraction of ten fitting, setting and inspection occupations into two grades: press fitter and the (essentially ancillary) crane drivers. In effect the job reorganisation had increased the task repertoire and job discretion of the fitters (now both 'labouring' and performing electrical work) at the expense of the semi-skilled grades: demanned and deskilled. The third WRS was linked to the pressline automation and reconstituted the work planning and direction dimensions. The computer monitoring system introduced with the new line had been adapted to provide details of individual workers' location and performance as well as the output rate of any particular section of the line. Because the system worked on a 'real time' basis the authority of shop managers as well as the line supervisors had been enhanced. The latter were now intermediaries in a more extended hierarchy of control. These WRSs were articulated to an authoritarian-unitary IRS philosophy (see Rose and Jones 1983) although there were several points of inconsistency and tension between the WRS and IRS (Rose and Jones 1983). Representational channels had deteriorated for most groups of workers with the exception of the engineering craft workers whose 'multi-skilling' required extensive bargaining and consultation arrangements. Demanning on the press line and other redundancy exercises and re-allocation of labour had been accomplished in a largely authoritarian and arbitrary style.

Offices

Three WRSs had been launched in the past two years as a result product and process changes in technology. But there was little evidence that these were linked, either by an engineering or an IRS logic. Clerical work was being re-organised as a result of a computerised stock control and distribution system. A new office equipment product aimed at a wider market and with fewer complex parts was being produced on an assembly-line rather than in the previous small-batch discrete work-station mode. Finally the ubiquitous CAD equipment was being introduced into the design and drawing offices. However changes in the latter area were (as yet) minor and most management and union attention was focused on the clerical and production WRSs.

Introduction of the assembly-lines had been eclectic and episodic. A pilot project at a nearby subsidiary plant had been an initial success but then fell victim to various worker protests. The new line in the main plant had involved operator control of stations, trade union consultation arrangements, job rotation, and a limited reduction (negotiated) in craft-maintenance manning rules.

In the clerical areas de-manning, and combinations of previously distinct occupational grades were accompanying convergence of supervisory with clerical and clerical with ancillary production jobs. It seemed that eventually this could lead to a fusion of operational and administrative functions. But the company policies were being implemented piecemeal on the apparent WRS policy of: first introduce the technology and then rearrange the work roles. In general task repertoires were being expanded but work planning and direction were perceived as reduced as a result of supervisory monitoring through an 'on-line' information system. Similar perceptions were evinced about a reduction in task-discretion. Both IRS and company philosophy on employee relations generally seemed to be in a state of flux though consultation and bargaining arrangements continued formally to be conducted along the previously orthodox 'familial pluralist' lines with elements of a change towards the style favoured in 'Automotive'. Redundancies for financial and administrative as well as technical reasons had reduced the total workforce by 20 per cent over two years with more losses feared in the near future.

(6) Sweets

As with three of the above companies WRS changes at sweets accompanied product and process changes. Corporate-level strategy was to move from a marketing-orientation to a production focus to improve quality and reduce costs and lead times. A massive investment in new plant had begun some time previously. Automatic was the main thrust of the changes. The aim was to leap several generations of productive equipment by moving from large and small batch methods with extensive manual transfer and manipulation (some of the equipment dated back to the 1940s) to fully computerised process technology conforming to Woodward's 'process' level of production. The scale of the changes meant that there were extensive redundancies and reclassification of both supervisory and production roles. These changes could augment the work-planning and self-direction potential of process monitoring and control occupations towards more coherent work groups. But the shift to a computer scheduling facility for the plant as a whole was enhancing strategic management monitoring and control and fusing manufacturing functions. The engineering department was becoming administratively closer to production management while at the task level plans were afoot to merge some maintenance with operating functions. The WRS strategy was being run in close tandem with a set of IR policies. The company had (nationally and locally) been renowned for its mild paternalism in employees' relations and this had been accompanied by adherence to orthodox bargaining arrangements at local level. A move towards more explicit consultation/communication exercises had been accompanied by a more general accentuation of employee-involvement ideas moving the management towards the 'technocratic-pluralist' pole of our classification of philosophy and representational policies. A major point of contact for the IRS and WRS involved a rationalisation of bargaining units as part of the reorganisation of craft-maintenance, technical and production work roles.

(7) Steel

Since this plant is fairly new (1966), and operating on the market-responsive 'mini-mill' concept, technological factors are of limited importance. The WRS emphasis is upon occupational mergers and inter-craft 'flexibility'; so functional re-organisation and the attendant inter-union negotiations are central. In the task re-allocations some of the process workers had increased their skill repertoire at the expense of the mechanical crafts while the shift to electronic controls was enhancing the discretion of electricians in work planning and direction of their tasks. Consultation was largely a device for by-passing detailed job-bargaining in a management IRS which emphasised the 'buying-out' of craft demarcations and the 'buying-in' of production-craft and inter-craft flexibility between tasks.

6 Managerial Strategies, New Technology and the Labour Process*

J. Child

Any consideration of managerial policies towards the labour process must today take account of the new technologies based on micro-electronics. The level of investment in new technology is substantial and is forecast to grow rapidly. It is already proving to be a vehicle for significant changes in the organisation of work, and therefore in the position of workers within the productive process. Four managerially-initiated developments, facilitated by new technology, are directed towards (i) the virtual elimination of direct labour, (ii) the spread of contracting, (iii) the dissolution of traditional job or skill demarcations, and (iv) the degradation of jobs through deskilling. These initiatives affect the ability of workers to control the conduct of their work through an exercise of discretion and skill, and each one has implications for the position of the workers concerned in the labour market.

New technology can play an important role in these changes to the organisation and control of the labour process. The rationales applied to investment in new technology are not necessarily focused primarily on the labour process, but the technology does carry with it a potential for change in that process. The introduction of new technology in ways that change the labour process is therefore looked upon as the unfolding of a managerial strategy. This concept is, however, controversial, and its use here must be clarified before proceeding to the main argument.

Managerial Strategy
Management normally exerts a major, if not the dominant, influence on

* I am grateful to Edward Heery, Stephen Wood, colleagues in the Work Organisation Research Centre, and participants at the Conference on the Organisation and Control of the Labour Process held at Owens Park, Machester in March 1983 for commenting on an earlier draft of this chapter. It draws in part on research funded by the Economic and Social Research Council.

the organisation of the labour process in enterprises funded by private capital, excluding those of a professional and/or co-operative character. Contrary examples such as the national newspaper industry in Fleet Street are sufficiently exceptional as to prove the rule (Martin 1981). Nevertheless, doubts are raised about the concept of managerial strategy which expresses this influence and the intentions behind it. Three of these doubts concern (i) the concept's implication of rationality, (ii) the extent to which the labour process is the main point of reference for managerial policy, and (iii) the relation between policy intentions and implementation.

The concept of strategy implies a rational consideration of alternatives and the articulation of coherent rationales for decisions. In practice, some studies of senior managerial decision-making have identified as inherent characteristics: vacillation, the pursuit of factional interests, and even randomness (e.g. March and Olsen, 1976; Mintzberg, Raisinghani and Theoret 1976). Rationality often appears to be bounded and focused on the next step rather than on the long term. This critique, valid though it may be, is, however, only significant for an analysis of changes to the labour process if the persistence of disagreement within management (perhaps deriving from specialist values and interests) leads to attempts to dilute or sabotage the implementation of decisions once reached. Otherwise, the more significant factor is the substance of the policy that emerges, whatever quality of thinking underpins it, and the claims of rationality and hence necessity which managers may make for that policy.

In some of the labour process literature it is assumed that managerial strategies are formulated with labour's role in the productive process primarily in mind (e.g. Braverman 1974; Edwards 1979). In practice, consideration of that role could be quite secondary, with the actions taken on employment and job content being merely consequential upon other decisions. Management's priorities for the creation of surplus value may well be directed towards improving the conditions of market exchange or of financing. Investment in new technology which is subsequently applied towards securing changes in the labour process could therefore owe its origin to an intention of strengthening a company's position in its product market, perhaps by permitting the manufacture of new or improved products, when circumstances allow finance to be acquired on acceptable terms. The force of this qualification is to indicate a need to examine carefully the intentions behind managerial policies and not to assume that they are necessarily formulated with a conception of the desired labour process prominently, or even clearly, in mind. This does not mean, however, that managerial policies directed primarily by other objectives will be inconsequential for the labour process.

The possibility of attenuation between managerial policy and its implementation has been identified as a third problem with the notion of managerial strategy towards the labour process. As Wood and Kelly (1982) point out, one cannot infer the successful implementation of a managerial strategy simply from its statement as a policy. Nor can the existence of a strategic intention necessarily be inferred merely from conditions at the point of production or of service provision. These might result from interventions by junior managers or from informal practices introduced by the workers themselves. Supervisors have, for example, been found to make frequent *ad hoc* changes to workers' deployment and duties, particularly when the task system is variable by dint of inconsistent materials, product changes, or equipment breakdowns. The discretion and skills exercised by supervisors themselves can depend upon informal accommodations reached with middle managers (Child and Partridge 1982). Thompson (1983) also recalls that an important manifestation of the defence of craft identity has been the persistent practice of 'clawing back' concessions to management on questions of control and skill within the workplace; this will further attenuate actual practice from managerial policy. In short, attentuation can result from control loss within organisational hierarchies.

However, accommodations and informal practices lower down in the hierarchy can be conducive to efficient working (Gross 1953), in which case they might persist for a long time without the intervention or even the awareness of senior management. They would, in effect, be filling gaps in the systems laid down by management or correcting their dysfunctional effects. It is when such practices result in low efficiency that this is likely to register among senior managers as a problem and 'corrective' action will ensue. There are bound to be limits to the deviation of implementation from policy, though these require further empirical investigation. The substitution of technology for manual intervention in the conduct of tasks, and the technological improvement of control data, will tend to reduce such deviation. Thus not only does investment in new technology embody managerial intentions, but its introduction into the workplace may facilitate the implementation of these intentions.

One response to these qualifications would be to insist on a 'stringent' definition of managerial strategy in labour process analysis. This would restrict use of the concept to cases where (i) it can be demonstrated that managers hold a coherent set of policy rationales, which (ii) are directed specifically at key labour process dimensions such as control, discretion and skill, and where (iii) there is an effective follow through from policy to implementation. Rose and Jones (this volume) also appear to follow this stringent definition when they question whether the concept of managerial strategy can be usefully applied to the situations uncovered by their case studies.

Rose and Jones note that managements in all the firms they studied were promoting greater flexibility in manning, though the industrial relations processes whereby this was progressed varied considerably. The firms they studied were located in different manufacturing sectors, and it is suggested later that there are likely to be considerable differences between sectors and between organisations in the character of managerial strategies and in their effectiveness. Thus while one sector of British industry such as shipbuilding, with its long tradition of demarcated craft control and a generally strong workplace organisation, may exhibit relatively imprecise managerial strategies which have had limited influence on the labour process, another sector such as banking exhibits a centralised and specific managerial planning of the labour process which is implemented very effectively through managerially-controlled pilot schemes and the imposition of precise work measurement, with little organised workplace opposition. Rather than rejecting the notion of managerial strategy because it is not always specific or effective, an alternative view would be to conclude that a model is required which allows for the possibility of variation in the nature of strategies and their implementation, and which draws attention to contextual factors pertinent to explaining such variation. In other words, the problem with the 'stringent' definition of managerial strategy lies in its failure to allow for the possibility that managerial strategies which are unspecific towards the labour process may still nonetheless have relevance for it. The influence of managerial strategy on the labour process may be more complex, variable and less direct than a stringent perspective allows. The alternative view is considered to provide a constructive basis for analysing the introduction of new technology, and is now outlined.

The point of departure is the observation that in capitalist economies corporate managerial strategies will necessarily reflect a consciousness of certain general objectives which are the normal conditions for organisational survival. These objectives are oriented to accumulation and are often expressed by senior managers in terms of 'profitable growth' (Child 1974). A portfolio of corporate strategies, amounting to what Spender (1980) has called a 'recipe', will typically be developed and will reflect the views of senior managers as to how the objectives can be realised in the specific context of the organisation. These strategies are not necessarily formulated with the management of labour and structuring of jobs explicitly in mind.

It is noted later, for example, that investment in new technology is reportedly undertaken to meet targets such as improving the consistency of product quality, reducing inventory, or increasing the flexibility of plant. The appreciation of the production process held by the managers who approve the investment may not even include a clear conception of how the labour process is organised and controlled. Senior managers, particularly in larger organisations, often exhibit good understanding only of the work of a relatively small group of colleagues and subordinates, such that a 'psychological boundary' exists between them and the labour process (Fidler 1981). At this elevated hierarchical level managers tend to deal in terms of statistical abstractions such as throughput volume, wastage rates, stock levels, delivery performance, unit costs, budget variance, and employment costs. Managerial policies on new technology need not therefore articulate explicit statements about the organisation of the labour process. Nonetheless, they effectively amount to strategies towards the labour process if the choice of a particular technology imposes certain constraints on its operation and manning, and if the strategic expectations attached to the new technology also impose constraints on labour process design. Moreover, management will influence the route by which these strategic intentions are operationalised, by selecting those specialists and subordinates who are to act as work organisation designers. Each of these, be they production engineers, industrial engineers, systems analysts, craft-trained line managers, or social scientists, will have their own relatively specific orientation towards the organisation and control of the labour process.

Managerial strategies therefore establish corporate parameters for the labour process which are unlikely to be inconsequential even when there is attenuation between policy and implementation. Purcell (1983) makes a comparable point in arguing that, within the modern large enterprise, managements have established corporate systems of centralised planning and financial control which have significant implications for the location of and control over bargaining about incomes and employment. The process whereby managerial intentions feed through to the workplace is therefore regarded as one in which managerial strategies play the role of 'steering devices' that have 'knock-on effects', to use terms suggested by Grieco (1983). This still allows for the fact that in different industrial sectors the extent to which strategies are formulated centrally or locally, unilaterally or bilaterally, can vary considerably. This perspective is also compatible with a recognition that the strategies may sometimes be unspecific and poorly understood, that they may be subject to reinterpretation and opposition by functional and junior managers, and that they may encounter worker resistance both informally in the workplace and through trade union action. Even in the absence of such opposition, the translation of policies and strategic decisions to the organisation of the labour process will require detailed working out by lower levels of management, by specialists (who might include external consultants) and possibly by shopfloor and office workers themselves.

The tightness of coupling between senior managerial intentions and their actual implementation in the organisation of the labour process is therefore regarded as a variable factor, which raises the question of the processes that may intervene in the transition from strategy to implementation. The flexible nature of new technology hardware and particularly its software may in fact permit a range of alternative working arrangements. The perspectives and values of middle managers, work organisation designers and workers who have the potential to influence the implementation process therefore need to be taken into account, including factors determining their relative influence.

The role of managerial strategy developed here in connection with the introduction of new technology is represented in Figure 6.1. Fundamental capitalistic objectives are seen to provide management's basic strategic motives. Strategies are developed as corporate steering devices, which are likely to inform decisions to invest in new technology. While it cannot be assumed that corporate strategies express an explicit view about the organisation of the labour process, they will at the least establish certain parameters within which implementation and actual changes to jobs, and employment relations, take place. The transition to implementation is subject to intervening processes and actions. In short, actors, processes and contextual conditions all have to be taken into account.

New Technology

The term 'new technology' is applied to a wide range of equipment utilising micro-circuitry and associated software. In some applications, microelectronics data handling capacity is combined with modern communications facilities to provide what has become known as 'information technology'. While there is as yet little agreement on the definition of these terms, it is possible to give examples of where new technology is being applied to work processes in manufacturing and services; these are listed in Table 6.1.

The newness of new technology lies not so much in the application of electronics to data processing, which has been commercially available since the 1950s, but rather in the radically changed nature of the equipment now produced. This has enormously increased the range of its practical applications. Microelectronic technology is distinguished by its (i) compactness, (ii) cheapness, (iii) speed of operation, (iv)

Figure 6.1 Representation of the role of managerial strategy

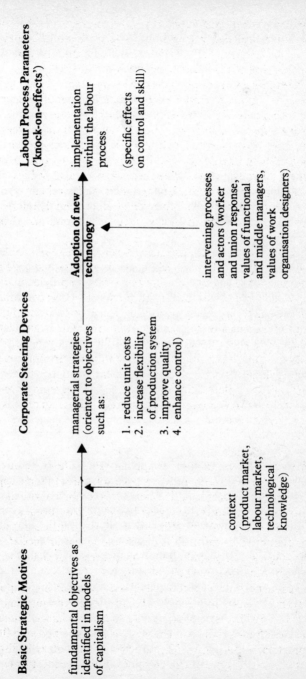

Basic Strategic Motives

fundamental objectives as
identified in models
of capitalism

context
(product market,
labour market,
technological
knowledge)

Corporate Steering Devices

managerial strategies
(oriented to objectives
such as:

1. reduce unit costs
2. increase flexibility
   of production system
3. improve quality
4. enhance control)

**Adoption of new
technology**

intervening processes
and actors (worker
and union response,
values of functional
and middle managers,
values of work
organisation designers)

**Labour Process Parameters
('knock-on-effects')**

implementation
within the labour
process

(specific effects
on control and skill)

reliability, (v) accuracy, and (vi) low energy consumption. When combined with suitable data inputting and communication facilities, the new technology permits information to be collected, collated, stored and accessed with a speed not previously possible.

Table 6.1   Examples of new technology applied to processes in manufacturing and services

---

Manufacturing
1. **Computer-controlled manufacture:** CNC machines, robots, flexible manufacturing systems, process plant monitoring and control.
2. **Computer-aided design (CAD).**
3. **Computerised stock control and warehousing:** Motor vehicle parts for manufacture and sale of spares. Also examples in service sector: retail store stocks, hospital pharmacies.

Services
4. **Financial:** automatic cash dispensers/tellers; customer records via VDUs, electronic funds transfer.
5. **Medical:** computer diagnosis, automated laboratory testing, intensive care monitoring.
6. **Retailing and distribution:** automated warehousing, stock control, electronic-point-of-sale (EPOS).
7. **Libraries:** computerised information systems, lending records based on use of bar-coding.
8. **Information services:** videotex (interactive and one-way systems via modified TV sets and telephone lines).

Office and managerial work
9. **Word processing and electronic filing.**
10. **Communications:** electronic mail and facsimile transmission, teleconferencing, networking (local area networks and to homeworkers via microcomputers and telephone lines).

The real cost of new technology equipment is falling, and its programming is becoming easier (though software costs are not falling in proportion). It is also becoming more versatile. It is not surprising therefore that investment in new technology is already proceeding on an impressive scale, and that this is shortening the innovation cycle both in products and processes. Forecasts vary and obviously have to be treated with particular caution in such a new and changing field. The figures in Table 6.2 do, however, provide an indication of the scale and rate of growth of investment in new technology.

Investment is central to the process of capitalist development, and new technology has today become a significant component of that investment. Few studies of the labour process, however, have yet had an opportunity to take account of this technology, though there has been plenty of speculation about its generation of unemployment and

Table 6.2   Examples of investment in new technology and its projected growth

Application	Market	Annual sales ($US billion)	
		1982	1986 predicted
1. CAD/CAM Systems	World	1.15	3.3
2. Robotics	W. Europe	0.17	0.76[a]
			(0.23)[b]
3. Microcomputers	U.K.	0.56	4.5
4. Total data processing	W. Europe	54.7	151.9
		(1981)	(1987)

Sources: 1. Financial Times, 13 December 1982
        2a. Financial Times, 16 July 1982
        2b. Financial Times, 5 April 1983: revised forecast, 1981 prices
        3. The Times, 1 March 1983
        4. Data International Corporation, 'The Impact of IT', Supplement to Management Today, June 1983

de-skilling. Braverman's analysis (1974) is already dated. The 'automation' he describes is more accurately termed 'Detroit automation', an advanced form of mechanisation including automatic transfer which has been applied primarily to motor vehicle mass production lines. It is not representative of present-day new technology based on microelectronics. Edwards (1979: 122–5) briefly discusses the potential of new technology for extending 'technical control'. He comments that the feedback systems involved 'constitute qualitative advance over Henry Ford's moving line' (p. 125), the older form of technical control which provides the main technological point of reference for Braverman. However, Edwards has little to suggest by way of consequences for the labour process except to say that the new 'technology of production' now becomes the workers' 'immediate oppressor' rather than the supervisor.

Thompson (1983) provides a carefully considered assessment of the application of new technology based partly on his own research in telecommunications. New technology in his view 'does add to the power of capital to restructure the labour process' (p. 115). Thompson concludes that there is a tendency to use the technology in furtherance of a general trend towards de-skilling. He sees this as an expression of management's motive for change, namely the desire to increase control over the labour process. New technology is also extending de-skilling into the area of office work. Nevertheless, Thompson argues that there is no *technological* inevitability about de-skilling. In so far as de-skilling is underway, it results primarily from competitive market pressures and in many cases predates the introduction of new technology. Examples may also be found of alternative policies, such as 'responsible autonomy' identified by Friedman (1977), while certain new skills are being created as well.

Thompson's analysis is reinforced by the conclusions which Jones (1982a) and Wilkinson (1983) derive from case studies of numerical control technology. Both are critical of 'deterministic and universalistic conceptions of the direction and nature of skill changes' which accompany the introduction of new production technology (Jones 1982a: 181). Jones, for instance, found that firms differed in the forms of skill deployment accompanying the use of numerical control machines. He attributes this variation to differences in product and labour markets, organisational structures and trade union positions. Although cautious about according too much influence to managerial intentions, Jones suggests that one clue as to why he found a variety of skill deployments may lie in evidence that the criteria applied to investment in numerical control equipment did not necessarily include the reduction of labour costs as a determining objective.

Several significant points are suggested by the available research and statistics on new technology. First, it is a major area of investment and one that has important potential for the labour process. New technology therefore links managerial strategy to the labour process, as Figure 6.1 suggested earlier. Second, changes in the labour process accompanying the introduction of new technology can follow a number of possible routes. Third, this choice of possibilities is facilitated by the considerable flexibility offered by new technology, particularly by its software.

This degree of flexibility virtually transforms the application of electronic technology, driven by software, into an aspect of organisational design. Changes to the labour process must for this reason be attributed primarily to non-technological factors, such as managerial strategies formulated in the light of market decisions; established ideological definitions of appropriate structures and working practices can also be expected to play a role. The increasing flexibility of technology renders it far less of a constraint upon, and more of a facilitator of, working practices which emerge from the political processes of management's relations with labour.

Jones presumably had in mind the ability of workers to defend existing working practices when he commented that 'management cannot construct, de novo, the conditions under which labour is to function' (1982a: 199). The significance of the introduction of new technology at the present time when the power of organised labour has reached a low ebb is, however, precisely that this gives management considerably more scope than hitherto to use the technology to impose changes upon the labour process. Managers can, and do, justify these changes by reference to competitive pressures and in terms of a need to utilise the technology effectively – in other words, an appeal to the ideology of market-driven technological determinism. In present circumstances, when managerial strategies associated with new technology have teeth, it is particularly important to examine what these strategies are.

Managerial Strategies and New Technology

Evidence from case studies (e.g. Buchanan and Boddy 1983) and surveys (e.g. Northcott, Rogers and Zeilinger 1982) suggests that the following objectives usually feature prominently in managerial intentions when introducing new technology: (i) reducing operating costs and improving efficiency; (ii) increasing flexibility; (iii) raising the quality and consistency of production; (iv) improving control over operations. There is clearly some interdependence between each of these strategic intentions. They are all directed towards enhancing opportunities to create surplus value, and enhancing the organisation's ability to absorb the risks of competition.

Improvements in *costs and efficiency* may be secured in several ways relevant to the labour process. New technology may permit reductions in manpower via a substitution for direct labour (as in the automatic spot welding of Austin Metro bodies-in-white: see Francis *et al.* 1982); or via partial substitution for labour as in word processing (IDS 1980) and in laboratory automation (Harvey and Child 1983); or via the more economical allocation of manpower on the basis of superior workflow information such as that provided by electronic-point-of-sale (EPOS) systems in retailing (Cosyns, Loveridge and Child 1983). New technologies can also reduce costs by permitting improved stock control, the reduction of waste due to operator error, and better plant utilisation via computerised scheduling. Advanced manufacturing systems offer a combination of these advantages on the basis of integrating the different elements of design, production, handling, storage and stock control (Lamming and Bessant 1983). They also offer greatly improved flexibility.

In an industry like engineering, many firms now have to compete on the basis of offering custom-built products produced in smaller batches and often involving complex machining. Achieving *flexibility* in production has therefore become an increasingly important goal. One of the most attractive features offered by new computer controlled technology is the ability to run a range of production items through a single facility with the minimum of cost and delay when changing from one specification to another. A somewhat comparable advantage in flexibility is now being sought in banking with experiments in computerising customer files and linking these to VDUs used by bank staff. By providing individualised customer profiles, this facility would enable staff to adjust rapidly to the financial circumstances and history of each customer, and on that basis to make decisions rapidly on whether to grant loans or to offer other services. Increased operating flexibility based on new technology is likely to be accompanied by managerial demands for a complementary flexibility in manning and the breaking down of traditional task boundaries, or by attempts to avoid reliance on direct labour altogether.

Improvements in *quality* can be gained from the introduction of highly accurate automated equipment conducting repeatable operations, or from the use of microelectronics for more precise process control. These examples substitute for human intervention. Quality can also be enhanced when electronic assessment complements human judgement, an example being some forms of testing in manufacturing.

The new technology is one of information processing which depends upon the quality of its data inputs. If accurate measurement can be obtained, the ability to communicate information swiftly across distances, and the capacity to apply computational or synthesising routines when required, clearly enhance the potential for managerial *control*. Senior managers may now no longer have to rely upon operators and middle managers for control data or for their interpretation, if these data can be captured directly at the point of operations. For example, EPOS systems in retailing can, via capturing data through the scanning of bar-coded or magnetically ticketed items, transmit control data on itemised sales, on throughput at each point of sale, and on stocks, directly to store managers and to central buying departments in a company's head office.

New technology is therefore being introduced to advance managerial strategic objectives, and it can be used as a means of facilitating the four types of change in the labour process which were listed at the beginning of the paper. In keeping with the representation in Figure 6.1, these changes are regarded as being in the nature of managerial strategies towards the labour process in so far as they are initiatives which stem originally from corporate objectives and decisions, whether directly and explicitly or not.

It will be evident that each of these managerial strategies effects a reduction in costs through the intensification of labour, whether directly through extending the labour power exerted or indirectly through improving the intrinsic performance of equipment. Moreover, by their very nature as interventions, they each constitute an extension of managerial control. However, the strategies provide different routes towards the increase of efficiency, and the perceived appropriateness of each is presumed to depend on specific circumstances of the kind outlined at the close of this paper. The way in which labour cost reduction is balanced with other objectives also appears to vary with each strategy. Another variable factor is the extent to which proponents have so far come forward publicly, or have been uncovered by researchers, to articulate specific statements of intent towards the labour process in connection with each strategy. Further evidence on managerial intentions is required. Finally, the provisional character of the present fourfold classification needs to be recognised. If found to be useful, it will certainly require considerable elaboration.

(1) Elimination of direct labour

Abolition of labour has been the dream both of engineers and social visionaries, though from quite different perspectives. The concept of factories without workers has already reached the experimental stage. It is predicted that the wholly automated factory with virtually no direct workers will have become a reality in most advanced industrial countries within five years.

There are two main technological routes to the elimination of direct labour, which though starting from different points in different industries, are becoming more similar. The process industries achieved an integrated flow of production many years ago and have operated with minimal direct labour forces. With increasing market pressures, employers such as chemical producers are turning increasingly to speciality products produced in batches. The ability of manufacturers to make several products and versions of the same product on a batch basis using the same basic plant is becoming particularly important. Computer controls linked to microelectronic sensors and intelligent data gathering instruments are essential to achieving the flexibility and they enable process producers to avoid dependence on human intervention outside the central control room (cf. Williams 1983).

A second main route to eliminating direct labour in manufacturing is via Flexible Manufacturing Systems (FMS). These are computer-programmed and controlled integrated production systems which bring to discrete item (i.e. non-process) production many of the continuous flow characteristics of process plants. The prospect of achieving greater flexibility in regard to batch changes on the same plant is often cited as a major attraction of FMS. Current interest in FMS is high, as witnessed by attendances at the three-day FMS Conferences in Brighton (October 1982: 500 manufacturing managers and senior engineers listening to 50 papers) and London (October 1983: 400 delegates and 70 papers). The first prototype fully automated FMS factory in Britain, which opened in Colchester at the end of November

1982, attracted considerable press comment (e.g. Guardian, 1.12.82, p. 7; Financial Times, 8.12.82, p. 31; Sunday Times, 12.12.82, p. 50). Three-quarters of the factory managers polled by MORI in December 1982 said they were considering the introduction of FMS (Sunday Times, op. cit.). While no doubt overstated, this is a clear expression of interest.

Discussions of FMS tend to emphasise the achievement of higher surplus value via the strategic advantage of being able to respond quickly to changes in market demand both in models and quantities ordered, and via the inventory/work-in-progress saving that results from dramatic reductions in manufacturing lead times. Saving labour has not been given much emphasis in public statements, perhaps for obvious reasons at a time of high unemployment. In fact, the incidence of labour saving can be very significant with even less than full automation. In the early examples of full FMS systems it is dramatic. The Colchester engineering factory, which produces a variety of shafts, gears and disks, is reported to run with three operatives rather than thirty (Sunday Times, op. cit.). A manning of one person instead of 200 is reported on the night shift of the Fanuc FMS plant outside Tokyo (ibid.), while there are now many examples of the labour savings achievable through the installation of robotics which is an integral part of FMS (e.g. Cane 1982; Francis *et al.* 1982).

There is evidence of a conscious intention among some managers and engineers to use FMS and process control as a means of extending managerial control over the labour process. For example, Peter Dempsey of Ingersoll Engineers, which by 1982 had planned over 100 manufacturing installations in 15 countries, stated in 'a keynote paper' on the first day of the 1983 FMS conference that 'ultimately [FMS] will mean wrestling manufacture away from human interference in much the same way as has happened in the oil refinery, sugar factory or cement plant'. Dempsey clearly viewed this as a managerial strategy rather than just a consequence of technology: 'FMS is a way of thinking. It is not about technology (Charlish 1983).' A line manager, who had led a project team to commission a new highly automated chocolate processing plant controlled by microprocessors, told the writer that 'we had through the commissioning period to decide how much flexibility [discretion] we can give the operator. Our objective was to reduce that to nil if possible.' This plant runs with a total complement of four people concerned with the process per se, only one of whom is an operator/controller who replaces the 23 operators previously required.

The managerial vision into which the elimination of labour through automation fits was developed in an interview with the recently retired technical director of a major international food processing company. (Although this company is itself a long way from full automation, it is nevertheless significant that largely under this man's influence a long-term plan was initiated in the late 1970s which has almost halved the labour force partly on the basis of introducing rationalising and labour-saving new technology.) His initial premise was that the technical relations of production were simple but that difficulties begin with the social relations – people mess things up. The object is therefore to eliminate labour, and in his view this should include labour at all grades. 'If you get rid of everybody, you've got an ideal factory, and most of your problems will disappear.' He saw automation as the key. It enables production levels to be maintained with less labour and with fewer plants. This permits an economy of space, even whole factories, which can be sold or put to other use. The rationalisation of factories reduces the managerial and service overheads, while the remaining units are smaller and less complex. They are therefore simpler to manage and are likely to enjoy a 'better' climate of employee relations.

The labour-elimination strategy can also be found in some parts of the service sector, where it simply manifests the logical conclusion of a widespread trend to shift the labour costs of service provision onto the customer (for instance, self-service in retailing). One example, which is conceptually developed and is already operational in some locations abroad, is 'lobby' banking. This could substitute for branch banks an array of automatic cash transaction machines which have already been developed to perform services such as cash dispensing, cash depositing, crediting of other accounts, balance notification and ordering of statements. Such satellite branches would eliminate the present job of tellers, back office staff and branch managers.

The theoretical implications for labour process analysis of situations where the production process or service provision employs little or no labour are intriguing. Labour is obviously embodied in the plant and processed materials used, but what if it is absent from the workplace as such? This as yet largely hypothetical but prospectively significant case indicates that it is the productive process which is analytically significant as the main source of surplus value, and that labour is not necessarily involved *directly* in that process. The more that this situation comes into being, the more attention will need to be directed to the social relations of exchange, distribution and re-distribution under capitalism rather than simply to the social relations of production in a narrow sense.

Automation has proceeded historically in the train of task simplification and routinisation. The archetype of this earlier stage was the degradation of work through deskilling of the kind associated with

Taylorism. As the employment of skilled craftsmen in direct production tasks became substituted by the employment of semi-skilled
workers, and as the number of alternative employments in the labour
market reduced through this process of change, so the market position
of the production worker changed. In terms of the classification first
developed by Mok (1975) and extended by Loveridge (1983), these jobs
had changed from a location in the 'primary external market' to one in
the 'secondary internal market'. In the primary external market, the
craft jobs provided long-term stable earnings and permitted high levels
of discretion – an advantageous 'primary' position founded upon
special skills widely marketable in the general labour market 'external'
to any one employing organisation. In the secondary internal market,
the new semi-skilled jobs enjoyed a relatively lower earning capacity
with less long-term security (a less advantageous 'secondary' position).
These jobs no longer utilised skills derived from specialised craft
training but were instead now defined increasingly on the basis of
specifications and training prescribed 'internally' by the particular
employer. The benefit for the worker of generally sought-after skills
commanding high value in the external labour market had gone.

The now emergent stage of direct labour elimination through the
means of advanced automation gives rise to a further shift in labour
market position for the workers concerned. In so far as they are
displaced from regular employment altogether, their location will have
shifted to the secondary external segment. They will have been forced
onto the general labour market 'external' to the particular employing
firm. Their position remains 'secondary' in that the absence of
generally marketable skills eliminates the availability of long-term
earning security as well as any opportunity to exercise discretion in the
performance of tasks if work is secured. The labour market position of
production managers displaced by the elimination of direct labour may
shift even more dramatically from a relatively privileged primary
internal position to one in the external market which will be of
secondary standing unless their abilities and experience can still
command a premium in the marketplace.

(2) Contracting
Contracting refers to an arrangement whereby the employer pays for an
agreed delimited amount of production or period of labour time, but
leaves the organisation, manning and sometimes the equipping of the
task to the worker or group of workers concerned. It has a long history.
An early form of labour management in Britain was the putting-out
system in which production was let out to physically dispersed
domestic workers by a central employer-merchant. Subcontracting to

groups of workers on a central production site became widespread in the nineteenth century (Gospel 1983). Some putting out persists to the present day in the form of homeworking (Cragg and Dawson 1981) while subcontracting is still a common arrangement in the building industry.

These historical forms of contracting involved manual workers who were engaged on productive activities which could be performed as discrete tasks or stages. In such cases, the expense of maintaining continuity of employment and a superstructure of control could be avoided, and with it an economic risk when faced with market uncertainties and competitive pressures. There are distinct possibilities that where manufacturing can be carried out in discrete stages, a comparable development could re-emerge with the aid of new information technology. Here a standardisation of language for specifying fabrication needs, combined with computer programming which can turn the specifications into production, may eliminate the need to incorporate the separate stages of manufacture within a single location serviced by a unified labour force.

It is noteworthy not only that employers today are displaying increasing interest in contracting arrangements, but that these are now being extended to office and managerial workers located at the core of bureaucracies. Arrangements for working from home while remaining part of a network connected electronically to a central office are clearly motivated by economic considerations, but their achievement relies heavily on new technology (Mandeville 1983).

Although the problem of controlling the growth of administrative and managerial overheads has been recognised for some time now (cf. Child 1978), it has not yet been resolved. A recent survey by the Institute of Administrative Management found that among 180 UK companies administrative costs had risen by 4 per cent in real terms during the five years to 1981 (Kransdorff 1983). Managements have in the past few years become acutely aware of overhead costs including those of wage and salary earners who had until recently come to expect long-term employment. Wage and salary earners incur many extra costs for the employer: heat, space, food, car parking, office and secretarial support, insurance costs and various requirements imposed by legislation. Additional investment in supervisory control is required to transform labour power into actual labour within the expensively serviced place of work. There is therefore a growing interest in the possibility of paying workers to work on their own premises on a contract basis. It has been predicted that fee paying short-term contracts will increasingly come to be substituted for long-term employment within organisations (e.g. Handy 1982).

Williamson (1975) analysed the development of hierarchical working relationships within large bureaucracies in terms of the lower transaction costs, including greater certainty and predictability, which often attended organisational as opposed to market relationships. New information technology, whether for transmission of data, facsimile documents or audio-visual exchange, is beginning to facilitate communication over distances and the precise logging (i.e. measurement) of the transmission. Long-range communication can take place with increasing ease and reducing real cost, and less reliance has therefore to be placed on the close proximity of working that justifies the 'office'. Taking into account as well the burden of wage and salary costs, the balance of transaction cost advantage is thus moving back towards the market relationship in which smaller units and even people working at home are linked electronically and through market contracts to form a whole system of work.

According to a recently reported survey of 255 among the largest 1000 UK companies, almost two-thirds believe that by 1988 they will be employing executives working from home (Cane 1983). Already, over 20 per cent of companies with a turnover of more than £500m a year have some executives working from home using personal computers. It is not stated how many of these computers are linked to the corporate office. Rank Xerox has initiated 'networking' arrangements with some of its specialists whereby they now work from their own homes on individualised contracts, and often have Xerox 820 microcomputers linked to the company's head office. The saving to the company is reported to be substantial since it estimates that a manager's or specialist's employment cost approaches three times his or her salary once overheads, secretarial and office services, and administrative back-up are taken into account. Under the 'networking' system, payment is only for a contracted number of days and/or services rendered and not for the non-productive time contained in full-time employment. Under such arrangements, the use of new technology increases the ability to record the networker's output, which further adds to managerial control.

Staff working at home under this kind of arrangement become self-employed contractors, and in fact Xerox encourages them to start up their own businesses or private practices to operate during the time not contracted to the company. In the case of high level specialists able to secure work on their own account, contracting therefore shifts them from the internal to the external labour market while retaining a primary standing. This standing would shift downwards towards a secondary status were the homeworkers not able to attract a market demand for their skills as consultants or private entrepreneurs. They, rather than their erstwhile full-time employer, now bear the risk of providing a secure income flow. They enjoy a greater control over how their work is actually carried out and over their pattern of working time, but the employer enjoys greater control over the conditions for extracting surplus value in that he can now specify the relation between work done and labour cost much more precisely – in addition to enjoying a much reduced overall labour cost.

Another strategic development in this category is already well established. This consists of contracting out whole areas of work, such as maintenance and services like cleaning and canteens which are regarded as peripheral to the core productive activity, in order again to save bearing the cost of a standing overhead for an activity which can be bought in more cheaply instead. New technology has some relevance to this strategy, particularly with respect to the external contracting of maintenance. Some new equipment has become so sophisticated and complex that its maintenance internally would require the employment of costly highly trained staff. On the other hand, with self-diagnostic systems and greatly improved reliability, the unanticipated need for major attention tends to reduce, and this may make it possible to use an outside contractor on a planned basis. Minor rectifications may now be adequately catered for by adding on the monitoring of plant condition and the replacement of standard parts and modules to the existing tasks of operatives, a form of 'polyvalence' discussed shortly. There is then less need to rely on specialised maintenance staff employed by the organisation staff who, as Crozier (1964) indicated, occupy a strategic position *vis-à-vis* the labour process. In so far as external contracting of this kind substitutes for internal employment, the labour market consequences are to move former employees from either primary internal (maintenance) or secondary internal (most other services) segments onto the external labour market, though after relocation they may become members of the internal labour markets of contracting firms.

(3) Polyvalence

The third managerial strategy is frequently adopted in connection with new technology but does not depend on it. This is a strategy of 'polyvalence', in the French sense of the term, denoting a situation in which workers perform, or at least are available to perform, a range of tasks which cut across or extend traditional skill and job boundaries.

Polyvalence may be reached along several different routes. One involves the removal of skill demarcations and is horizontal in nature. In some cases the requirement for specific job skills which once commanded a premium in the external market has disappeared, because of technological change. The jobs concerned are extended to take in other tasks as a result. Lithographic workers in some provincial newspapers provide an example. In other cases, the route will be through the drive by employers to remove demarcation between skills which are still required. The intention here is to reduce employment costs and to increase the flexibility of manpower deployment. The fusion of electronic and mechanical features in the design of new technology is often cited by managers as a rationale for seeking polyvalence of this type among maintenance workers. In the service sector, a similar argument has been pursued in terms of integrating the application of specialist skills to meet the total needs of the customer, once new technology can provide the appropriate information system support. An example is provided shortly from banking, while Heery (1983) describes a development of this kind in local authority 'Neighbourhood Offices'.

A second main route to polyvalence is through enlarging the task competences of the worker in a job requiring relatively limited skills – usually an operative or routine office job. The dimension of this enlargement – how many additional tasks and how much additional responsibility or control – can vary and so correspondingly will the training required. A 'vertical' element of upskilling may be involved in job enlargement, but in other cases tasks requiring little skill are simply added together, and this may even be done in the hope of salving some worker job satisfaction in the wake of deskilling.

The job definition and routes of possible advancement for the polyvalent worker will in the main be highly specific to the employing organisation, thus locating him or her firmly in the internal labour market. The standing of the polyvalent worker in the internal labour market will depend on the level of the skills which are now combined and on the discretionary content of the job. Whether or not polyvalence represents advance or regression, upskilling or degradation, will be a question of the route by which the worker has travelled to it.

The polyvalence strategy is often combined with the development of a 'responsible autonomy' type of control (Friedman 1977). 'Job enrichment' is a case in point, combining an extension of tasks with an increment of autonomy with regard to matters such as checking the quality of completed work. This will often form part of an employment policy which reinforces the internal labour market, through (i) the provision of opportunities to acquire new skills and tasks which are defined in the local organisation's own terms, (ii) opportunities to advance at least some way up a grading ladder defined in terms of an organisational scheme of job evaluation, and (iii) emphasis upon long-term employment opportunities, involvement in communications and participation arrangements, corporate ceremonies and events, and other elements designed to build commitment to the corporate objectives defined by management. We are not, of course, very far from the so-called 'Japanese philosophy of management' here, though it is one which has characterised certain Western companies for some time (cf. Ouchi 1981). It approximates to the more sophisticated form of 'bureaucratic control' identified by Edwards (1979).

As well as offering the employer potential cost advantages by way of flexibility and reduced levels of manning, the polyvalence strategy is also an approach to control over the labour process which may be more effective than blatant and direct controls (as in close supervision) because it emphasises the consensual and 'positive' side of the employment relationship. This strategy endeavours to tie the worker into the internal labour market of the organisation and to render his or her skills specific to that organisation. In so far as it succeeds in increasing the dependence of workers on employment in the particular organisation and reduces their marketability elsewhere, then the polyvalent strategy enhances management's power in the employment relationship and hence its potential for control. Thus while, in the British situation at least, the initial stages of polyvalence may sometimes be forced through by confrontation with trade unions (though it is more often to be found in non-union situations), the strategy once it has reached a mature stage will tend to develop a more advantageous ground for managerial initiative. It may indeed generate a degree of acquiescence if policies of fostering normative commitment meet with success. It also has to be recalled that the 'responsible autonomy' which tends to complement polyvalence, is a control strategy with its focus typically on output measurement. For instance, the allocation of responsibility to a worker or work group for a more 'complete' set of tasks – what is sometimes called a 'whole task' such as complete assembly of a TV set – can make it easier for management to identify accountability for sub-standard performance. The application of new microelectronic monitoring devices and information transmission systems facilitates performance measurement, and may thereby make a transition from direct personal supervision of the labour process to a responsible autonomy format that much more acceptable to management. In effect, new technology can substitute supervision at a distance for supervision in the workplace.

Polyvalence as a strategy is not necessarily pursued in connection with new technology – it may, for instance, take the form of a general managerial drive against craft or custom-and-practice demarcation and against multi-unionism. However, it can be associated with new technology in several ways: (i) as a policy to maintain the use of workers' capabilities when these would otherwise be underutilised because new technology takes over from the use of skills; (ii) in circumstances where new technology is introduced to enhance the organisation's capability of competing – either on the basis of quick response and small job quantities, where flexibility in manning is therefore at a premium, or on the basis of introducing new technology to enhance the quality of service provided by staff whose range of tasks is thereby extended; and (iii) in cases where the new information processing capabilities accompanying plant investment permit polyvalence to a greater degree than before.

Wilkinson (1983) provides an example of the polyvalence strategy in a situation in which new technology might otherwise have resulted in deskilling. This was a firm manufacturing lenses and spectacles in which job rotation was introduced as a means of preserving the intrinsic content and interest of jobs concerned with lens preparation where the introduction of new computer-programmed machinery had reduced the skill and judgemental component of individual tasks. This policy of job rotation was supported by the careful selection of new recruits to ensure a certain level of competence and considerable attention was given to training. These measures in turn provided possibilities for future promotion to supervisory jobs. A craft-oriented management in this firm had adapted its policies on job design to the introduction of new technology so as in some degree to offset the reduction of skills, but also in a manner which tied the definition of those skills and opportunities for personal advancement more closely to the firm's internal labour market.

Banking provides an example of the second way in which polyvalence is associated with new technology. In one of the largest clearing banks, new technology is currently being considered as a means of enhancing the capacity of staff located behind desks in the lobbies of branches to offer a superior level of advisory service to customers. The idea would be to equip each desk with a VDU unit linked to a file containing customer details. It is argued that immediate file access of this kind would not only facilitate updating, but more significantly it would permit the member of staff to take on a marketing function by suggesting in the light of the customer information how the bank could be of service in terms of arranging insurance, providing a loan and so forth. It would also provide the staff member with data relevant to a judgement *not* to offer certain services – such as a further loan. The bank is already developing the concept of 'personal bankers' to deal with all non-cash transaction services to customers coming into bank branches; this new job is located at a grade above that of counter tellers, and it is claimed that the exercise of additional skills (including interpersonal ones) that it requires will provide a basis for further future promotion into posts such as back-office supervisor. If new technology is introduced in the manner described, then this is likely to enhance the polyvalence of the 'personal banker' role. The definition of this new job and the skills it requires is specific to the bank in question, though in the banking industry barriers already exist to the ready movement of workers from one bank to another through the external labour market. What should be noted with this example is that the new technology involved could just as readily be used to *reduce* the skill and control of the bank worker in dealings with the customer, by means of incorporating programmed decision hierarchies of a standardised form which serve as instructions to the worker over responses to the customer, given the latter's computerised profile. In the case of banks, such decisions are indisputably the direct product of managerial strategy: they are taken centrally, in detail, and with very little employee or union participation (Child *et al.* 1984).

A food company provides an example of the third type of connection between pursuit of the polyvalence strategy and the introduction of new technology. Having reduced its workforce considerably, the management of this company is now attempting to use the possibilities offered by microelectronics for integrating the monitoring of production workflow and the condition of equipment into a central control room (plus features such as the self diagnosis of faults and ready replacement of faulty circuits) in order to introduce a new shopfloor role which combines operative and routine maintenance tasks. The new role offers some opportunity for upgrading once appropriate training has been successfully completed. Members of this particular management display a remarkable degree of consistency and unanimity in describing their labour strategy in connection with new technology: they see its purpose as enhancing flexibility and economy, of manning, by (i) workers taking on additional responsibilities, and (ii) a concomitant opening up of the job grading structure. These two thrusts are bringing management into direct confrontation with unions in a multi-union situation. The situation clearly illustrates the conflict between internal labour market managerial perspectives and those of occupational interest organisation representatives holding to external labour market definitions of their members' jobs.

(4) Degradation of jobs

A central argument in Braverman's book (1974) is that the conflict of classes around economic interest promotes a continual search by the capitalist for ways to control and cheapen the production process. While it may be his dream to eliminate the dependence on labour altogether, his desire for control and cost reduction are seen in the meantime to motivate a long-term trend towards the degradation of existing jobs.

The main features of this strategy are the fragmentation of labour into narrowly constituted jobs, with de-skilling and a use of direct control methods either through close supervision or structuring by technology. Of all the developments discussed in this paper, the degradation of jobs can be the most confidently identified as a managerial strategy – it has a long history, has been widely discussed and practised, and for many years found a place in managerial, engineering and even personnel literature (though never without its critics). It was pupil to F.W. Taylor's main theme: that skill, knowledge and hence control should be separated from the worker. Work study techniques were developed to operationalise this maxim, while the moving conveyor technology closely associated with Henry Ford added a 'technical control' over the pace of work and the physical location of the worker (Edwards 1979).

Managers are able today to use new technology in an attempt to avoid reliance on the skills and judgement of workers, and to regulate their performance more precisely. While this may be perceived by managers and engineers as a stage towards automation, a degradation strategy often has more effect on the intrinsic quality of jobs rather than on their quantity. It permits cost reduction through a substitution of less qualified workers, a minimisation of training and a closer managerial definition of performance standards. These changes reduce worker control over the labour process and facilitate an intensification of work, but degradation will nevertheless probably involve fewer reductions in absolute manpower than polyvalence and certainly fewer than full automation.

Many examples of the pursuit of job degradation alongside the introduction of new technology are now recorded in the literature. Those concerning the use of numerical control have borne out Noble's (1979) contention that some managements have made a conscious choice to employ new technological possibilities for the purpose of job degradation even when there was an availability of alternative technologies or alternative modes of work structuring which could be used effectively with the technology (e.g. Jones 1982b; Wilkinson 1983). Another relevant example is newspaper production where new technology has been introduced in ways that have degraded and in some cases eliminated traditional skills. This has generated defensive measures by alarmed craft unions which appear to have poor prospects of long-term success (Cockburn 1983; Gennard and Dunn 1983). Degradation has also accompanied the introduction of new technology into areas of routine office work, such as local government treasurer's departments (Crompton and Reid 1982). However, a trend towards job degradation was already underway in office work well before the introduction of electronic technology, with the use of an advanced division of labour and close supervision within large open-plan offices (e.g. de Kadt 1979).

Policies of job degradation are even evident in areas of service provision where in the past the quality of the service has been associated with staff discretion concerning the appropriate response to individual customers' needs and covering, if necessary, a wide range of transactions (advice, purchases, services). Two instances, in retailing and banking respectively, may be illustrated from studies undertaken by the writer and his colleagues.

The major introduction of new technology within retailing consists of electronic-point-of-sale (EPOS) systems, which are fronted by electronic cash registers incorporating devices to scan bar-coded individual sales items. The cash registers are linked to a retail company's computer which will (in an advanced application) contain the prices to be applied to each item of sale – 'automatic price look-up'. With the exception of relatively few accounting and systems staff (who may be located at a head office rather than in local stores), the way EPOS has generally been applied so far is to reinforce a work degradation strategy. In the case of supermarkets, for instance, the system now permits management to impose much greater control over check-out 'girls'. Indeed, one of the claims made by those who supply EPOS systems is that they eliminate various forms of check-out fiddling. (This also applies to the loss of goods from stock.) Also because EPOS systems make readily available much more precise information on customer flows, they enable management to direct the deployment of staff more closely with regard to hours of working and job allocation within the store. There is a consequent intensification of the check-out operator's work. An interesting feature of EPOS is that it is also being used in a way that degrades jobs of higher standing within the organisation. The information it provides on sales profiles and stock levels permits routine programming (such as automatic re-order routines) to be applied to some buying decisions for which management had previously to depend upon the judgement of buyers. In a similar way, the new information now reduces the dependency of store general managers upon the assessment of conditions and trends by departmental or section managers. The latter's role then tends to be reduced to that of a supervisor and in supermarkets there may be very few section staff left to supervise now that EPOS can eliminate the need to price-label individual items or to inspect the stock level of shelves visually. (Elimination of item price-labelling, of course, reduces the *level* of staffing as well.)

In the new or refurbished branches of one of Britain's largest banks, the traditional job of teller has been divided into routine and less routine components. While a relatively small number of staff now concentrate on dealing with non-routine customer requirements in a role that has actually been upgraded through taking on additional 'marketing' functions, the larger number of lobby staff now occupy jobs which have been degraded. They are required to specialise only on the handling of small cash transactions (and not even those involving large amounts of coin) and on customer balance enquiries. This policy has been developed by the bank's central management in order to speed up routine transactions for the customer and at the same time to intensify the work of the counter teller. It has been assisted by the introduction of new technology in the form of keyboard operated automatic electronic cash dispensers, in conjuction with a very old technology of pneumatic tubes to transmit cash deposited rapidly to a secure area.

The implications of job degradation for the labour market position of the workers concerned were summarised when discussing the elimination of direct labour through automation, for which degradation can be the forerunner. The application of techniques such as work study and clerical work measurement to the narrowing and deskilling of jobs is typically formalised in job descriptions and gradings which are particular to the employing organisation. They serve to locate the worker more firmly within the organisation's internal labour market, and along a historical path towards an increasingly secondary position. The worker's power to negotiate favourable terms and conditions as an individual is vitiated both by deskilling itself (the decline towards secondary status) and by the particularisation of his or her skills away from substantive definitions or norms of experience which are recognised and command general value on the open external labour market. It is not suprising that workers who experience degradation often come to regard collective action as the only means of defending their position and securing a tolerable livelihood.

Discussion

Four managerial strategies have been identified to which the introduction of new technology can be allied. Each reflects objectives relating to the pursuit of capital accumulation under conditions of market competition, and represents in different forms an intensification of labour. All have definable implications for the labour process and for the labour market position of the workers concerned. When pursued severally by the management of a particular organisation, these strategies increase the segmentation of its labour force into different skill and status categories as well as increasing the pool of labour in the external labour market. Both these results weaken the capacity of workers to mount an organised resistance against management and its use of new technology, or even to formulate common policies on the subject. The internal and external labour market consequences of managerial strategies towards the labour process will therefore tend to reinforce management's ability to pursue those strategies, unless wider contextual factors change significantly.

In so far as these managerial strategies are effectively implemented, they will generate variation in the labour process. The factors that influence the choice of strategy, and that determine whether workers seek and are able to resist its implementation, are therefore salient to an explanation of the specific form taken by the organisation of the labour process. There are some pointers in the literature to these operative factors, and following the lead they provide, it is possible to outline the conditions which are likely to encourage each managerial strategy.

An extremely complex framework would be required for a full analysis of variations in the managerial strategies pursued towards the labour process and in the success with which they are implemented or resisted. It is possible only to suggest a bare outline here, which is approached along two planes or dimensions. First, as the previous discussion began to indicate, there are several levels of relevant contextual analytical unit: the mega socio-economic system, the nation or society, the industry or sector, the enterprise or organisation. Second, there are conceptually distinct influences, including government policy, institutional and cultural features, product and labour market conditions, organisational and task variables.

It is accepted that the capitalist labour process will embody capitalistic objectives expressed in modern enterprises through management as the agent of capital. This implies a contrast with labour processes and modes of organisation in non-capitalist mega systems: in principle with socialism but in practice with what Thompson has labelled 'state collectivism' (1983: 223n). While there is a common reliance on hierarchical work organisation and the managerial function in both mega systems, the formal status of the worker in the production system is different as are the official organs which express that formal position. Managerial policies connected with the use of new technology are prima facie expected to reflect this fundamental difference.

Within the capitalist system, a divergence is apparent between countries in features that influence managerial strategies and the organisation of the labour process. Sorge *et al.* (1983) illustrate this clearly through comparing British and West German companies in the extent to which the organisation of computer numerical control usage is designed to build upon workers' existing skills rather than to substitute for these. Though other factors such as size of company are also found to be relevant, Sorge and his colleagues conclude that the tradition of craft reflected in the scale and quality of present-day German vocational training helps to account for the greater tendency in the German firms to rely on workers on the spot to control and edit machine programmes as opposed to confining this to specialist programmers – in other words a polyvalent rather than a degradation policy. This tradition of craft and practical industrial knowledge is strongly represented in most German line management, and is likely to encourage a polyvalent strategy. Research adopting a cross-national perspective, and which is sensitive to the mode of industrial and social development in each country, points to a variety in capitalist labour processes and in the employer strategies which importantly shaped these. Littler's analysis (1983) of the managerial strategies adopted in Britain, Japan, the United States and Germany is particularly suggestive of the components of this variety.

The analysis of variety in managerial strategies has to be refined further, to more specific locations within a nation's system of productive relations. Littler (1983) cites Britain as the country most removed from what he calls the monopoly capitalism model of employment and labour relations incorporating a marked development of internal labour markets. At the same time, as he admits, within that one country, internal labour markets developed unevenly between different sectors. British banks and large chemical companies had, for example, developed internal labour markets at an early period, while these remained absent for a long time in other sectors such as textiles. Spender's research on strategic recipes (1980) has also indicated their industry-specific nature. Individual large firms will today typically straddle several industries and be internally divided into quasi-autonomous divisions or business units. A variety of managerial strategies towards employment is therefore not unexpected within the same company. Moreover, if managements are sensitive to the labour market position, skills and expectations of specific groups of workers, it is to be expected that they will adopt different strategies towards each group. Differentiated employment policies will therefore be evident even at the level of a single plant, such that particularly valued groups may be upgraded and encouraged to acquire new skills (polyvalence) while others are possibly degraded, eliminated or placed on limited contracts. In short, similarities and differences in managerial strategies need to be analysed at various system levels.

The second analytical dimension relevant to managerial strategies brings in the substantive factors which are likely to promote variety in labour process organisation. The major factors to emerge from available research and discussion are government policy, institutions, culture, product and labour market conditions, organisation and task. The first three of these factors are predominantly national in scope. The importance of *government policy* illustrated by the conclusion that legislation provides the most significant single stimulus to industrial democracy in the European countries (IDE 1981). Governmental encouragement has also been a major factor behind the West German vocational training programme previously mentioned. The role of government as promoter of certain applications of new technology is substantial and takes it effectively into the role of sponsoring certain managerial strategies. Thus the Colchester prototype FMS factory was largely funded by a £3m British government grant, and £60m has been set aside to meet FMS development and capital costs. Through the medium of policies for education and training, for recognition of professional privileges, and for industrial relations, governments play a substantial role in the development of the *institutional framework* which a number of studies have shown to impinge significantly on the organisation and manning of the labour process (e.g. Maurice, Sorge and Warner 1980; Child *et al.* 1983). *Culture* is the third factor which is primarily identifiable at the national level. While its ontology and role is subject to considerable debate, the thesis has been strongly argued that culural values such as those concerning the equality of individual worth within society and interpersonal trust will influence the strategies adopted by management: thus a low evaluation of workers' individual worth and trustfulness will encourage job degradation (cf. Hofstede 1980).

Market conditions can be both general and specific. Ramsey (1977) and others have pointed to the way that managerial strategies are adjusted to general business cycle conditions. In periods of recession and weakened labour power, it is suggested that strategies of labour elimination and degradation are likely to predominate, and that management's ability to enforce any chosen strategy will be greater. Conversely, the ability of workers to resist managerial strategies and to impose their chosen occupational definition of the labour process will be greater in periods of market buoyancy and labour shortage. Friedman (1977) examined the more specific labour and product market conditions of three British industries to reach the conclusion that these in large measure distinguished between the adoption of 'direct control' and 'responsible autonomy' strategies. The former tends to incorporate job degradation while the latter may incorporate polyvalence of the job enrichment type where a higher level of discretion is added. Labour supply conditions may also differ, of course, for particular groups of workers within a single firm. Even today, certain categories of skilled and specialist workers are claimed to be in short supply: the scarcity value of such workers is likely to be reflected not only in levels of pay but also in their ability to secure greater control over working practices.

Organisational and task factors are specific to the particular unit of production. Among *organisational factors*, company traditions can exert an important influence. They frequently have their origins in the ideology of an entrepreneurial founder who set out both a strategic perspective on the task of the organisation and a philosophy on the form of the labour process to accomplish it. 'Fordism' as a labour process to accomplish the strategy of opening up the latent mass motor car market is simply the best known example out of very many. In this way, some companies have developed a mass production culture which encourages a trend towards job degradation, while others have maintained a bespoke tradition to which retention of craft skills and even polyvalence is more naturally related. Size of organisation tends to be associated with this particular strategic choice, with mass producers usually being larger. A close relationship between larger size and greater speciali-sation has been found in many studies conducted in a wide range of countries and organisational types (cf. Child 1973; Hickson *et al.* 1979). This means that larger size will encourage job degradation, over and above any mass production 'effect', through two processes. First, larger workforces will tend to become more internally specialised thus encouraging a narrowing of skills. Second, larger organisations will tend to employ more 'staff' specialists including industrial engineers and machine tool programmers who will work to control the labour process by narrowing the discretion of, and tasks performed by, workers.

There is some consensus among organisational theorists that the most significant *task dimensions* for an understanding of how work is organised are those relating to uncertainty and complexity (cf. Perrow 1970; Van de Ven and Ferry 1980). The number of exceptions encoun-tered in performing the task and its general variability, a lack of clarity about what is required and about cause-effect relationships are all factors contributing to uncertainty. Complexity is increased by factors such as the amount of relevant information to be absorbed in carrying out the task, the number of steps involved, and the number of contri-butions required from different sources. A third relevant dimension is the cost of making an error, whether this falls primarily on property or on the person.

An analysis of the introduction of new technology into medicine, banking and retailing conducted by the writer and colleagues (Child *et al.* 1984) concluded that task uncertainty and the cost of error were particularly significant for enabling service providers to preserve the integrity of their jobs. New technologies will normally have a superiority in receiving, storing and providing rapid access to complex data, so long as these are in a structured form. Moreover, tasks involving uncertainty and risk require the exercise of judgement: the best way of carrying them out is not transparent. This 'indeterminacy' has considerable ideological potential for the defence of the worker's control over the labour process, as professional workers in particular have demonstrated (Jamous and Peloille 1970). In short, the greater the uncertainty and risk in tasks to be performed, the less likely are strategies of labour elimination or job degradation to be adopted. Since an organisation will normally contain a range of tasks with different degrees of uncertainty and risk, this is another factor encouraging a diversity of management strategies towards the labour process within the firm.

Each of the four managerial strategies is likely to be pursued under different circumstances and in relation to different categories of workers. Within the purely British context, relevant product market, labour market, task and organisational influences may tentatively be identified, drawing from the framework just set out.

The *elimination of direct labour* through automation entails considerable investment in new equipment. Leaving aside process production where the properties of the materials is a major consideration, this strategy is most appealing to a management whose firm competes on the basis of embodying complex machining in products manufactured in small batches and subject to variability in specification. Investment of this order is also more likely in a recessionary period but when market opportunities are apparent and an upturn in demand is expected. In so far as FMS developments have so far involved new facilities, the relevance of labour market characteristics has not been clear. However, labour elimination strategies are more likely to be pursued and to succeed in existing establishments when the negotiating position of workers is weakened by unemployment, especially if severance terms are generous or alternative employment is offered elsewhere within the company or locality. Labour elimination would appear to suit tasks of which the performance dimensions are well understood, but which are complex and where precision is required. It is, finally, the strategy most likely to find favour in an organisation with a strong professional engineering (as opposed to a craft) culture.

Contracting is a means of reducing the risk incurred in serving product markets which display unstable or seasonal patterns of demand. It commits the employer to maintaining a portion of his employment costs for a limited period only. The spread of contracting is likely to be facilitated by slack labour markets, in which a sufficient number of people come forward who are prepared to work on limited contracts and themselves bear the risk of providing a long-term income flow. Contracting is also more practical where there is a technical possibility of segmenting distinct tasks or stages in production, which can constitute a specific contracted obligation. Finally, the organisation with high overheads and whose management has a strong (probably traditional) sense of a 'core' organisational competence, is the more likely to favour contracting.

It may be recalled that *polyvalence* takes the two forms of (i) removal of demarcations and (ii) job enlargement. Product market conditions in which quality of product or service is a significant competitive factor are likely to encourage both forms. An important impetus to removing demarcations may come from competitive pressures bearing on production costs, while job enlargement policies have been more common in buoyant product market conditions. The labour market factor is also relevant here. The removal of demarcation is likely to be seen as a threat to job control and will therefore be more readily introduced when organised worker opposition is weak. In contrast, job enlargement has typically been introduced in tight labour markets as an attempt to reduce high levels of absenteeism and labour turnover. The type of task conducive to a polyvalent strategy is one in which the use of worker discretion and judgement is believed to be functional, and one which permits flexibility of physical movement, of time budgeting and possibly of sequencing. The type of organisation more likely to contain polyvalent strategies will have small work units (plants, departments or offices), a craft or professional tradition, and an emphasis on the training and development of workers. It may well have inherited a paternalistic tradition.

A *job degradation* strategy is likely to be stimulated by competitive pressures in product markets, but where the basis of that competition is keenly priced standardised production. Slack labour markets, with a pool of readily available compliant cheap labour from the 'secondary external' sector, are also conducive to the adoption and successful imposition of this strategy. Favourable task characteristics include repeated standard routine operations, the methods for which can be readily defined and performance assessed without undue difficulty. The type of organisation in which this strategy will tend to be found is large and without a strong craft or professional tradition. It may well have a history of autocratic management which maintained a considerable social distance from the workforce, and did not encourage opportunities for workers to gain advancement within the company.

These propositions suggest that the use of new technology to advance particular managerial strategies can usefully be understood in terms of contextual factors of a market, task and organisational nature within a particular country. Governmental, institutional and cultural factors come into account when broader cross-national comparisons are attempted. The analysis presented here implies that a study of job redesign within the labour process needs to be sensitive to specific historical and contemporary features which shape the patterns of its variation around the course of capitalist development.

References

Braverman, H. (1974), *Labor and Monopoly Capital: The Degradation of Work in the Twentieth Century*, New York: Monthly Review Press.

Buchanan, D.A. and Boddy, D. (1983), *Organizations in the Computer Age*, Aldershot: Gower.

Cane, A. (1982), 'The factory with no workers', *Financial Times*, 14 July.

Cane, A. (1983), 'More expected to work from home', *Financial Times*, 1 September.

Charlish, G. (1983), 'FMS – A way of thinking', *Financial Times*, 3 November.

Child, J. (1973), 'Predicting and understanding organization structure', *Administrative Science Quarterly*, **18**, 168–185.

Child, J. (1974), 'Managerial and organizational factors associated with company performance', *Journal of Management Studies*, **11**, 175–189.

Child, J. (1978), 'The "non-productive" component within the productive sector: a problem of management control', in M. Fores and I. Glover (eds.), *Manufacturing and Management*, London: HMSO.

Child, J. and Partridge, B. (1982), *Lost Managers: Supervisors in Industry and Society*, Cambridge: Cambridge University Press.

Child, J., Fores, M., Glover, I. and Lawrence, P. (1983), 'A price to pay? professionalism and work organization in Britain and West Germany', *Sociology*, **17**, 63–78.

Child, J., Loveridge, R., Harvey, J. and Spencer, A. (1984), 'Microelectronics and the quality of employment in services', in P. Marstrand (ed.), *New Technology and the Future of Work*, published for the British Association by Frances Pinter.

Cockburn, C. (1983), *Brothers: Male Dominance and Technical Change*, London: Pluto Press.

Cosyns, J., Loveridge, R. and Child, J. (1983), *New Technology in Retail Distribution – The Implications at Enterprise Level*, Report to the EEC, University of Aston Management Centre.

Cragg, A. and Dawson, T. (1981), 'Qualitative research among homeworkers', London: Department of Employment Research Paper, No. 21, May.

Crompton, R. and Reid, S. (1982), 'The deskilling of clerical work', in S. Wood (ed.), *The Degradation of Work?*, London: Hutchinson.

Crozier, M. (1964), *The Bureaucratic Phenomenon*, London: Tavistock.

de Kadt, M. (1979), 'Insurance: a clerical work factory', in A. Zimbalist (ed.), *Case Studies on the Labor Process*, New York: Monthly Review Press.

Edwards, R. (1979), *Contested Terrain*, London: Heinemann.

Fidler, J. (1981), *The British Business Elite*, London: Routledge and Kegan Paul.

Francis, A., Snell, M., Willman, P. and Winch, G. (1982), 'Management, industrial relations and new technology for the BL metro', Imperial College, Department of Social and Economic Studies, November.

Friedman, A.L. (1977), *Industry and Labour*, London: Macmillan.

Gennard, J. and Dunn, S. (1983), 'The impact of new technology on the structure and organization of craft unions in the printing industry', *British Journal of Industrial Relations*, **XXI**, 17–32.

Gospel, H.F. (1983), 'Managerial structures and strategies: an introduction', in H.F. Gospel and C.F. Littler (eds.), *Managerial Strategies and Industrial Relations*, London: Heinemann.

Grieco, M. (1983), Contribution to discussion, Conference on Organization and Control of the Labour Process, Owens Park, Manchester, March.

Gross, E. (1953), 'Some functional consequences of primary controls in formal work organizations', *American Sociological Review*, **18**, 368–373.

Handy, C. (1982), 'Where management is leading', *Management Today*, December, 50–53, 114.

Harvey, J. and Child, J. (1983), 'Green Hospital, Woodall, Biochemistry Laboratory: a case study', University of Aston.

Heery, E. (1983), 'Polyvalence and new technology', unpublished working paper, Department of Sociology, North East London Polytechnic.

Hickson, D.J., McMillan, C.J., Azumi, K. and Horvath, D. (1979), 'Grounds for comparative organization theory: quicksands or hard core?, in C.J. Lammers and D.J. Hickson (eds.), *Organizations Alike and Unlike*, London: Routledge and Kegan Paul.

Hofstede, G. (1980), *Culture's Consequences: National Differences In Thinking and Organizing*, Beverly Hills, Calif.: Sage.

IDE International Research Group (1981), *Industrial Democracy in Europe*, Oxford: Oxford University Press.

Incomes Data Services (IDS) (1980), *Changing Technology*, Study No. 22, London.

Jamous, H. and Peloille, B. (1970), 'Changes in the French University-Hospital System', in J.A. Jackson (ed.), *Professions and Professionalism*, Cambridge: Cambridge University Press.

Jones, B. (1982a), 'Destruction or redistribution of engineering skills? the case of numerical control', in Stephen Wood (ed.), *The Degradation of Work?*, London: Hutchinson.

Jones, B. (1982b), 'Technical, organizational, and political constraints on system re-design for machinist programming of NC machine tools', paper for IFIP Conference on 'System Design for the Users', Italy, September.

Kransdorff, A.A. (1983), 'Now for the white-collar shake-out', *Financial Times*, 18 April, 10.

Lamming, R. and Bessant, J. (1983), 'Some management implications of advanced manufacturing technology', unpublished paper, Department of Business Studies, Brighton Polytechnic.

Littler, C.R. (1983), 'A comparative analysis of managerial structures and strategies', in H.F. Gospel and C.R. Littler (eds.), *Managerial Strategies and Industrial Relations*, London: Heinemann.

Loveridge, R. (1983), 'Labour market segmentation and the firm', in J. Edwards *et al.*, *Manpower Strategy and Techniques in an Organizational Context*, Chichester: Wiley.

Mandeville, T. (1983), 'The spatial effects of information technology', *Futures*, February, 65–72.

March, J.G. and Olsen, J.P. (1976), *Ambiguity and Choice in Organizations*, Bergen: Universitetsforlaget.

Martin, R. (1981), *New Technology and Industrial Relations in Fleet Street*, Oxford: Clarendon Press.

Maurice, M., Sorge, A. and Warner, M. (1980), 'Societal differences in organizing manufacturing units: a comparison of France, West Germany and Great Britain', *Organizational Studies*, **1**, 59–86.

Mintzberg, H., Raisinghani, D. and Theoret, A. (1976), 'The structure of "unstructured" decision processes', *Administrative Science Quarterly*, **21**, 246–275.

Mok, A.L. (1975), 'Is er een Dubbele Arbeidsmarkt in Nederland?', in *Werkloosheid*,

Aard, Omvang, Structurele Oorzakenen Beleidsatternatieven, The Hague: Martinus Nijhoff.

Noble, D.F. (1979), 'Social choice in machine design: the case of automatically controlled machine tools', in A. Zimbalist (ed.), *Case Studies on the Labor Process*, New York: Monthly Review Press.

Northcott, J., Rogers, P. with Zeilinger, A. (1982), *Microelectronics in Industry: Survey Statistics*, London: Policy Studies Institute.

Ouchi, W. (1981), *Theory Z: How American Business Can Meet the Japanese Challenge*, Reading, Mass.: Addison-Wesley.

Perrow, C. (1970), *Organizational Analysis: A Sociological View*, London: Tavistock.

Purcell, J. (1983), 'The management of industrial relations in the modern corporation: agenda for research', *British Journal of Industrial Relations*, **XXI**, 1–16.

Ramsey, H. (1977), 'Cycles of control: workers participation in sociological and historical perspective', *Sociology*, **11**, 481–506.

Sorge, A., Hartmann, G., Warner, M. and Nicholas, I. (1983), *Microelectronics and Manpower in Manufacturing*, Aldershot: Gower.

Spender, J-C. (1980), Strategy-Making in Business, Unpublished Ph.D. Thesis, University of Manchester.

Thompson, P. (1983), *The Nature of Work*, London: Macmillan.

Van de Ven, A.H. and Ferry, D.L. (1980), *Measuring and Assessing Organizations*, New York: Wiley.

Wilkinson, B. (1983), *The Shopfloor Politics of New Technology*, London: Heinemann.

Williams, E. (1983), 'Process control boom near', *Financial Times*, 16 May.

Williamson, O.E. (1975), *Markets and Hierarchies*, New York: Free Press.

Wood, S. and Kelly, J. (1982), 'Taylorism, responsible autonomy and management strategy', in Stephen Wood (ed.), *The Degradation of Work?*, London: Hutchinson.

7 Automation, Management Strategies, and Labour-Process Change*

Rod Coombs

This chapter is concerned with the relationship between job redesign and technical change in the labour process. The paper argues that the development of the debate since Braverman (1974) has overemphasised the role of changes in work organisation and underemphasised the role of technical change, such that the interactions between these, and other factors have been wrongly analysed. This argument revolves around two theoretical devices. The first of these is a revised taxonomy of the elements of the labour process and of the factors that may precipitate change in these elements. The second device is a typology of mechanisation which relates to the first device. This second typology is used to propose a historical periodisation of mechanisation which forms a context within which changes in work organisation can be re-examined.

The chapter is structured as follows. Part one reviews some of the theoretical and empirical problems raised by the labour process debate and presents the revised taxonomy of the labour process. Part two presents the typology of mechanisation and uses this typology to interpret the historical progress of mechanisation. Part three presents some data on the diffusion of mechanisation. Part four discusses the implications of the analysis for the debate over Kondratieff 'long waves' and over the implementation of new technologies in production processes.

Part One

1.1 The labour process debate

Despite the service done by Braverman in re-charging the concept of the labour process, there were many weaknesses in his work which have

* I am grateful to Bryn Jones and David Knights for comments on an earlier draft of this chapter.

led to a number of criticisms. The criticisms are now well-known and can be briefly summarised. First, Braverman's notion of de-skilling is too monolithic; it asserts that managers are always trying to de-skill workers, will always be successful in the long run, and that there are few counter-tendencies. There is now factual evidence to contradict all of these propositions. Secondly, Braverman's reference point for de-skilling is a romanticised account of nineteenth century engineering craft skill. This is historically limited, and cannot be successfully applied in other areas. Thirdly, he neglects the objective need for managers to utilise the cooperative character of labour in a production process. This results in a failure to acknowledge the alternative ways in which that cooperation can be achieved, and their potential effects on work organisation. These criticisms and many others have been well documented by various authors. Littler (1982) reports most of the substantial contributions to this process of evaluation of Braverman.

Recent empirical and historical studies of job redesign and labour process change (Jones 1982; Kelly 1982; Littler 1982) have shown two things. First, Taylorism was a more complex phenomenon than Braverman supposed. Its development and diffusion was not as linear as presented in *Labour and Monopoly Capital*. In fact it encountered several obstacles including resistance from supervisors as well as workers. Further, there have been, and may still be, circumstances in which Taylorism may be 'reversed' and fragmented jobs recombined (or redesigned) in response to specific pressures by some or all of the participants in the historical evolution of particular patterns of work organisation. Secondly, and rather more fundamentally, it has been cogently argued that job fragmentation and/or job redesign *as management strategies* are not the coherent, planned strategies for control and production optimisation which the labour-process literature has suggested. This argument criticises the over-emphasis on foresight amongst entrepreneurs and managers, and the objective efficacy of organisational structures as means of achieving strategies even if they were to exist. A feature of both of these criticisms is the emphasis on the capacity of workers and their organisations to respond to proposed changes in work organisation and in so doing force a compromise or bargain which makes the outcome diverge from any management strategies.

This last point raises a more fundamental issue in the labour process debate, recently discussed by Edwards (1983). A discussion framed in terms of management strategies, albeit vague ineffective ones which are anyway confronted by worker responses, assumes that there is an objective basis for conflict over work organisation. In fact, available conceptions of work organisation in production processes do not establish any necessity for conflict. Rather it is the embedding of these in specific social and economic conditions which engenders conflict. Therefore, as Edwards (ibid.) points out, a theoretical conception of the labour process which *assumes* conflict is making very particular claims about the status of the labour process in the broader theoretical description of capitalism as a mode of production. Braverman's relatively orthodox Marxist position establishes this theoretical link via the concepts of exploitation and surplus value. As we have seen, this results in a view of the historical evolution of the labour process in which managers continually seek control through job fragmentation in order to increase relative surplus value. We have seen further that this view cannot explain observed 'departures' from this trend. It should be added that this view is also incapable of allowing sustained worker resistance to job fragmentation, nor can it explain the opposite phenomenon: the regular presence of 'consent' over work organisation as described by Burawoy (1979) and further analysed by Knights and Collinson (chapter 9 in this volume).

For the purposes of analysis of the development of the labour-process debate in this paper, research can be divided into two camps. On the one hand there are those who have done important empirical work on the variability of labour process change, but have not yet clearly deduced the logical implications of this work for the theoretical status of the labour process. On the other hand there are those who have concentrated on the theoretical link between labour process change and the development of capitalism as a system. These approaches need to be reconciled in order to progress. Endless Marxist exegesis will not explain particular conjunctural changes in work organisation or initiatives in job redesign. Nor will further demonstrations of infinite particularistic variations of labour processes determine whether these are representative aspects of more basic *trends*; still less will it show whether there are any reasons for them.

What is needed therefore is an account of the production process and its components in *historically specific capitalist economies*, not in 'capitalism in general'. Yet this account should give sufficient credence to the general principles of capitalism to prevent it from becoming a purely contingent account. All societies create surplus in order to enable them to reproduce themselves; capitalist societies are sufficiently distinct from other societies that it would be perverse to forgo using capitalism as a term to describe one very particular way in which a surplus is created. The real work then becomes that of comparative analysis over time and between countries and industries. This is only now beginning to emerge.

For the purposes of this chapter it still remains to clarify the basic

features of an account of production which conform to the requirements mentioned above. Some further requirements can also be
clarified.

It is clear that an account of production is needed in which the
relationship between profits (at the level of the enterprise) and the
'personal efficiency of labour' is not one-to-one. If other factors are
allowed to affect the level of profit, then the efficiency of labour, and
factors such as management strategies that act upon it, are not
theoretically required to change everywhere and always in the same way
and as a result of the same pressures. In the traditional Braverman
perspective this diversity is unnecessarily excluded. This follows from
his conceiving the process of exploitation in the way suggested by the
classical Marxist labour theory of value, and by effectively reducing
class relations to those that are present at the point of production. Both
of these faults can be corrected. Edwards (1983) has argued, using the
work of Cohen (1979), that it is possible to have a perfectly sensible
concept of exploitation *without* using the labour theory of value.
Exploitation would still exist even in conditions where workers had
reduced their efficiency below the point at which exploitation is positive
in the classical Marxist sense. This in itself does not predict the
existence of conflict in work relations. But if we then acknowledge that
the employment relation is constituted not just at the level of the work
place, but also at the levels of the labour market, property relations and
the state, then we have an adequate basis for conceptualising a labour
process in which conflict is neither required nor excluded, it is simply
permitted. Whether it does occur will partly depend on other factors
which affect both the levels of profit and wages, and the levels of
satisfaction of workers and managers with their respective qualitative
relationships to the conduct of the labour process.

As Nicholls (1983) has pointed out, what managers are primarily
interested in is final outcomes of the labour process. Their concern with
its actual content, where it exists, flows from an instrumental concern
with productivity, quality, and predictability. As mentioned in the
introduction these outcomes can be affected by changes in technology as
well as by the changes in work organisation which have been the focus of
so much recent labour process writing. In what follows we offer an
account of the production process in which technology and other factors
are capable of affecting outcomes (productivity etc.) along with processes
which moderate the efficiency of labour. Thus our account will be
consistent with the requirements above in that work organisation change
will play a part in the process of profit seeking, but particular strategies
for changing work will not be rigidly required (à la Braverman) in order
to maintain the theoretical integrity of capitalist production.

1.2 *An account of the production process*

The model is summarised in Figure 7.1 but some explanation is required to accompany it. Firstly, the production process is described in relative autonomy from the capitalist institutions of private ownership, competition, and control. The connections between the two spheres are the function of operational management, which is central to our problem, and the institutions of the labour market and the capital market, which have been omitted from the diagram for the sake of clarity but which are essential to the context. In this section we shall begin by describing the production process and the factors that affect its productivity. From there we shall move to the descriptions of the way the outputs of the production process are assessed and the alternatives for capitalist institutions to intervene in the production process.

The production process consists of four main elements which interact and are also conditioned by other factors. First there is the technical efficiency of the capital equipment. Whatever the manner of its actual operation it is clear that different configurations of technology will, *ceteris paribus*, have different intrinsic maximum physical productivities. Secondly there is the range of tasks that must be performed by workers and the manner of their combination into specific jobs. This division of labour is partly constrained by the technology itself, but there is a range of flexibility within which it is possible for workers and/or managers to exercise (consciously or not) some choice. Thirdly there is the personal efficiency of labour. This will be partly conditioned by the technology and the division of labour. (For example machine pacing and line balancing clearly set some limits.) Some variation in efficiency will also exist, however, and this will be open to influence by a whole range of factors which come under the general heading of the nature of the employment relation. Examples are the nature of the labour markets for particular jobs or firms, the payment system, the possibility for, and effectiveness of, direct supervision. Fourthly there is the coordination function. By this we mean that part of the management function which is not specifically concerned with production *for profit* but which is concerned with the direct continuity and rational conduct of connected activities. In practice, of course, certain jobs will combine this function with that of policing the wage relation and property relations but the function is nevertheless distinct and belongs in the production process proper.

Given certain inputs, in the form of a stock of machinery, raw materials and energy, these four elements *together* create output with a particular efficiency measured in terms of productivity, quality and predictability. Productivity here could be measured against labour

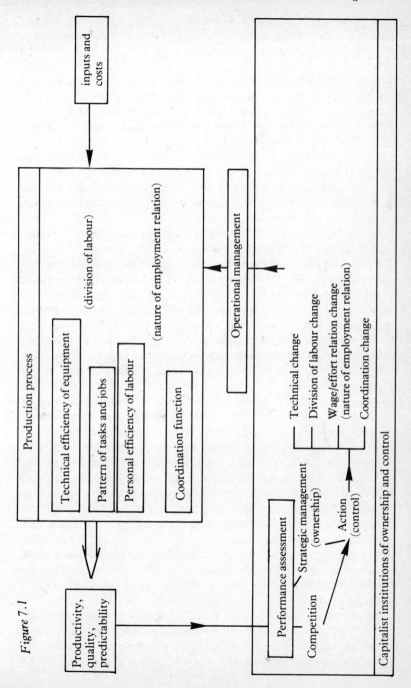

Figure 7.1

time, units of energy, 'social surplus embodied in capital stock' or any other numeraire. In capitalist societies, however, the inputs have a set of associated money or opportunity costs, and the output has a certain potential to be realised as money. It is of course not guaranteed that this potential will be realised, but that is a different matter. It is also true that the realisable value of output does not necessarily exceed that of the inputs, but, as mentioned above and as argued by Edwards (1983), exploitation will still exist because *any* output will still be owned by the firm rather than by the workers.

We move outside the production process now to the institutional context. Any productive unit will have its output assessed in some way. In the simplest and most abstract case a one-product firm will have its performance assessed directly by the process of competition. (This assumes for the time being that markets work in the long run, in the sense that the more efficient producers will survive either by making larger profits or by offering lower prices and taking a larger share of the market, or by some combination of these processes.) More generally, a productive unit will be continuously monitored by those exercising an ownership or strategic management function. These people will be estimating likely competitive success on the basis of past experience and indirect indicators of output.

The model suggests that if strategic management assess performance unfavourably a range of actions are open to them, through operational management, to alter the performance of the production process. At this point however, it is important to register the fact that strategic management may not choose any of these corrective 'strategies'. For example, in the simplest case they may be incompetent! More interestingly, they may not be concerned in the short term with the performance of a particular production unit because they may be insulated from unwanted effects. This insulation could come from monopoly position, from profits being made by other units (or even on the financial markets), in short by any particular environmental factor which attenuates the pressure to adopt a 'strategy' of change in the production process. This could be summarised in economic terms by observing that our account has little in common with the neoclassical theory of the firm but rather more in common with a behavioural theory of the firm in which there is satisficing behaviour at the strategic as well as the operational level.

Of course in the long run it would be inadmissable to argue that pressure for change in the production process will be delayed indefinitely. But it is important to register the non-necessity of instant Taylorist responses in order to establish the contrast with the Braverman position. In the long run there is always the probability that competition in product, capital, and resource markets will force management to identify and attempt to alter some aspects of the production process. Figure 7.1 shows that they can attempt to act in any of the four major components of the process. They can change the technology, the division of labour, the employment relation, or the process of coordination. It is important to recognise the diversity of factors which surround these possible changes. Some of them will involve search costs, (technical change), some of them will encounter resistance, there will be no obvious 'best solution' in any area, and all of them will interact with each other. For example a new technology may alter the options in the division of labour, or a change in the division of labour may exclude a future possible technical change. Furthermore there can be a large number of actors in the situation who may take relatively independent initiatives in these areas.

It should also be noted that management may respond to pressure on production efficiency by changing the *product* or by radical diversification. This is of great importance in analysis of broader industrial change, but is not considered directly in this chapter.

It will be clear by now that the great variety of reported labour process change is perfectly consistent with this model of the production process. The coupling between a unit of capital and its production process is sufficiently flexible for great empirical diversity to emerge. However, the coupling between units of capital through the market, while capable of great mediation, is nevertheless strong enough to ensure that, in the long run, production processes get more efficient rather than less efficient (judged according to cost criteria, whose relationship to other criteria will not be discussed here but is obviously variable and complex).

This account of the link between the production process and the capitalist process of competition is quite simple and does not contain anything remarkable. It merely emphasises what is evident from an economic viewpoint; that firms are concerned with the minimisation of total costs in the long run (or, more generally, the ensuring of a satisfactory difference between costs and prices). Any activity that reduces costs is welcome provided it does not threaten or undermine the large institutional features of capitalism such as the nature of the wage relation. This contrasts with the position commonly found in labour process literature which is more restrictive and assumes that all change in the production process necessarily changes the position of labour. This has led to an analysis of the issue of control over the labour process which has been removed from the context of the wider production process. As a result some have seen an inevitable de-skilling dynamic, and others, seeing the occurrence of increases in worker autonomy (as in work re-design experiments) have been forced to conclude that these events are either aberrant or else *only* Machiavellian alternative strategies of control. They may be both of these on some occasions, but on others they may be the result of entirely different factors; these are issues to be investigated empirically rather than theoretically decreed.

It must be admitted however that the 'openness' and lack of determinism in this alternative account would not be of any practical value if it could not be used as a framework in which to investigate the possibility of *trends* in the structure of the production process. If, for example, we could not use it to give an acceptable account of Taylorism, Fordism, or the other major trends of that type, then its theoretical superiority over the labour process perspective would be a Pyrrhic victory. In the next section the second theoretical device is introduced. This allows us to identify major phases in the technological development of the production process and consider such phenomena as Taylorism and Fordism in this context. It is this interaction between the technical and the organisational aspects of the production process which has been badly represented in the labour process literature.

Part Two

2.1 Technological change and the labour process
It is ironic that the labour process literature and the industrial sociology literature has placed great emphasis on the importance of technology, and yet has, for the most part, ignored the substantial body of analytical and historical literature on the mechanisms of technological change. The implicit, and extremely unsatisfactory position which has gained ground since the work of Braverman is one which makes technology a fairly plastic instrument in the hands of managers. The classic example of this is the account by Braverman, and the subsequent account by Noble (1977), of the development of NC machine tools in which there is a tendency to see the technology as reflecting *only* the desire of managers to increase their control of the labour process and reduce their dependence on workers' skills. Generalising from this sort of example gives an attractive image of technology being shaped by capitalist relations of production, and this is a powerful antidote to the de facto technological determinism adopted by much of social science.

It is of course true that technology is shaped by some of the forces mentioned in these accounts, and emphasis on this is an important corrective to determinist accounts which fall back on a heroic theory of innovation. But it is equally dangerous to assume, in the way that much labour process literature does, that technology is shaped by considerations of work control alone. This is much too superficial a treatment of what is in fact an enormous analytical problem which has occupied a great many writers for many years and is only now approaching a coherent solution. This problem is the relationship between the relatively autonomous advance of scientific knowledge, partially shaped as it is by funding patterns, and, on the other hand, the complex array of needs, market forces, political forces and pure accidents which select between alternative technological applications of scientific knowledge. To argue that NC tools have been developed to de-skill workers without having an explanation of where a key component like the transistor comes from is hardly satisfactory.

Paradoxically, therefore, it is the Bravermanian account itself which lapses into determinism, though of a different kind. By having a monolithic account of the labour process which incorporates an inexorable de-skilling dynamic, he makes technical change a passive reflection of this trend. Consequently it is difficult for this approach to explain adequately the development of the later CNC machine tools which can, given certain circumstances, reverse some of the de-skilling attributed to ordinary NC machine tools. Clearly some other and more complex mechanisms must have been at work in the evolution of this technology.

The underlying problem here is the theoretical status of terms such as mechanisation and automation. They are often used in a fairly common-sense manner as though the former simply means the removal of manual labour and the latter means the removal of mental labour. They are seen as fairly simple historical trends which are shaped by the pressure to increase productivity and, latterly, to increase control. This glosses over the real complexity of the development of production technology. There is a pressing need to give a more thorough account of the twists and turns in this history, and to relate them to the specific technical possibilities and inducement mechanisms which have participated in the process.

Braverman's treatment of mechanisation and automation is based on the work of Bright (1956). Bright presented a hierarchy of 17 'levels' of automation in which machine-effected functions become more and more complex and gradually displace human faculties. He argues that movement up the lower levels of this spectrum usually entails increases in human skill, but that the higher reaches of the automation scale progressively remove the need for human skill. It will readily be seen how comfortably this approach fits with the general intellectual project of Braverman. The problem with Bright's scheme is that it conflates into a single scale the mechanisation of quite different aspects of the production process, thus obscuring the possibilities for complex and uneven development of mechanisation. The later work of Bell (1972) is a superior starting point for the study of this problem.

Bell argues that manufacturing activities consist of combinations of three different but related functional activities which are susceptible to different levels of mechanisation. These three activities are the transformation of work-pieces, the transfer of work-pieces between transformation sites, and the control of the first two activities. Therefore a particular machine or group of machines can, for example, exhibit high control mechanisation and low transfer mechanisation or *vice versa*.

Bell used these categories to analyse engineering production systems and found that the three dimensions of mechanisation could be 'calibrated' and that the different types of machines in engineering could be accurately specified with respect to these axes. Furthermore he found that as new machines appeared they too could be situated in this three-dimensional space but that the direction of evolution was not constant. He did not, however, explore the historical data in any detail. Bell's work pre-dates the labour process literature, but he in fact had already shown, using this framework, that when new machines are introduced, their skill-effects depend on the way in which the new functions associated with the machines are combined into packages to make jobs. These jobs are not simply determined by the technology itself but are open to some elements of choice and negotiation. Bell's three dimensions of mechanisation are a useful framework within which to study more generally the development of the technical components of the labour process. They are consistent with a view of technical change in which the technology of production and the division of labour interact, rather than a view in which one determines the other. In the remainder of this section we shall argue that the general terms mechanisation and automation be scrapped and replaced by the terms primary, secondary and tertiary mechanisation. These will refer to, respectively, the mechanisation of transformation, transfer and control. The support for this proposition takes the form of a reinterpretation of the history of production technology in which these three phases of mechanisation are presented as the successively dominant forms over a period from the middle of the nineteenth century to the present. A specific attempt is made to account for the factors which mediated the transition from one phase of mechanisation to the next. We shall subsequently consider the implications of this interpretation for the analysis of management strategies toward the *organisation* of work.

2.2 Phases of mechanisation in the history of production technology*

The transition from manufacture to machino-facture is the starting point for this discussion. In the third quarter of the nineteenth century the striking feature of the development of production technology is the generalisation of steam-powered machino-facture across several sectors of industry. Landes (1969) has shown that the steep spine of the steam engine's diffusion curve runs from the 1840s to the 1870s. This can be regarded as a period in which *primary mechanisation* was dominant over secondary/tertiary mechanisation. A series of incremental innovations added to the power and efficiency of steam engines and the machinery they drove, but this avenue of technical change eventually encountered diminishing returns. The decades around the turn of the century were a period in which the instrinsic superiority of the internal combustion engine and the electrical engine began to tell on the position of steam power. Eventually, the electrical engine was regarded as superior to the internal combustion engine for prime movers in factories. The reasons for this are too complex to enter into at this point, but the significance for the develoment of the labour process was great. During the earlier phase of the dominance of primary mechanisation, the main performance characteristic of manufacture which was subject to continuous improvement was the *speed and scale of transformation*. The increases in motive power were assisted by changes in steel quality, lubrication techniques, ball bearings and a host of other innovations (see Landes 1969: 293). But the increase in speed and scale of transformation, stimulated by foreign as well as domestic competition, eventually served to expose the increasing inadequacies of the *transfer system* for moving work between transformation operations. This situation can be summarised as the emergence of a 'bottleneck' in the evolution of manufacturing systems, which was likely to result in inventive and innovative effort being focused on its resolution. This general phenomenon is discussed in more detail by Rosenberg (1976). Two of his 'inducement and focusing devices' were present at this time: imbalances between interdependent parts of production processes, and groups of workers exercising degrees of control over production processes which are dysfunctional to managers. The imbalances have already been referred to. In the German *Platzarbeit* systems, for example, work could spend longer moving from one machining area to another than its actual machining time. The general control conflict emerged from the combination of two conditions. Firstly, the craft machinists were given a considerable material support for their

---

* This section is a summary of Coombs (1982), chapter 4.

bargaining position by their skill and the objective importance of their position. Secondly, this was reinforced by the technical circumstance of the absence of interchangeability amongst parts in most industries, which placed great reliance on the skill of the 'fitter'. This latter problem was gradually resolved by a series of machine tool innovations (see Landes 1969: 305–15) which gave sufficient accuracy for interchangeable parts.

The control problem was approached through the now well-documented phenomena of systematic management and Taylorism. The importance of this development in the USA during this period is discussed by Littler (1982: 175) who also relates it to 'problems of work flow'. The combination of systematic work organisation, interchangeability of parts, and specific machines for the more efficient transformation *and movement* of work-pieces, comprise a phase of labour-process change which can be characterised as *secondary mechanisation*. The process of electrification, referred to above, was important by virtue of the great flexibility and mobility of electricity as a power source. It enabled more machinery to be sited with more freedom and therefore relaxed some of the restrictions of plant re-organisation.

At this point in the argument it is worth emphasising that this interpretation differs from the conventional 'second industrial revolution' diagnosis of this period. The technical and organisational changes are not simply the result of the 'arrival' of better steel, electricity, etc. They are also the result of their applications being shaped by the particular bottlenecks and imbalances caused by the prior evolution of the labour process and its constituent technologies.

The two classic forms of secondary mechanisation, the 'continuous flow' industries and the assembly-line system, achieved significant diffusion in inter-war America. In Europe their diffusion was more restricted, but its role, especially in newer industries, was still clear. The beginnings of mass markets for consumer durable items were important stimuli to this process. The interaction between changes in supply and demand at this time have been given special emphasis in the work of Aglietta (1979). It is clear that the Second World War gave a great impetus to the further elaboration and diffusion of secondary mechanisation. In Europe in particular, the post-war boom involved a further diffusion of these production systems into both new and old industries. At the same time, however, a specific limitation of secondary mechanisation began to emerge. In production processes where transformation and transfer are subject to some degree of mechanisation, it is inevitable that engineers' attention will begin to focus on the way in which these pieces of equipment are controlled. Indeed it is difficult to imagine a mechanised transfer system in which control is not mechanised to some extent, although the very early version of Ford's moving assembly line did use a considerable amount of human control. In general, however, the effectiveness of the transfer and transformation system and their potential for increased speed, reliability and coordination depend on using more sophisticated controlling devices. A representative example of the initial improvements in control mechanisation is the system of activating a machine by a switch tripped by the arrival of the work-piece. This is a common way of controlling sequences of transformation actions in a transfer line for machining parts.

This type of mechanisation of control, of which the instrumentation in the chemical industry is another example, constituted a third phase of mechanisation which can be termed tertiary mechanisation. It effectively reduced the labour requirement still further in those parts of a process where it can be achieved. It is important to point out that this is not a black and white distinction. There are levels of control mechanisation (which have been documented in the case of machine tools by Bell) and there is progressive change in the balance between machine and labour in the control activity. This tertiary mechanisation was given a considerable impetus by the application of the mathematical principles of feedback which were first thoroughly elaborated in the 1930s, and by the arrival of reliable electronic components in the early post-war period. It was, however, still fairly inflexible mechanisation of control in that it could not be adapted to cope with high levels of product variety. This has since become a new limitation and this point is discussed in the conclusion.

It is important to add the rider that this analysis holds in its simple form only at the most general level. In particular industries at particular times the evolution of the dimensions of mechanisation has, of course, been specific to particular circumstances. The most obvious case is that of new industries which emerge with many of the lessons of older industries already incorporated into their production processes. But from the point of view of the overall direction of technical change and the structure of output in the capital goods industries, the above analysis is a powerful framework of interpretation.

To summarise the argument thus far; there have been three major technological 'regimes' in the evolution of the production process. The first of these, from the middle of the nineteenth century to the end of that century, emphasised using machinery to accomplish transformation tasks. The second regime, from the turn of the century until the Second World War, placed the emphasis on the use of machinery to accomplish transfer tasks. The third phase, which began during the War and is still continuing, has stressed using machines to achieve control functions.

It is important to emphasise that control is used here in the technical sense employed by Bell. It is related to, but not the same as, the sense in which control is used by labour-process writers. Their use extends the term to include control of workers as well as of activities. It is appropriate from now on to distinguish these meanings more clearly. Control means the direction of an activity such as the movement of a work piece. This could be a relationship entirely between machines or it could involve some human function. The 'control' of how a worker performs a task is better described by the term 'constraint'. Thus we can speak of a system of work organisation and associated technology *constraining* a worker's actions, while the performance of a particular action may be *controlled* by technology, by the worker, by a manager, or by some combination of all three.

The three regimes of production referred to above each represent a particular type of technical component of the broader production process described in the taxonomy in section 1 of the chapter. As such they set limits around, but do not determine, the prospects for improvements in the performance of the production process with each regime, as assessed by the process of competion and the judgements of strategic management. We are speaking here of the production process at a very high level of abstraction and generality. Clearly not all industries and processes have followed this sequence exactly, and some have been 'born' with earlier stages already largely accomplished. However, at this high level of generality the chronology of the regimes can be summarised in Table 7.1.

In the short term and medium term, particularly during the early period of each regime, performance tends to improve quite readily as a result of incremental improvements within the framework of the regime. Steam engines, for example, improved their (narrowly defined) technical efficiency dramatically in the 1840s to 1970s. In the long run, however, each regime encounters some instrinsic limit rather in the manner suggested by Wolff's law. As diminishing returns are encountered in the search to increase performance on the basis of the existing regime, attention gradually becomes focused on radical solutions. This view of technical change is closely related to the theory of 'natural trajectories' and 'selection environments' developed by Nelson and Winter (1977) in their attempts to synthesise a model of technological innovation with a behavioural theory of the firm.

Before moving to a discussion of how these phases may relate to work organisation change and management strategy, two vital observations about the chronology are appropriate. Firstly, there is a broad similarity between the timing of the phases of mechanisation and the timing of the 'long waves' in the development of the world economy

Table 7.1

	Primary mechanisation	Secondary mechanisation	Tertiary mechanisation
1850	beginning		
1875			
1900	spreading across sectors and maturing technically	beginning	
1925		substantial diffusion in some sectors, increasing technical maturity	
1950	continuing but increasingly likely to occur together with secondary or tertiary mechanisation	being generalised across a wide variety of industries	beginning in some industries and slowly becoming more flexible
1975			flexibility increasing

which have recently been the subject of fresh research. This correlation is clearly in need of investigation. In a separate paper I have discussed the mechanism that may connect these two phenomena (Coombs 1983). The argument is complex, but some elements of it are relevant to this chapter and will be mentioned in part four. For the present it is important to note the following point which leads to the second observation on the chronology of the phases. It seems that in long wave 'upswings', such as 1850–1970 or 1900–20, the *initial*, experimental part of a phase of mechanisation is underway. In the downswing of a long wave, with slack demand putting pressure on production costs, the bottleneck in the regime of mechanisation becomes more apparent. From 1900 onwards, these processes are overlaid. Each upswing is then characterised by the experimental part of a new regime and the widespread diffusion to all sections of the mature regime from the previous long wave. This leads to a specific diagnosis of the technical character of the commonly discussed upsurge in 'automation' in the post-war boom of the 1950s and 1960s. It is the simultaneous generalisation of secondary mechanisation and the initiation of tertiary mechanisation. This hypothesis is supported by the data presented in part three of this chapter. We return now to the mainsteam of the argument.

2.3 The implications of phases of mechanisation for changes in other parts of the production process

It is now possible to insert this account of phases of mechanisation into the analysis of the labour process and the production process presented in part one of this paper. It will be recalled that the conclusion of the analysis in part one was that managers' responses to shortfalls in performance in the production process could take a number of forms. It is possible to operate on the technical efficiency, the division of labour, the personal efficiency of labour, the coordination function, or on some combination of these elements. It is even possible that no *coherent* action will be taken at all. If we assume, however, that some action is taken by some enterprises, how are these possible actions affected by the existence of these historical regimes of mechanisation? It seems reasonable to argue that, if the technological trends are taken *for the moment* as given, the effects on other parts of the production process might be as follows.

In the upswing of a long wave, when the development of a regime of mechanisation is in its initial phase, the efficiency of some production processes will be susceptible to considerable improvement as a result of the permissive character of the technical change. This will clearly result in some associated changes in the division of labour, but it may well *reduce* the need for managers to address the question of the personal efficiency of labour. This tendency would be powerfully reinforced by the favourable conditions of market growth facing new industries in the healthy macroeconomic climate of a long-wave upswing. In other words, though work organisation will be by no means static in this situation, any changes would be more likely to be derived from developments in technology, rather than the other way round.

In the downswing, however, the picture could be quite different. If performance improvement in some production processes is proving hard to achieve using the old technological paradigms, it becomes important to look across a wider spectrum of possibilities for change. In these circumstances, any management strategies for change in the production process which do emerge are more likely to *combine* technical, organisational and other dimensions. These other dimensions could be concerned with the personal efficiency of labour and with the broader character of the employment relationship. The downswing is thus a period in which managers' and engineers' views on the subject of 'desirable' job redesign and desirable employment relationships could well enter into the process of shaping those new technologies which are developed at the time. Thus in the process of mutual determination between the division of labour and technology itself, the balance may shift back and forth as the regimes of mechanisation, and the long waves, progress. This argument is offered therefore as a set of historical constraints within which the more limited argument about management strategies in work re-organisation should be situated. Those who argue that there is an enduring strategy of job-fragmentation, those who argue that there are occasional strategies of increasing worker autonomy, and those who argue that there are no strategies, only particular contingencies, should consider their arguments in the light of these overarching structures of technical possibilities.

To recognise these three major functional activities in manufacturing, (transformation, transfer and control) and their successive but overlapping periods of mechanisation is not to impute any deterministic character to this sequence. But it would be perverse to deny the great weight of evidence that the sequence was more likely to take that order rather than any other. It seems reasonable to state that the progressive mechanisation of these activities, in the order observed, was a general requirement of the historical development of production in capitalist society. What was not pre-ordained was the exact manner in which that process occurred. It is our view that the mechanisation process has been loosely articulated with the long waves of economic expansion and contraction (see Coombs 1983). The concept of a management strategy towards workers' mode of participation in the labour process must therefore be integrated with this insight. It seems that 'the labour process' *as a concept* has been expected to bear too much weight in previous literature and the concept of the production process outlined in this chapter therefore seems more useful.

Before discussing the implications of these arguments for current developments in production we briefly consider some data which support the view of phases of mechanisation developed above.

Part Three

The diffusion of mechanisation technologies since World War Two
A major difficulty with previous discussion of mechanisation has been the difficulty of measuring its extent. One aspect of the problem already referred to is that of establishing satisfactory definitions. The disaggregation into primary, secondary and tertiary mechanisation provides a partial solution to this problem. Another difficulty is that

mechanisation means different things in different industries, where different technologies are in use. Again however, the generic processes of transformation, transfer and control, go some way toward solving this problem. The data presented here refer to secondary and tertiary mechanisation in the UK and USA in the post-war period. The data have been constructed by examining the machinery sections of the Census of Production at the most disaggregated level, and assigning each type of machine to one or other of the various categories. The data therefore represent the changes over time in the proportion of total capital goods output in each of the three categories. This data supersedes that presented in Coombs (1981), where secondary and tertiary mechanisation were not distinguished. The data are presented as follows.

The main tables (Tables 7.2 and 7.3) show the value of output in each census year of a variety of machines and components used in a large range of industries. Each entry is an aggregation of a much more detailed list of equipment in the original data. Some of the entries have one of the following labels attached to them.

MH = mechanical handling technologies
CF = continuous flow technologies
H   = 'hard' automation (dedicated technology for volume
         production)
C   = control technologies

The attachment of these labels reflects a series of complex judgements based on literature describing the production technologies of all the potential user industries and conducted at a level of disaggregation several stages more detailed than presented here. The justifications for these judgements are to be found in Coombs (1982), chapter 5. Tables 7.4 and 7.5 aggregate the data in Tables 7.2 and 7.3 and give a summary of the share of MH, CF, H and C in total capital goods production over time. In the graphs (Figures 7.1 and 7.2) MH and CF are combined to give a curve for secondary mechanisation, and C and H are combined to give tertiary mechanisation. The data show that in both countries secondary mechanisation was already a significant fraction of capital goods output (10–15%) immediately after the War, and that the increase over the post-war boom is modest. In contrast, the tertiary mechanisation curve rises rapidly from zero to a level near that of secondary mechanisation. The total of secondary and tertiary thus shows a rise to 30% or more of capital goods output. The data therefore support the diagnosis made earlier. Post-war 'automation' was in fact two quite distinct phenomena occurring simultaneously. Transfer technologies of an established character were being generalised across a

Table 7.2 Summary tables of US Census of Production data (millions of US dollars)

		1947	1959	1958	1963	1967	1972
34C	Fabricated platework	660.0	1089.4	1613.9	1580.8	2589.4	3265.7
	CF: Heat exchangers, pressure vessels etc.	37.6	303.5	324.4	302.7	716.0	825.9
35A	Steam engines and turbines	119.0	426.2	753.9	589.1	1059.3	2079.7
	Farm machinery	844.4	1060.3				
	Tractors	778.8	1070.8	2172.5	2542.1	4077.3	5484.5
	MH: Blowers and elevators	—	37.0	39.0	28.0	42.0	52.0
35B	Construction machinery			1989.2	2624.2	3766.6	5653.6
	Mining machinery	932.4	1159.2	277.7	336.2	521.5	729.8
	Oilfield machinery			496.1	572.7	660.7	980.0
	Elevators			165.2	248.2	248.2	412.2
	MH: Cranes	248.0	268.7	361.1	464.8	656.5	961.0
	MH: Conveyors			165.5	224.2	385.3	825.6
	MH: Hoists, cranes, monorails	108.8	112.9	276.6	458.7	780.7	446.0
	MH: Industrial trucks etc.			333.8	414.8	655.4	1004.8
35C	Machine tools	1615.4	3561.6	3264.4	4411.8	7355.0	6872.6
	H: 'Hard' machine tools (see text)	13.5	70.2	27.3	119.7	308.9	233.1
	C: NC Machine tools (see text)				111.0	381.4	380.6
35D	Special industry machinery						
	Food products machinery	335.9	371.4	399.8	517.3	689.9	867.2
	CF: Dairy and milk products plant	62.0	81.2	64.6	71.6	77.7	114.8
	CF: Bakery equipment (see text)	10.2	10.2	9.1	44.5	38.2	22.0
	CF: Other food products plant (meat, sugar, packing and bottling, see text)	127.3	115.2	129.0	220.7	284.8	615.1
	Textile machinery	391.8	304.0	322.2	499.1	652.6	738.1
	Woodworking machinery	151.3	163.4	174.4	220.8	274.4	441.6
	CF: Paper industries machinery	134.7	176.1	280.1	347.6	515.1	381.4
	Printing trades machinery	195.1	228.7	270.6	403.2	656.0	736.6
	CF: Roll/web-fed presses	24.2	26.4	42.6	70.0	131.0	147.3
	C: Electronic typesetting machines				4.0	24.9	88.7
	Special industry machines NEC	462.2	604.5	726.4	988.4	1670.3	2367.1
	CF: Chemical industry machinery	87.3	102.7	118.4	152.4	284.5	212.5
	CF: Plastics-working machinery	19.6	37.6	50.8	137.1	247.6	434.1
	CF: Petroleum refinery equipment	22.4	18.9	20.6	36.5	53.4	40.2
	H: Cigarette-making machinery	20.1	14.3	14.8	5.3	6.9	3.6
	H: Clay-working machinery	6.9	7.8	10.5	11.4	16.5	19.5
	CF: Cement-making machinery	8.1	4.2	3.8	8.5	8.1	19.2
	H: Concrete block-making equipment	17.8	22.5	21.0	5.4	7.3	6.8
	CF: Glass-making and working machines	21.5	16.5	21.4	36.0	45.0	52.3
	H: De-greasing equipment				47.2	97.9	93.5
	H: Lamp-making etc. machinery				171.3	314.8	715.5
	CF: Processing ovens				41.4	66.8	84.9
35E	General industrial machinery						
	Pumps and compressors	524.3	867.4	1001.8	1249.2	1947.5	2355.6
	Ball and roller bearings	352.5	533.7	636.7	961.0	1292.2	1418.7
	Blowers and fans	129.9	274.0	252.8	299.4	499.1	682.0
	Industrial patterns	77.7	236.5	121.2	159.9	233.7	234.4
	Power transmission equipment	426.7	595.0	622.7	883.4	1283.4	1568.0
	CF: Industrial furnaces	84.6	154.2	184.8	237.7	415.9	341.1
	General industrial machinery NEC	321.0	429.0	467.3	664.3	899.8	1132.8
	H: Non-food packing machinery				46.4	72.9	139.5	177.4
35F	Office, computing and accounting machinery						
	Typewriters	140.1	141.6	188.5	265.5	508.1	1075.9
	Calculating and accounting machinery	284.9	501.3	1038.8		630.8	687.7
	C: Computers				2468.4	4048.8	6228.0
	Scales and balances	51.4	59.4	70.9	90.0	131.4	174.8
	H: Automatic scales etc. (see text)				24.9	39.2	44.3
	Office . . . etc. NEC				275.8	417.7	—
36A	Electrical measurement and distribution machinery						
	Transformers	326.7	628.9	638.3	692.2	113.6	1436.1
	C: Industrial electric controls	171.2	333.8	447.2	633.3	1071.4	1245.6
	Welding apparatus	107.6	160.0	233.2	324.9	432.9	570.0
	Electrical apparatus NEC	107.8	227.1	213.0	250.5	398.5	442.9
36E	C: Industrial X-ray equipment	0.7	3.2	5.6	12.0	24.8	24.8
38A	C: Industrial process instruments	168.3	280.8	403.3	522.4	749.8	740.6

CF — continuous flow
MH — mechanical handling
C — control
H — hard automation

Table 7.3   Summary table of UK Census of Production data (£ million)

	1954	1958	1963	1968	1972	1975	1979
Agricultural machinery	38.7	48.4	57.8	72.0	81.9	155.9	244.5
Metalworking machine tools	87.7	109.0	151.1	210.5	230.1	418.4	713.3
T/H: Transfer machines	7.5	12.0	5.2	9.6	8.6	20.4	44.6
T/H: Automatic lathes	5.0	5.2	9.8	12.9	16.1	22.7	27.1
C: Copy/plug-board lathes				1.5	13.0	21.0	14.8
T/H: Automatic presses					2.5	5.0	6.9
C: Physico/chem formers				0.7	3.6	2.8	11.8
NC and machining centres				1.9	11.2	23.7	65.6
Pumps, valves and compressors			143.7	275.2	352.7	679.4	1227.3
C: Automatic process control valves					9.6	18.8	26.5
Industrial engines	67.6	82.0	85.5	118.8	142.9	335.4	476.5
Textile machinery	62.0	52.1	95.7	142.9	173.4	260.9	270.3
Construction and earth moving equipment	57.7	69.6	130.9	217.3	308.0	577.6	922.2
Mechanical handling equipment	62.4	87.1	138.7	218.0	329.4	674.2	1151.5
MH: Cranes	19.3	30.0	35.4	46.8	79.3	144.1	202.1
MH: Conveyors	10.5	14.1	39.7	55.7	71.6	149.8	289.4
MH: Industrial trucks etc.	5.7	7.5	17.8	53.7	85.3	198.8	364.1
Office machinery	28.2	46.3	61.6	74.7	127.1	158.6	148.8
T/H: Doc handling	0.4	0.7	3.8	10.2	9.9	15.4	44.7
C: Point of sale systems							2.9
Mining machinery			63.8	83.8	118.0	281.0	566.3
MH: Power cutters and loaders	0.5	3.6	10.0	11.4	27.9	71.4	126.1
MH: Conveyors	5.0	7.7	10.8	19.4	27.4	55.8	107.2
Printing, bookbinding and paper goods machinery			35.8	52.0	73.8	150.1	256.0
CF: Roll or web-fed presses		0.2	8.8	12.9	8.4	2.5	0.5
T/H: Bag and box making	0.3	0.7	2.9	6.3	18.7	30.1	54.7
Food and drink processing and bottling machinery			34.0	54.2	112.7	193.9	331.5
CF: various processing (see text)	24.4	23.3	33.9	54.0	59.4	94.3	178.0
T/H: Packing and bottling machines					43.2	77.5	130.3
Miscellaneous (non-electrical) machinery	374.3	490.3	263.8	364.2	350.6	548.5	968.5
T/H: Bottling, packing etc.	7.5	14.0	21.7	31.6			
T/H: Vending machines	0.1	1.2	2.0	11.2	5.3	7.2	25.4
CF: Brick and tile-making	1.2	1.0	2.5	3.7	7.6	14.1	18.0
CF: Cement-making	1.5	0.7	0.7	2.2	0.8	1.2	0.5
CF: Chemical, petro-chemical	3.5	4.5	8.1	12.8	19.1	39.0	48.4
CF: Glass-working and bottle-making	0.9	1.2	3.2	3.5	4.6	4.6	8.8
CF: Rubber and plastics working	2.6	7.1	16.7	30.7	33.9	54.1	95.7
T/H: Cigarette-making	4.8	4.1	11.8	16.7	16.5	31.4	59.0
CF: Rolling mills	5.3	13.4	16.9	17.9	12.3	14.7	11.4
Industrial (including process) plant and steelwork	107.8	139.0	97.5	94.8			
CF: Parts used in turnkey process plants				15.0			
kilns, refuse, sewage and water treatment, heat exchangers, evaporators, nuclear vessels etc.					186.8	356.2	542.1
General mechanical engineering	234.3	358.6	383.3	485.0	129.1	213.9	310.4
Ball and roller bearings					326.5	608.7	1066.0
Precision chains and other machinery							
C: Document copying equipment			4.8	39.1	60.6	93.7	200.0
C: Process measuring and control instruments and systems	9.5	24.0	45.0	72.5	151.5	249.7	451.4
Electrical machinery Generation and transmission	211.9	301.5	120.1	176.5	200.0	357.1	591.9
Switchgear and control gear			139.2	169.1	170.0	302.2	518.2
C: Computers		6.9	41.8	119.2	344.2	486.9	1056.4
Tractors	59.8	79.2	170.4	192.8	273.3	584.4	964.5

Table 7.4   Re-aggregation of UK data

		1954	1958	1963	1968	1972	1975	1979
1.	Total machinery production (£m)	1401.9	1894.0	2214.5	3247.6	4242.6	7686.7	12977.6
2.	Hard automation							
	Value	25.5	36.7	55.2	87.3	108.5	202.5	367.3
	% of total	1.8	1.9	2.5	2.7	2.6	2.6	2.8
3.	Mechanical handling							
	Value	41.0	62.9	113.7	187.0	291.5	619.9	1088.9
	% of total	2.9	3.3	5.1	5.8	6.9	8.1	8.4
4.	Continuous flow							
	Value	147.2	190.5	188.3	247.5	332.9	580.7	903.4
	% of total	10.5	10.1	8.5	7.6	7.8	7.6	7.0
5.	Control							
	Value	9.5	30.9	91.6	234.9	593.7	868.6	1829.4
	% of total	0.7	1.6	4.1	7.2	14.0	11.4	14.1
6.	3 + 4 as % of 1	13.4	13.4	13.6	13.4	14.7	15.7	15.4
7.	2 + 5 as % of 1	2.5	3.5	6.6	9.9	16.6	14.0	16.9

Table 7.5   Re-aggregation of US data

		1947	1954	1958	1963	1967	1972
1.	Total machinery production ($m)	10019.7	14784.9	20339.2	26969.1	42677.1	53645.5
2.	Hard automation						
	Value	58.3	114.8	120.0	458.1	940.9	1293.7
	% of total	0.6	0.8	0.6	1.7	2.2	2.4
3.	Mechanical handling						
	Value	356.8	418.6	1176.0	1590.5	2519.9	3289.4
	% of total	3.6	2.8	5.8	5.9	5.9	6.1
4.	Continuous flow						
	Value	659.5	1046.7	1414.7	1954.9	3132.3	3703.0
	% of total	6.6	7.1	6.9	7.2	7.3	6.9
5.	Control						
	Value	340.2	617.8	856.1	3751.1	6301.1	8708.3
	% of total	3.4	4.2	4.2	13.9	14.8	16.2
6.	3 + 4 as % of 1	10.2	9.9	12.7	13.1	13.2	13.0
7.	2 + 5 as % of 1	4.0	5.0	4.8	15.6	18.0	18.6

wider number of industries and allocation. Control technologies were being newly developed and diffused in a smaller number of industries and applications. The momentum of both diffusion curves shows signs of slackening in the 1970s. It is also worth noting that the rise of the tertiary mechanisation curve is earlier in the USA than in the UK.

Figure 7.1   *Diffusion of secondary and tertiary mechanisation technologies as a percentage of total machinery produced in the UK*

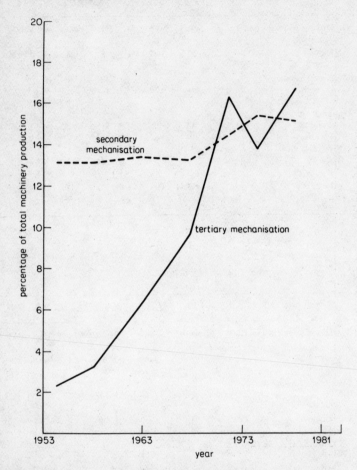

Although the data only cover a section of the period covered by our argument, they are consistent with the view of successive phases of mechanisation. They also show that the re-structuring of the output of the capital goods industries in the early stage of a phase is on a very large scale, with a major fraction of production being re-allocated to the new technologies over a relatively short period of time. Once the technology has reached an 'equilibrium share' of capital goods output, it is clearly continuing to have an important effect on the productivity of those industries which are consuming it.

Figure 7.2   *The diffusion of secondary and tertiary mechanisation*
technologies as a percentage of total machinery produced
in the US

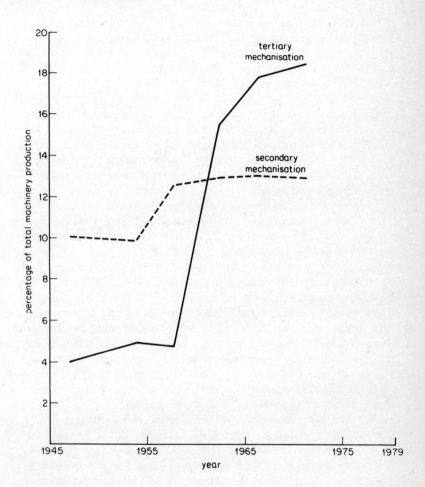

Part Four

Conclusions

Elsewhere (Coombs 1983) I have argued that the phases of mechanisation described in this paper are linked to the Kondratieff long wave.
The debate over the mechanism of the long wave has become complex
in recent years and the earlier determinist viewpoints are being replaced

by more elaborate multi-causal models. One of the main points of discussion has been the role of technical change, particularly at the lower turning point: the movement from depression to recovery. Some authors see clustered innovations as the driving force of the transition (Mensch 1979). Some see a major shift in the rate of profit as a result of changed positions between the classes as permitting the recovery, and allowing a technical revolution in production machinery (Mandel 1975). Others argue that new industry life cycles drive the upswing but that the assembly of the necessary technical and economic factors for their initiation is essentially serendipitous (Freeman, Clarke and Soete 1982). Finally, a fourth group of authors have emphasised the intricate connections between changes in labour markets and employment conditions and major institutional and political innovations which create a new 'social structure of accumulation' to permit the recovery phase (Gordon, Edwards and Reich 1982). The debate among these positions can be taken a step further and partially resolved by incorporating the analysis of production process change summarised in this paper. The essence of the position presented in Coombs (1983) is as follows.

The economic circumstances of a long wave downswing intensify the pressure towards rationalisation in the production process. This is a reflection of stagnant or declining demand and intensified competition. The rationalisation available is limited by the fact that the room for improvement in the technologies developed in the upswing is becoming less significant. Some of the more radical possibilities on the horizon are often ruled out by the scale of the investment required and the uncertainty which militates against such investment. As the downswing continues, however, some experiments with new forms of rationalisation emerge, often involving changed work practices which may be easier to negotiate against the background of increasing unemployment. Over a prolonged period then, an array of inducement mechanisms begin to operate which shape and may even trigger some form of technical and/or organisational change in the fundamental features of production systems. The actual movement into recovery is likely to be the result of the type of major social and political change discussed by Gordon *et al*, which permits the shift in perceptions of long-term profit prospects and increases the optimism of investors. During the recovery and boom, some of the new production technologies will become 'best practice', and new growth industries may be involved closely with them both as users and producers of the equipment. Thus it is argued that there is some induced innovation in the movement from depression to recovery but this is not the full-scale 'depression trigger' hypothesis of Mensch. New technologies do not accomplish the transition but they are partially shaped by it and contribute to the complex and historically unique character of each lower turning point.

In the remainder of this chapter these ideas are used to illustrate our main argument on the need to relate work organisation changes more closely to technical changes. No more than a sketch is possible at this stage, and further research, particularly on national differences, is necessary to determine the limits of the ideas.

Littler has shown that during the Great Victorian Depression in the last two decades of the nineteenth century substantial changes in work organisation were underway. These took the form of the decline of the internal contract system and experiments in systematic management (Littler 1982: chapter 7). Our argument has shown that this was also the time when the early benefits of primary mechanisation were diminishing and a pressing need was developing to mechanise transfer operations. It has already been argued that during the upswing of the first two decades of the twentieth century the technical process of secondary mechanisation began to develop rapidly and Taylorism accompanied this process (at least in the USA). The principles of transfer mechanisation and Taylorism were therefore 'invented' and shaped by the pressures of the downswing, but their innovation and diffusion required the more dynamic environment of the upswing.

In the interwar period, which was dominated by the long wave downswing, the connections between secondary mechanisation and Taylorism were extended and deepened during the process of widening diffusion. This is really the period when 'Fordism' became mature and clearly recognisable (Littler 1983: 14). It is often held, correctly, that a major constraint of Fordism is its inflexibility in the face of the need for product differentiation. This constraint was not the first one to be faced however. It has been argued above that, in the interwar period, the pressures towards rationalisation led to a series of technical rather than organisational changes which we have characterised as tertiary mechanisation. Fordist work organisation was not challenged during the transition from the interwar period to the post-war boom; on the contrary it was more widely diffused. What began to change over this period was the degree of machine-effected technical control of transfer and transformation tasks within Fordist job structures. It is also important to note, of course, the major changes in the employment relationship which took place over this period, often institutionalised through major legislation, which contributed to a stabilisation of labour markets in the core industries (see Gordon, Edwards and Reich 1982).

It is interesting to speculate that Braverman's perception of an enduring tendency to de-skill – by which he meant precisely the removal of technical control tasks and their associated planning and discretionary characteristics – may have been fundamentally shaped by this prolonged period during which the general direction of work organisation change was Fordist. Rather than perceiving Taylorism as a particular period in the evolution of work, Braverman saw de-skilling as extending from the mid-nineteenth century to the time when he was writing and therefore as endemic to capitalism. Thus he overlooked both the importance of pre-Taylorist forms of work organisation and the prospect of a later crisis in Fordism. As pointed out earlier, this error was linked to his linear view of the progression from mechanisation to 'automation'.

In the post-war boom of the 1950s and 1960s then, Fordism was given a new lease of life by the initial phase of tertiary mechanisation. The reductions in *quantity* of direct labour were more important than changes in the *quality* of labour in the productivity increases of this period. In the 1970s, however, the real problems of lack of flexibility have begun to emerge. As the long wave upswing has subsided, markets have become more characterised by replacement demand in many sectors. This leads to a flurry of product differentiation in order to gain marginal increases in market share and places great strains on traditional mass production techniques. The traditional views of the links between batch size and unit costs are being eroded by the variety of new technologies which are emphasising flexibility and re-programmability. 'Neo-Fordism', while not yet a mature technical paradigm, is beginning to reveal some of its principal features in the experimental automation of small batch production. The potential work organisational changes which interact with these changes have been shown to be variable by the empirical work on the labour process which was discussed earlier in this and other chapters. It would be a mistake to believe that there is anything pre-ordained about the outcomes of these changes. We are entering the period in the long wave downswing when the volatility of these technical and organisational changes is at its greatest, and it is therefore not surprising that solid, clear 'strategies' do not seem easy to find in individual case-studies. Nevertheless, choices are being made, and will continue to be made, within a general constraint created by the further progress of tertiary mechanisation.

The argument of this chapter can therefore be summarised as follows. There is a situation now, in the downswing of the long wave, in which there are diminishing returns to the types of production-process improvement used in the 1950s and 1960s. The type of improvement now needed is one that not only continues the downward trend in unit labour costs, but also increases the degree of flexibility of the production process. This may be achieved by a variety of alterations which include the use of new technology, the re-organisation of work and changes in the other elements in the production process. The actual combination of solutions which will emerge is not yet clear nor is it pre-determined. It does not necessarily involve de-skilling, although it may in some operations, nor does it necessarily involve reversals of the Fordist division of labour. This diversity and openness of the possible changes is not in any way theoretically inconsistent with an account of the evolution of the capitalist production process. What this chapter has argued is that both the general process of capitalist competition *and* the specific intensifications of that process by long wave downswings create change in the production process as a *whole*. In some periods the changes have concentrated on the technical element of the process; in others they have included changes in the organisation, the division of labour and the employment relation. Often the two types of change have been related. There is however no specific capitalist dynamic to work organisation change of the form claimed by the early labour-process literature. The historical dynamics of the phases of mechanisation, however, do appear to be fairly robust. Their evolution has been shaped by the intrinsic likelihood of transformation being mechanised before transfer, and transfer before control by the long phases of accelerated and retarded growth in the capitalist economy, and by specific interactions with other elements of the production process, notably the division of labour. Now that all three dimensions of mechanisation have been established, future changes can combine elements of all three types.

Over the next decade we can therefore expect to see increasing attempts to make production systems more flexible as well as more productive, but through a number of different 'strategies' involving both technical and organisation change. The 'new technology' does form a nucleus for this process of change, but it is not yet itself mature and it does not *determine* the work changes. There is a range of action within which future technical and organisational change is still un-certain and subject to a variety of influences.

In conclusion it must be pointed out that the role of production process change in long waves discussed here is not put forward as an alternative to the role of new technology in new products, which has been analysed by Freeman *et al.* (1982), nor have we gone into detail on issues of institutional innovation such as those mentioned by Gordon *et al.* (1982). These are to be seen as complementary components of an account of long waves, together with the arguments concerning production process change put forward in this chapter.

References
Aglietta, M. (1979), *A Theory of Capitalist Regulation*, London: NLB.

Bell, M. (1972), *Changing Technology and Manpower Requirements in the Engineering Industry*, Sussex University Press.
Braverman, H. (1974), *Labour and Monopoly Capital*, Monthly Review Press.
Bright, J. (1956), *Automation and Management*, Harvard University Press.
Burawoy, M. (1979), *Manufacturing Consent*, University of Chicago Press.
Cohen, G.A. (1979), 'The labour theory of value and the concept of exploitation', *Philosophy and Public Affairs*, 8(4), Summer.
Coombs, R. (1981), 'Innovation automation and the long-wave theory', *Futures*, 13(5), 360–371.
Coombs, R. (1982), 'Automation and long wave theories', Ph.D. thesis, University of Manchester.
Coombs, R. (1983), 'Long waves and labour-process change', paper presented to the Round Table on Long Waves, Maison des Sciences de L'Homme, Paris, March.
Edwards, P.K. (1983), 'Control, compliance and conflict: analysing variations in the capitalist labour process', paper presented to UMIST/ASTON Labour-Process Conference, March.
Freeman, C., Clark, J., and Soete, L. (1982), *Unemployment and Technical Innovation*, Frances Pinter.
Gordon, E., Edwards, R., and Reich, M. (1982), *Segmented Work, Divided Workers*, Cambridge University Press.
Jones, B. (1982), 'Destruction or re-distribution of engineering skills? The case of numerical control', in S. Wood (ed.), *The Degraduation of Work?*, Hutchinson.
Kelly, J.E. (1982), *Scientific Management, Job Redesign and Work Performance*, Academic Press.
Landes, D. (1969), *The Unbound Prometheus*, Cambridge University Press.
Littler, C. (1982), *The Development of the Labour Process in Capitalist Societies*, Heinemann Educational Books.
Littler, C. (1983), 'Taylorism, Fordism and job-design', paper presented to UMIST/ASTON Labour-Process Conference, March.
Mandel, E. (1975), *Late Capitalism*, NLB.
Mensch, G. (1979), *The Technological Stalemate*, Ballinger.
Nelson, R. and Winter, S. (1977), 'In search of a useful theory of innovation', *Research Policy*, 6, 36–76.
Nicholls, T. (1983), 'Marxists, economists and sociologists on labour productivity', paper to UMIST/ASTON Labour-Process Conference, March.
Noble, D. (1977), *America by Design*, New York: Knopf.
Rosenberg, N. (1976), *Perspectives on Technology*, Cambridge University Press.

8 The Ghost in the Labour Process*

Tony Manwaring and Stephen Wood

A NEED

I find myself a prisoner of necessity
Trapped in a bable of noise
Machinery conflicting with thought

Hands flat on blackened steel
Heads bowed, back deformed
Half my life flows through stitches

Yet I have pride in the completion
Joy in the creation
Embroidery pleases the senses

And I am lost in the contradiction
Of loving and yet loathing
This need for creation

Sally Flood

'Nineteen Eighty–Three'
Lancashire Association of Trades Council, 1983

The object of this chapter is to discuss the active role of workers in the labour process. The emphasis is on the role of subjectivity and what we shall term tacit skills. For, as others have argued, even unskilled workers require some knowledge to do their jobs; the absolute divorce of conception from execution as Taylorism proposed is an impossibility and Taylorism cannot successfully reduce workers to automatons. The acknowledgement of the 'ghost' in the machine' – of mind dependent on, but also responsible for, the actions of the body (Koestler 1976: 202) – seems essential if we are not to reduce the mental activity inherent to the labour process to the operation of a kind of automatic

* We would like to thank Sheila Cochrane, Tony Elger, Paul Edwards, John Kelly and Maxine Molyneux for their very helpful comments on an earlier draft of this chapter.

telephone exchange in the brain. As this contrasts with the work of Braverman (1974) who exorcised the 'ghost from the machine' we shall first look at the relative neglect of workers' participation in the productive process and hence justify our focus on tacit skills or working knowledge, as Kusterer (1978) calls it. We develop the notion of tacit skills after the introduction, drawing heavily on insights gained by us in two empirical studies in which we have recently been involved, one of recruitment, the other of industrial relations in the British motor industry. We then go on to relate this idea to the recent work by Burawoy (1978), Kusterer (1979, 1981), and Cressey and MacInnes (1980), in which the role of workers' subjectivity has been given prominence. A full recognition of the necessity of workers' active participation in the labour process and exercise of tacit skills has a number of implications for the conceptions that Marxists in particular have all too often treated as settled. We will in particular draw out the implications of our argument for debates about work humanisation and job design. Whilst sceptical of the feasibility of statements about long-term trends in skill, we shall nevertheless make some brief comments about deskilling in our conclusions. Working knowledge does not in and of itself refute the deskilling thesis, but it does provide a different vantage point, one in which the central notion is that work is both degrading and constructive, both crippling and enriching.

Introduction
We are deliberately using the word 'tacit' to get away from two sets of conceptual problems that often bedevil work on skills. First, the Braverman position which treats the reduction of workers to automatons as an imperative of capitalism. Second, Kusterer's argument which begins by recognising the importance of 'working knowledge' and then assumes that this automatically enables workers to be autonomous from management. There is a danger, certainly in Braverman's analysis, that the mind is reduced to conscious thought. Not enough attention is given to what Koestler described as the 'obvious, trivial fact that consciousness is not an all-or-nothing affair but a *matter of degrees*' (Koestler 1976: 205).

There are three main dimensions to tacit skills that we want to highlight. First, that the performance of 'routine' tasks involves a process of learning by which skills are acquired through experience. The example of driving to which writers such as Kusterer often refer shows the way in which routines are developed through the interaction of both conscious and unconscious processes. At the early stages of learning such skills too much conscious thought may be counter-productive, leading to poor judgement and uncoordination. The transformation of learning into successful routines is a process of internalising patterned movements and reduced awareness. The learning of dance routines, typing, operating presses and so on all involve a relation between the mind and body so that they can be repeated and successfully performed without full awareness. The second dimension of our concern with tacit skills is that there are different degrees of awareness required to perform certain activities. The tacit routine skill of which the worker has little awareness can be contrasted to the problem of coping with unfamiliar situations for which existing routines are inadequate. To return to the motoring example, driving on a familiar road may require little direct awareness, overtaking on a motorway may become a kind of semi-aware routine, whereas overtaking in a dangerous situation requires much fuller awareness. Tricks of the trade, such as workers using cigarette papers as wedges in machines in which parts have been worn down, are an example of this heightened awareness. The third dimension of tacit skills relates to the collective nature of the labour process and the necessity for workers to develop cooperative skills. There are many such skills required in the production process, including congeniality, 'mucking in', timekeeping and obedience. We wish, however, to draw attention to the significance of workers' appreciation and awareness of how their jobs relate to the production process. The integrated nature of production makes this very important. It involves an ability to spot the problems that can arise in jobs which are related to each other, problems which are rooted in transfer systems, differential capacity levels and variable production rates. The example of working in a sausage plant illustrates this well; a former meat-chopper told us how he had to learn to 'read' the line ahead of him in order to set an appropriate pace for his work so that the flow of the whole line was synchronised.

The existence of tacit skills underlies many of the characteristics of workers valued by the managers we talked to in our study of hiring practices. The importance of experience in proficient production is reflected in the quest for workers who can 'fit in', even if they only need short training times. This rationale makes sense in the light of the important distinction, which one manager stresses, between 'making widgets, making widgets *efficiently* as part of a production system, and making widgets efficiently as part of an *ongoing* production system'. This rationale is also compatible with workers experiencing an element of freedom; the feeling that much of what they do is working from 'inside outward', to use Koestler's terminology once more.

It is easy to infer a simplistic economism or pragmatic acceptance on the part of many workers in remarks such as 'doing a fair day's work for a fair day's wage' and 'all I want is to be left alone by management'. But this is to miss the importance of the fundamental psychological process by which workers develop an identity in relation to the labour process. An understanding of the role of tacit skills will then have implications for a wider study of the political consciousness of the working class. Nevertheless, our object in this chapter is mainly limited to exploring the implications of tacit skills for recent debates about the labour process.

Tacit skills are seen as especially important in the context of the debate surrounding Braverman's deskilling thesis according to which management control and the degradation of workers are seen as basic preconditions for productive efficiency.[1] Accordingly, management is assumed within capitalism to monopolise knowledge and deprive workers of any skills and initiative. It is taken for granted that, without this process of deskilling and assertion of managerial control, management would be faced with a recalcitrant work force which would undermine any attempt to realise the productive capacity of capital. As such the process by which management gains control of the labour process – in Braverman's terms through 'Taylorism' – at once reduces conflict, incorporates workers into capitalism and secures the capitalists' exploitation of both workers and capital. The implication of this is that it is not necessary for managements to gain consent for their actions or cooperation from their workforces; passivity and total alienation are fundamental requirements of monopoly capitalism.

There are several consequences of this argument, many of which have been discussed elsewhere. First, that methods of management other than Taylorism have no place within capitalism, and that human relations and other non-Taylorist theories of management do not produce alternatives but are simply cosmetic measures to habituate workers to their meaningless productive roles. Second, that the working class is reduced at worst to a totally passive acquiescence to capitalism, or at best it can develop an economistic consciousness. Resistance to managerial control can only take the form of economistic trade unionism as it can only influence the exchange and not the use of labour power. A traditional Leninist analysis of politics is presumably maintained by Braverman, according to which the working class cannot develop a revolutionary or even class consciousness independently of a vanguard party. Thirdly, that divisions within the working class are largely artificial and certainly not based on any genuine skill differentials. Any differences in occupational status within the working class are illusory and socially created by managements perhaps – as in Edwards' (1979) theory – as part of a process of divide and rule to enhance their control.

Braverman's neglect of the role of subjectivity in the labour process arises from both his method – his decision to limit his study to what he called the objective process of change – and his assumption that the Taylorist divorce of execution and conception could and has been achieved. The first wave of reactions to Braverman stressed the latter but did not question the validity of his method, but just indicated his analysis was one-sided. Later writers tended to equate subjectivity with worker resistance and emphasised the importance of overcoming the neglect of class struggle. Friedman (1977a, 1977b) and Edwards (1979) went on to link this to the need to acknowledge alternatives to Taylorism. These alternatives were seen as attempts by management to counteract or come to terms with such resistance. More recent work has gone even further and pointed to the need to get away from an objectivist and technicist conception of work organisation. It points to the importance of the sexual division of labour, the failure of management to gain absolute domination, the limits and contradictions in Taylorism, the variety of forms of work organisation and Braverman's idealisation of craft work both as a definition of unalienated work and as a benchmark against which the content of twentieth century jobs should be measured.

The dangers of 'Bravermania' (Littler and Salaman 1982), in general, have been exposed, notably the excessive focus on the labour process and neglect of wider economic issues and functions of management other than control; the association of skill solely with craftsmen and artisans and hence de-skilling with the erosion of craft control; and the use of a zero-sum model of control and power, with the associated danger that management is treated as ultimately omniscient and absolutely dominant. In discussing workers' potential participation in the current economic system we are not, however, here concerned to take the focus right away from the labour process. Rather, we take as our departure point the need to reconsider and develop our notions of skill.

Conceptualising Skill

In order to develop our analysis of skill we take as a starting point Polanyi's theory of tacit knowing. Polanyi developed this in order to challenge mechanistic concepts of thought. He stressed the personal knowledge which is the foundation of the development of ideas in science as well as art. He argued that, '*All* knowing is personal knowing – participation through indwelling' (Polanyi and Prosch 1975: 44). The importance of subjectivity in all human action is Polanyi's central concern. By breaking down such action into its constituent elements, Polanyi shows that all human action involves some degree of skill. The description of any labour as unskilled is therefore relative, not absolute.

According to Polanyi, any practical skill involves a process of tacit knowing. Once the motions that make up the skill are learnt, they are known tacitly. In exercising that skill, the worker does not direct attention to his or her individual motions. Instead the worker's awareness is focused on the outcome of these motions. The very process of exercising a skill must necessarily involve some degree of skilful performance. But because the actions involved are known tacitly, the degree of skilful performance involved can easily be forgotten.[2]

Polanyi's theory of tacit knowing provides a useful starting point from which to consider the concept of skill and related issues of 'deskilling'. An immediate implication is that we must be sensitive in the way in which we classify work as skilled. One of the most frequently quoted findings of the Blackburn and Mann study of the Peterborough labour market is that '87 per cent of our workers exercise less skill at work than they would if they drove to work. Indeed, most of them expend more mental effort and resourcefulness in getting to work than in doing their jobs' (Blackburn and Mann 1979: 280). The value of using driving as the benchmark is that it is a highly skilled tacit activity. The sheer range of activities involved is revealing – both feet, both hands; awareness of traffic behind, in front and on the side; awareness of many different kinds of road users (pedestrians, bicycles, lorries, milk-floats), each of which travel at different speeds; awareness of road conditions (camber, road-works) and weather; and finally, awareness of the vehicle itself.

It is not only academics who use the analogy of the car. Kusterer (1978: 50) remarks, 'over and over again, operators use the analogy between operating one of their machines and driving a car':

> Cars are basically the same, but every car is different. . . . At first when you're learning, you just learn rules about driving. But as you get to know how to drive, you get a feel for the car you're driving – you know, things like how it feels at different speeds, how well the brakes work, when it's going to overheat, how to start it when it's cold. . . . Then if you think about old cars like these machines, been running three shifts for twenty years, some of them, like maybe you've got a car with no horn, that wants to turn right when you hit the brake, that don't start right unless you pump the gas a special way – then maybe you can start to see what it's like trying to run those junky old machines they've got down there. . . . Now a good operator is like when you put her on a new machine she knows these machines so well, she's got a feel for it, she picks up right away what she's got to do different on this new machine than she was doing on the other one.

This quote illustrates the ambiguity of using driving as a reference point. Kusterer (1978: 50–51) goes on to argue, 'The main point that they were all trying to make is that it is not enough just to know how to start, stop, clean and maintain their machines. That level of knowledge – knowing the "rules about driving" – is about the level that the women reach by the end of their three-day training period. The next higher level of knowledgeability, which is the real *sine qua non* of successful machine operation, requires that the operators learn the idiosyncracies of their individual machines.'

Tacit skills refer to the feel and discretion which form the basis for subjectivity in even non-skilled work and are vital to efficient performance in all work situations. The importance of such tacit skills emerged in studies carried out by the present authors of recruitment practices and selection criteria in local labour markets in Britain and of the motor industry:

A firm involved in rolling metals, in particular steel. A number of rolling mills are used, the construction of which dates back to the 1930s in some cases. No mill is alike, so skills can only be acquired by working with those who have had experience on that mill. Efficient production requires that the idiosyncracies of the mills are understood so that production can occur despite them. Apocryphal tales are told of the employees who so understand their mills (often dubbed 'her') that kicks and nudges are needed to get the mill to work.

The plant produces products made of brass, and has had a reputation for high quality which it is essential to maintain. Technologies have been largely unchanged for generations. For the personnel manager, stamping is a 'monkey job'. The best stamper should 'not have a lot of intelligence or they would go mad'. Locked into the logic of equating education and intelligence with technical skills it might appear that anyone, providing they were well motivated, could do the job. This is not the case. 'Our stampers have specialised knowledge though they are as thick as tin.' At critical moments the exercise of this knowledge is vital. Sometimes the 'job' (i.e. piece being stamped) sticks because, for example, the die billet is too big, so the die has to be oiled, the quality of the final product depends on the quantity and application of oil. This knowledge is made more important because the product is made of brass, as wastage results in high costs.

An assembly line worker in the motor industry, who describes his work as a 'shitty job' acknowledges that, 'The attitude of those who get jobs here is that it is good money, so they stay for a couple of years to get enough to get married.' However, this apparent 'instrumentalism' co-exists with his recognition that 'people believe this company is better than elsewhere. There is a certain degree of pride in the product despite the alienation . . . it wouldn't take a lot to bring that pride out. When the new model came out, workers agreed it looked really nice.' The pride in the product co-exists with a pride in the work itself: 'It may seem strange to say and I may be unusual, though I don't think I am. I enjoy the feeling of producing something. There is a certain basic satisfaction though you don't think of it like that . . . that something concrete is being made by my labour.'

Of course, simply because workers say they have pride does not mean that they exercise skills. They could merely be trying to create involvement. Yet the way the previous speaker talked of the jobs he had done reveals the exercise of tacit skills:

(a) Assembling oil pumps for four years, he got continuously quicker. When he was sick they had to replace him with two men. This speed builds up by learning certain basic motions and establishing a work rhythm. Poorly machined parts disrupt this rhythm so that new motions have to be learnt. He reflected, 'I'm not sure precisely why I got faster. It is difficult to explain what a skill is . . . little flicks of the fingers and tricks you pick up.'

(b) A job where he had to pick up twenty-six bolts and washers out of a pallet and place them on the front cover of the engine. After six months he would always automatically pick up the right number.

(c) Using torque bars – at first he would wait for the bar to click but later learnt to wait for his elbow to click. (In Polanyi's terms, this is an interesting phenomenal transformation, in which one's body becomes the tool to which awareness is directed.)

(d) Working on assembling oil pumps there is a pipe which can be used to hang the pump; he was supposed to take each pump to the rack and place it there but instead flicked it down the rack from where he sat. . . . 'It is an automatic unthinking understanding.'

This assembly worker was frustrated at the way line management ignored the knowledge he and his colleagues had.

> You think of the understanding that we have got. Senior management comes down to sort out a problem. We know what the answer is but they don't ask us . . . it happens all the time.

Yet the recognition of tacit skills was admitted by one senior production manager of another car manufacturer.

> I have lost count of the number of times we have a quality or productivity problem which the engineers discuss in their offices and the fellow on the shopfloor solves. Once there was a water leak on the bulkhead. One welder knew all along what was wrong. The welding gun had to be used in an awkward position which often meant knocking the weld. These kind of problems can't be identified from drawings.

These examples bring out a number of features of tacit skills which deserve emphasis. Whilst workers and personnel managers can describe jobs as lousy or as 'monkey jobs', they are also aware that these descriptions do not do full justice to the range of skills required. It is probably correct to argue that 'most workers are objectively capable of acquiring the skills necessary for most jobs; we estimate that 85% of workers can do 95% of jobs' (Blackburn and Mann 1979: 280). But it does not follow that non-skilled manual jobs differ only in the 'different levels of human debasement they involve' (ibid.). The problem with such conclusions is that tacit skills are often taken for granted. Basic working motions are learned which have, however infrequently, to be supplemented by new motions required to deal with unexpected situations. As workers learn to cope with these new situations, a further body of specialised knowledge (often tied into particular machines) is acquired and taken for granted. Polanyi uses the example of riding a bicycle to emphasise that such knowledge must be learnt empirically:

> We cannot learn to keep our balance on a bicycle by trying to follow the explicit rule that, to compensate for an imbalance, we must force our bicycle into a curve – away from the direction of the imbalance – whose radius is proportional to the square of the bicycle's velocity over the angle of imbalance. Such knowledge is totally ineffectual unless it is known tacitly, that is, unless it is known subsidiarily – unless it is simply dwelt in.
>
> (Polanyi and Prosch 1975: 41).

An important implication of this conception of tacit skills is that the exercise of skill should not necessarily be seen as a conscious activity.[3] Once a range of techniques and motions necessary for efficient performance of a job have been learnt then awareness need not be focused on those individual motions. It is only when new situations arise which require new techniques and motions that awareness changes. The worker must again focus awareness on the specific motions needed to perform the new task. Once these new motions have been learnt the awareness of the outcome of the motions can be re-established.[4] Another important dimension to this, as we said in the introduction, is the *collective* character of the production process.[5] Payments systems which use collective bonus payments illustrate this:

> Consider for example a firm employing semi-skilled women in assembly operations which has changed from a payment system based on time rates to one based on piece-rates. Production has increased by as much as thirty per cent with a largely unchanged workforce. The personnel manager accounted for this by the way in which the new payments system had been introduced. It was not just individual incentives that were stressed. Of great importance was the 'piece-work environment' that had been created, which was reflected in a kind of collective pride in the output figures which were being achieved. The collective nature of this pride is a necessary result of the interdependence of the production process. (If one section's output dropped it affects other sections.)

Efficient performance should therefore be seen as a process of developing more comprehensive responses to deviations in the normal work situation; or, more accurately, of widening the boundary of what is considered as normal. This process is gone through in all kinds of human labour. Even artists rely on what Arthur Koestler termed 'codes of perception' – he quotes John Constable, 'The art of reading Egyptian hieroglyphics' (Koestler 1977: 378). For Koestler artists must acquire a vocabulary – 'not only to express themselves, but to read meaning into appearance' (ibid.: 379). Thus Constable learned to distinguish between ideal types of cloud formation, to acquire a 'cloud vocabulary'; and Renaissance artists used Greek model to indicate emotion by gesture or attitude (ibid.: 378–381).

The final problem surrounding the conceptualising of skill is the distinction which is frequently made between technical skills and non-technical or social skills. Blackburn and Mann (1979: 280), for example, argue that when personnel managers talk of a worker's quality 'they were worried, not about intelligence or manual dexterity, but about worker *cooperation*. Responsibility, stability, trustworthiness – such are the qualities by which (reasonably enough) they wish to select and promote'. The stress we would place on tacit skills suggests that such qualities as a cooperative attitude are vitally important but are often taken for granted because of both the nature of tacit skills and the informal way in which they are learnt. However, in using tacit skills as a concept we would also wish to question the very designation of certain skills as 'non-technical', because this greatly over-simplifies the nature of the 'ideal' sought by personnel managers and the production system underlying such conceptions. Such 'non-technical' skills are often specific technical requirements of particular job situations (Wood forthcoming). The personnel manager who remarked, 'he is the nicest lad in the world, but he couldn't do most of our semi-skilled jobs', expressed a common sentiment. Thus, whilst in the selection process managers may give far more weight to personal characteristics and attitudes than qualifications or overt skill attributes (Blackburn and Mann 1979; Edwards 1979; Nolan 1983: 305), it does not follow that the procedures used are simply designed to elicit modes of behaviour 'consonant with the form of control in the firm' and are unconcerned with 'the actual work tasks themselves' (Edwards 1975, 1979). For, above all, workers are recruited for a labour process, and not simply a management control system. Factors such as 'personality' were seen by the managers we interviewed in our study of employers' hiring practices as important but what constitutes a 'good' personality is highly contingent upon the kind of job, and the situation in which it is located and to which the person is being recruited, as the following examples illustrate:

> An electrical engineering firm (employing about 2000 people). The factory is divided into a number of sections as a simple result of the structure of the building in which it is located – the building is divided into seven floors. On each floor there are marked differences in the dress and manner of the women

performing assembly operations. These differences can be only partially explained by differences in the kind of work being done, in particular the technologies utilised. Sections engaged in the sub-assembly of electrical devices were associated with a cleaner, quieter and less frenetic work environment than those engaged in the production of, for example, distributors. Even in sections engaged in similar kinds of work such differences persist. They lead the personnel manager to be sensitive to potential 'personality clashes'; such clashes referred not to the differences between individuals but to differences which may arise between the 'personality' of the new recruit and the section as a whole.

One medium-sized enterprise (of about 500 employees) producing electrical fans. The factory has two offices, one of which was burnt down in a fire. The personnel manager was not aware that there were important differences in the kind of person she would like to recruit for the two offices – the one rebuilt after the fire and the new office built after the fire. These differences stemmed from the fact that those working in the 'new' office had now smartened up, mimicking and feeling proud in the smartness of their surroundings.

Personnel managers in retail stores are aware that the kind of person they think is 'ideal' would not be thought so in other stores. What constitutes a good employee in an up-market store, aiming largely at middle class customers, is not the same as at the store catering for a traditional working class clientele. The gradations are quite fine, the personnel manager in the store which lies just behind the up-market chain of stores expect, and is prepared to accept those rejected from the up-market chain. Indeed, such a rejection is almost a criterion of recruitment. The differences to which personnel managers refer include appearance, speech and performance at school. What is 'good' in the context of one level of store might be inappropriate in another.

The precise nature of the 'social' skills required often therefore vary with the requirements of specific jobs; they are, in effect, as job related as any 'pure' technical skill.

Implications of Tacit Skills: cooperation in the labour process

The point is made by Aronowitz (1978: 37) that 'subjectivity or consciousness depends . . . upon the contradictions of the social system that produce the necessary conditions for self-activity' derives from the fact that subjectivity has a material basis within the labour process, because of the productive capacity of labour. Management must draw upon and harness the tacit skills of workers in all labour processes to maximise productive efficiency. The basis for a form of creative cooperation exists within the labour process, facilitated by the interdependent needs of management and workers and constrained by the differential resources of power which either can draw upon. A conflict of interests cannot necessarily be presupposed, so that there may not be any need to 'manufacture consent', in Burawoy's (1979) terms.

To understand this more clearly we can look more deeply into Burawoy's argument, beginning first with this treatment of Braverman. Burawoy argues that Braverman is mistaken in identifying the progressive separation of conception from execution as the essence of capitalist relations in production. This separation takes place because a fundamental antagonism between labour and capital has already been assumed as the economic relationship of capital to labour is taken to be zero-sum – the gains of capital are always at the expense of labour (Burawoy 1978: 255).

However, Burawoy implies that Braverman places us in a vicious circle having denied subjectivity: according to him the existence of de-skilling and degradation of work proves that a conflict of interests exists and is perceived so that a 'de-skilling technology' must be introduced. Burawoy breaks into this circle by trying to develop a theory of interests; for him, the essential feature of the capitalist mode of production is not the separation of conception from execution which he sees as one aspect, but is the 'dilemma of capitalist control . . . to secure surplus value while at the same time keeping it hidden' (ibid.: 261). He arrives at this conclusion by having stepped outside the capitalist mode of production, by comparing it with feudalism; in the latter, the surplus is visible and the relations of exploitation 'transparent', whereas they are 'opaque' under capitalism. Because there is a real but limited freedom under capitalism, the worker enters into the 'hidden abode' of production 'freely' and will not perceive the relations of exploitation as such. This will only be revealed if capital pushes labour too hard – if the line speed, for example, is raised above some tolerable level. Otherwise, there is space within the 'fundamental antagonism' for the reconciliation of labour and capital through the ideology of work, that is the production of an experience of relations of work. The 'day to day adaptions of workers create their own ideological effects that become focal elements in the operation of capitalist control' (ibid.: 273).

Burawoy (1981) does nevertheless argue that capitalism depends on the creative participation of direct producers. Capitalists cannot and must not eliminate that spontaneous cooperation of workers necessary for production (ibid.: 91). As a result the more effectively management separates conception from execution, the more necessary it becomes for workers to recombine conception and execution on the shopfloor in order to keep production going (ibid.: 92). No longer is subjectivity treated as if it were external to the labour process, or reducible to ideology, for there is the possibility that the role of subjectivity is 'internal' (to use Cressey and MacInnes' term) to the production process. However, Burawoy does not appear to take this step. He still finds it necessary to explain 'how workers [can] be persuaded to cooperate actively in the production of their *prisons* of labour' (ibid., our emphasis). True, the problem is no longer to explain workers compliance; rather we must 'examine the labour process in terms of the production of consent and the organisation of struggles'. For Burawoy this is achieved through game-playing, the product of informal rules imposed on and tolerated by management, at least until they become too counter-productive. Such games will be tolerated by management because they do not 'necessarily threaten the organisation of work' (ibid.: 93) and serve to minimise the extent of conflict in the labour process by securing the acceptance of workers and management to the ground rules of capitalist production. 'One cannot play a game and question the rules at the same time; consent to rules becomes consent to capitalist production' (ibid.: 92). Informal practices are an essential feature of the adaptation of the work environment by the working class. For Burawoy in many cases management frequently puts up with these because the costs of challenging such practices would be too great in terms of lost production and disaffection.

It is necessary to go beyond Burawoy's analysis in two ways. First, the importance of tacit skills suggests that some informal practices may also be essential to the maximisation of productive efficiency. Second, we cannot assume that a conflict of interests is necessarily perceived by management and workers. Burawoy writes as if workers have fallen prey to a form of false consciousness, the ideological wool being pulled over their eyes as they willingly march into their 'prisons of labour'. Yet Burawoy also accounts for consent in his earlier article by the fact that, in the capitalist labour process, necessary and surplus labour time are indistinguishable at the level of experience. 'Moreover the continued reproduction of wage labour depends on the production of surplus value and a rising rate of exploitation may increase productivity and finance increases in purchasing power. In terms of use value, relations between capital and labour are non zero-sum.' So that, through the dispensation of concessions, and increases in standards of living, associated with an advanced capitalist economy, the interests of capital and labour are concretely coordinated (1978: 256).

The merit of this argument is that it stresses the material basis of the ideological identification of interests. But, is Burawoy saying anything other than the consent is being bought? This is part of the explanation, but not the whole. Because of the tacit skills exercised by workers, they do have a 'real' role in the production process. Despite the monotony they experience, theirs is a crucial contribution, in the form of the production of use-values which others can consume.

Through membership of the social community of the workplace, other needs are also met. Moreover, the nature of the detailed division of labour is such that labour becomes more collective in form. A whole range of skills are called upon in production, including those of management. And here we should distinguish between the role of different functions of management, emphasising those responsible for production, coordination, and the rectification of breakdowns. To repeat, cooperation is internal to the labour process. Consent may not have to be 'manufactured', for cooperation lies in the structure of capitalist production. Ubiquitous conflict cannot be presupposed, and we need not evoke false consciousness to explain the failure of the working class to live up to our theoretical expectations. The reliance on tacit skills and need for cooperation in the labour process suggest that management cannot be regarded as an all-powerful omniscient force which can perfect a complete understanding of what it wishes to impose and of how to impose that plan.

Nevertheless, knowledge only partially guarantees power. There is an equal danger of overreacting to Braverman and assuming, as Kusterer (1978) does, that the very existence of tacit skills proves that an element of workers' control exists and that deskilling has not taken place to a significant extent. Yet, Kusterer rightly draws the conclusion that workers are not completely degraded by work. The knowledge they gain in order to do their jobs provides them with some of the 'satisfaction and self-respect that comes from learning, growing and making a useful contribution to society in the labour process'. 'Work is a duality of both constructive and destructive, humanity-affirming and humanity-denying aspects. In fact the struggle to remain involved, to combat alienation is more than just an individual struggle for survival. It is an essential part of the class struggle. Day in and day out, exercising and realizing its capacities, the working class authentically upholds the values of productive labor and dignity of productive laborers' (Kusterer, 1978: 92–3). As such, an involvement in one's job is not a form of false consciousness but a reflection of the material circumstances of the production system.

Management's Work Humanisation Programmes
In this section we will briefly relate our argument to the recent discussions about work humanisation and particularly such management initiated schemes as job enrichment. Within the Braverman management-control problematic work humanisation programmes are essentially marketing strategies which are part and parcel of the ultimate managerial practice, scientific management. Indeed

Braverman (1974: 39) likens them to 'the marketing strategy followed by those who, having discovered that housewives resent prepared baking mixes and feel guilty when using them, arrange for the removal of the powdered eggs and restore to the customer the thrill of breaking a fresh egg into the mix, thereby creating an 'image of skilled baking'. Leaving aside the question of what guilt workers experience when working, the implications of this seductive analogy are that changes in working practices induced by post-Taylorist ideas are essentially cosmetic and that workers, like their counterparts in the home, will be deceived by them. Some of those who have investigated recent experiments have drawn similar conclusions (Blackler and Brown 1978; Nichols and Beynon 1977): 'attempts to improve the quality of working life by job redesign . . . serve as little more than an unobtrusive device to control others' behaviour' (Blackler and Brown 1978: 12). It matters little whether such ideas result in any changes in work organisation, for at best such changes will be trivial. As one worker told Nichols and Beynon (1977) 'You move from one boring, dirty monotonous job. And somehow you're supposed to come out of it all 'enriched'. But I never feel 'enriched' – I just feel knackered.'

But it is misleading to infer from their minimal psychological impact that such schemes are essentially artificial (see also Kelly, chapter 3 in this volume). First, the danger in dismissing them as trivial is that we are applying an absolute standard, rather than measuring their significance against the past and current economic structures and issues which form the relevant reference point for the workers concerned. Braverman, as we have seen, works with a romanticised view of the unalienated craft worker whose work is inherently meaningful in human relations terms and compared with Taylorist innovations. Second, we cannot assume a passive worker who is totally gullible to the human relations marketing strategy. There is nothing in the above quotation from one of Nichols and Beynon's respondents to suggest that he or she was duped by it (see also Knights and Collinson, chapter 9 in this volume). Workers can and do resist and modify attempts by management to change working practices through supposed increases in their job satisfaction (Roberts and Wood 1982). Third, we must not lose sight of the significant role that work restructuring plays in attempts by management to solve economic crises through increases in efficiency and productivity. This last danger is especially prevalent in Friedman's work in which non-Taylorist methods are seen as attempts during periods of labour scarcity to come to terms with its associated increase in the political power of labour.

Firms are continuing to introduce flexible work groups, to reduce demarcations between craft and production workers and redesign and combine jobs (Kelly and Wood 1984). There is no evidence (certainly in Britain and the USA) that the job redesign which managements have tackled in the recession has only been along strictly Taylorian lines. In fact it has been suggested that attempts to analyse such changes in terms of the simple Taylorist versus work humanisation dichotomy is too limited (Kelly and Wood 1984). Equally it can be suggested that management's attempts to motivate workers and change jobs through participative methods cannot be fully understood in terms of a simple coercion versus cooperation dichotomy; management is not simply coercing workers to identify with corporate goals. It may be necessary to distinguish (cf. Roberts and Wood 1982: 82) between job design in which there is explicit reference to increasing intrinsic job satisfaction (job enrichment or work humanisation programmes) and those which are not, for example attempts to increase the flexibility of labour or self-inspection of operatives. But the latter cannot simply be seen as Taylorist or neo-Taylorist; that is as solely concerned with increasing in a simple way managerial control. They may have genuine, albeit very limited, enrichment components.

Many of the changes in working practices, at least in Britain in the last few years, may have been made without recourse to notions such as job enrichment or explicit reference to intrinsic job satisfaction. It is doubtful if such notions ever dominated the bulk of job redesign programmes even before the recession (see Kelly, chapter 3 in this volume). They have always been concerned with labour flexibility, control or quality and the introduction of new technology, albeit not in such an explicit manner as they are currently. Management's desire to come to terms with the possible drudgery of repetitive work has, at least in Britain, been a minor aspect, if not a totally absent element in work design. Yet, work humanisation has been given a fresh impetus and dimension by the importation from Japan of quality circles – small groups usually of between five and ten employees who work together and meet regularly to discuss and solve job-related problems (see also Littler, chapter 2 in this volume). In such techniques the modern theories of human motivation are in fact linked to productivity and the economic performance of the firm. The necessity of experiments such as quality circles have arisen primarily from the weaknesses of Taylorism and the need for a flexible and knowledgeable workforce. Such experiments are best seen not as developing out of an opposition to Taylorism, but in relation to it with all its limits, constraints, and contradictions (Wood and Kelly 1982; Kelly 1982). Certainly this latest technique, Quality Circles, is not a complete rupture with Taylorism (Galjaard 1981). But its very existence illustrates our central point. For as Heckscher (1980: 80) has argued, worker participation schemes reflect the fact that Taylorist methods have never succeeded in reducing workers to automatons. Participation schemes reflect both the collectivism of production and the need to harness the tacit skills of workers. Managements are developing techniques by which they 'are able to manage both the workers and their work as an integrated whole' (Galjaard 1981) and with specific methods like Quality Circles are attempting to intensify the cooperation of workers so that it contributes to 'the development of standards for managerial control'. They acknowledge the need to create jointly aspects of the labour process. As such participative schemes are not necessarily cosmetic or necessarily manipulative. The issue, as Elger has said, is that they are minimal joint creations within the context of capital's domination, and it is this aspect that deserves exploration. Workers do have an interest in the success of their enterprises and this explains, at least in the British context, the way in which they have been able to harness workers' skills to successfully improve productive efficiency (Bradley and Hill 1983). Equally the contradictions surrounding this interest would help to explain their failure in many situations where management have tried to introduce them and the conflict which undoubtedly surrounds them in many plants and the way they may not have altered the degree of trust between management and workers (ibid.; Knights and Roberts 1983). For example at one car plant, workers reacted to the management's call for greater participation by pointing out that in a car plant twenty miles away, schemes to improve quality and worker cooperation had not saved the plant from closure. The key question then is not whether work humanisation schemes deceive workers but how they react to them. As Roberts and Wood (1982) have shown, different workforces may react differently to the same management initiative; some are able to resist parts of the programmes, turn others to their advantage, and in certain situations go on the offensive. Such reactions reflect knowledge and traditions broader than Kusterer's working knowledge or what we have called tacit skills. Precisely what constitutes this knowledge is at the heart of the debate about class consciousness and trade unions.

The Labour Process as a Joint Creation

We will now move from a consideration of work organisation to an understanding of how work organisation is shaped by the capital-labour relationship. Braverman began with what he regarded as the decisive features of the capital-labour relationship and then drew out the implications for work organisation with an almost deterministic logic. We have started from a different point, emphasising the limits which exist on management's capacity to plan detailed aspects of the production process. Given the need for workers' tacit skills, it is tempting to suggest that the labour process could more accurately be depicted as a 'joint creation' than the product of managerial whim. What is at stake is just what *kind* of joint creation develops through the organisation of particular labour processes and the tension inherent in the capital-labour relationship. Moreover the factors that condition the kind of labour process which is developed cannot adequately be accounted for by the competition of firms and managerial strategies on the one hand, and workers' struggles over wages and working conditions on the other. The analysis must also move beyond the factory gate to consider the relations of the workforce to the community and the significance of divisions shaped by the contours of sex, race and age.

Braverman based much of his analysis on the division between conception and execution in the labour process. One implication of tacit skills might be to argue that this division has little analytical utility. As Aronowitz has written, 'Even the most degraded labour involves considerable mental operations. Execution is a type of conception and conception a kind of execution' (1978: 141). Burawoy has similarly argued that workers have to re-unify conception and execution because of management's attempts to force through their divorce. The problem is to avoid the implication that the kind of joint creation which is being described is one in which capital and labour are equal partners.

Cressey and MacInnes (1980) describe the labour process as being 'internally contradictory': at the level of exchange value (Braverman's starting point) capital is concerned with the minimisation of labour costs, but at the level of use value, capital must provide labour with the means of production and (to some extent) rely on labour for its effective use. By recognising the central importance of workers' active contribution to production, Cressey and MacInnes are able to challenge the conclusions which follow from an analysis which only traces through the implications of struggle over the surplus. At the level of exchange value capital and labour appear locked in a remorseless battle over the share of the surplus which goes to profits or wages. But the capacity of labour to create value can transform this zero-sum game. Capital needs labour if anything is to be made and sold.

The distinction between use-value and exchange-value often has a polemical function, as well as an analytical function, which can confuse as much as it reveals. The distinction is used polemically to criticise capitalism as a system of production which is geared to exchange rather than need. Even conflict at the level of exchange-value cannot be presupposed. Higher productivity can finance increased purchasing power even though the rate of exploitation may also increase. Moreover, whilst individual firms will seek to minimise labour costs, at an aggregate level there must be sufficient purchasing power to guarantee profitable production.

Profitable production presupposes labour's contribution, but capital and labour are not equal partners in the creation of the labour process. The footholds labour can secure are inevitably unstable and insecure foundations from which to challenge the priorities of capital accumulation. As Braverman indeed argued, the power to develop and reconstitute the labour process is a crucial prerogative. It is a power held by capital as a social relation, though often not by individual firms because of their different financial, organisation, product and labour market constraints. The joint creation of the labour process occurs within the context of capital's domination (Cochrane 1982). Major firms have access to financial resources which may dwarf even those of governments. Workers, as wage-labour, remain vulnerable in bargaining with their employers.

The capitalist-labour relationship shapes the context in which tacit skills are exercised. There are important limits which constrain the ability of workers to exercise their bargaining power to establish a different order of priorities. The conception of skilled jobs as an entirely social construction suggests that skills are virtually pulled out of the hat by the skilled worker or workers with key leverage in the production process. Their power, so the argument goes, enables them to define jobs as skilled, independently of their real technical content. Whilst this bargaining over skilled status is an important phenomenon, the existence of tacit skills shows that skills are never irrelevant for job definition (Penn 1982; More 1982; Wood 1982). The issue is what motions and competences, techniques and knowledge are *selected* through bargaining and then defined as skilled. This will hinge on social divisions within the workforce as well as the role of employers. The most obvious such division is between the sexes. The result may be that the link between pay and skill level is partially severed; for example, women semi-skilled machinists at one major motor company earn less than unskilled labourers who could not expect to do the women's job without training. This kind of process of social construction results in expectations which are built into grading structures. Subsequently, the grading structure is used to legitimise the expectations, thereby reinforcing the underlying social divisions.

An analysis which is concerned only with the global social relations of capital and labour can often overlook the specific circumstances which face firms and workforces. While firms may consider relocating production if they are faced with a well-organised workforce, in many cases they will choose not to. They must trade off losing access to the valuable resource of a community of skills against the uncertain benefits of 'green labour'. If there is a shortage of capital because of the ownership structure of the firm, technological change may be held back. If there is a shortage of labour, but product demand is buoyant, profitability may best be ensured by preserving existing work practices rather than seeking to employ new workers or sparking off a conflict which could result in lost orders. Similarly, the differential strength of union branches within firms may result in different forms of task organisation and a different distribution of wages and skill content (Littler 1982a).

The interests and power of particular workgroups cannot be read off from the 'global' capital-labour relationship. Semi-skilled workers are placed in a strategically vital position in the labour process; they occupy a central role and can bring to a halt a heavily interdependent production process in which they have responsibility for costly capital equipment (Rubery 1978). But, it does not follow that they can exercise the same bargaining power as can skilled workers. Tacit skills are tied to the firm or industry (and often locality) unlike the craft skills of the apprentice trained worker. Workers with such skills may therefore be expected to identify with the competitive success of 'their' firm. Their bargaining alliances may be with other semi-skilled workers, rather than skilled workers (Armstrong 1982). A further limit on workers' exercise of power arises in the case of workers with good career prospects. For example, computer operators may not use their collective power because of their individualistic concern, and reliance on employers for references. The circumstances of particular workers may suggest actions which run counter to collective responses so that the political consequences even of de-skilling cannot be assumed.

Capital's dependence on tacit skills need not necessarily be reflected in the form of higher wages or skilled status in grading ladders. The global category 'labour' ignores the different sections of the workforce with which management bargains. The wages received by women and blacks are often lower than those of white men. Because of women's employment at home and at work, their participation in the labour force is labelled marginal and their wages secondary. As a result, even where women are seen as exercising increased skills gained from longer experience on the job, this is frequently not reflected in higher wages (Manwaring 1984).

Conclusions

We began this paper by emphasising the neglect of subjectivity in the earlier attempts to reorientate Marxist debate towards the labour process – it being either deliberately excluded by a methodological decision in the case of Braverman, or seen as relatively unimportant in the long term development of capitalist work organisation in the case of Zimbalist (1979). Subsequent developments have tended to equate subjectivism with workers' resistance and hence view it as important for overcoming Braverman's neglect of class struggle. The dangers of continuing to treat workers as victims, at least for a certain time period, of managements' control and reducing them to mere ciphers are still evident in post-Braverman writings. For, although Friedman (1977a) is aware of contradictions, and Edwards (1979) of potential limits to bureaucratic control there still is a tendency to reproduce what Littler and Salaman (1982) term the 'panacea fallacy', i.e. the assumption that even if one system of labour control does not provide a total solution to management's problems at a given time a new one could and will be found to provide such a solution. Once we get away from a zero-sum model of control it becomes much more difficult to sustain such an argument.

Equally the existence of workers' knowledge cannot in and of itself be seen as workers taking control from management or even as a form of workers' control. The importance of the concept of tacit skills is that it points to the role of subjectivity within the labour process, the vital significance of an active workforce, in a way which reveals the limits to managerial competence and omniscience. However, this does not rule out the successful implementation of control procedures. That managements are not omniscient does not mean that their control is necessarily precarious. The important point about relating the notion of tacit skills to recent debate about the role of cooperation in the labour process, is to question the reduction of employers' strategies to a desire to control or to suppress workers' inherent resistance. The relationship between capital and labour is contradictory for each side relies on the other as well as being in conflict with it. This is not to portray the labour process as a haven of consent, but to stress the possibilities for and limits of both cooperation and conflict which together form the immediate experience of work. Moreover we must be aware of the danger when using terms such as consent of assuming that there is a conscious act of will by workers whereby they accept as legitimate, managerial demands, a danger which Edwards (1983) suggests Burawoy may fall into.

As our discussion of job design and work humanisation and particularly Quality Circles suggests, there is equally a danger of drawing too close to the human relations variant of cooperation and implying that a consensus exists between managers and workers when it may very well not. Quality Circles attempt to achieve more than just the enlargement of workers' knowledge for managerial gain. They attempt to draw on and develop the cooperative nature of the labour process. One cannot read off from their successful implementation a consensus, for the logic of our argument points at most to a kind of overlapping of interests between labour and management.

In reacting to the one-sided views of much recent Marxist analysis we must guard against exaggerating the other side – the active element in the labour process and workers' cooperation and consent. Part of the answer lies, as Edwards (ibid.) implies, in developing more refined concepts and to bear in mind at all times important distinctions between terms such as cooperation, consent and compliance. The material basis for cooperation between capital and labour through tacit skills and mutual economic and other benefits does not deny the value of presupposing a fundamental conflict. But it rules out presuming ubiquitous conflict as a starting point or notions such as the incorporation of the working class to explain the relative absence of conflict.

In highlighting the complex relationship between cooperation and control, we point to the need to unravel a host of elements in the labour process debate before they can be satisfactorily resolved or re-assembled. We cannot uncritically accept Taylor's central distinction between conception and execution as an analytical tool for under-standing the development of the labour process or skill levels, as Braverman did (Elger 1982; Wood 1982), or even for grasping the practice of Taylorism. It is also necessary to differentiate between different notions of skill, as well as between a loss of skill and a loss of control (cf. Beechey 1982).

The deskilling thesis is, or course, not refuted by the recognition of workers' knowledge. But, if the level of skill is relative 'deskilling' should be understood as a relative process. Littler (1982a) usefully distinguishes between *specialisation*, in which the range of skills required is narrowed but in which the skilled status of particular jobs may be increased, and *fragmentation*, in which the level of skill required is reduced. Specialisation overlaps with another differenti-ating feature of skill, the level of discretion in different jobs, and therefore the degree of autonomy open to the worker. Our conception of tacit skills suggests that there must always be some autonomy. Management can never predict all deviations. Deskilling through fragmentation can be understood as a process which limits the boundaries of what can be expected as the normal range of deviation. Few of the critics of Braverman have argued that there has been any general upgrading of the skill of jobs in the twentieth century – although some have rightly pointed to the increasing literacy rates and other skills which workers have developed, either because of their collective organisation or the increasing complexity of modern tech-nology. In investigations of Taylorism, even where severe reservations are made about Braverman, de-skilling is given prominence. For example, Littler (1982a) concludes that the employers' strategy in Britain and even more so in the USA was based on Taylorism and bureaucratic control, but this superseded the powers of the contractors and traditional foremen and centralised managerial control. Littler confirms that this deskills part of the workforce. To be sure, this process is sporadic, uneven and takes different forms. But it is clear that those who are thrown out of work due to economy-wide forces often are forced to take work which requires less skill. The issue is as much about how the process of de-skilling is generated, and from what starting point, as it is about its extent or counter tendencies. Sensitivity to the particular circumstances facing individual firms and workforces does not deny the importance of the tensions which are inherent in the capital-labour relationship. But it does leave one wondering whether any development of industry is shaped less by fundamental forces than by a mosaic of short-term resolutions as firms muddle through in a bid to survive.

The object of this chapter has been to describe tacit skills, indicate their importance and point to some of their implications. Like much of the recent contributions to discussions of the labour process, in highlighting the significance of tacit skills the aim has not been to foreclose debate. Nor have we been able to generate the kind of overarching perspective provided by Braverman. Rather debate has again been opened up into wider and more fundamental directions.

Notes

1.   The debate has been mainly in USA and Britain. See, for example, Aronowitz, 1978; Beechey, 1982; Burawoy, 1978; Coombs, 1978; Cressey and MacInnes, 1980; Elger, 1982; Friedman, 1977b, Jones, 1982; Kelly and Wood, 1983; Lee, 1982; Littler, 1982a, 1982b; Littler and Salaman, 1982; Mackenzie, 1977, 1978; Stark, 1980; Thompson, 1983; Tomlinson, 1982; Wood, 1982; Wood and Kelly, 1982; Zeitlin, 1979; Zimbalist, 1979.

2.   'Any practical skill', for Polanyi, 'consists in the capacity for carrying out a great number of particular movements, with a view to achieving a comprehensive result', (Polanyi and Prosch 1975: 37). He analyses the 'essential structure of knowing as an art' by distinguishing between three aspects of tacit knowing. These can be illustrated by the example of tactile cognition: of using a probe, for example, or some other tool. The first aspect is the *functional relation* of subsidiary items (in this case the feeling of the probe held in the hand) to the focal target (the end of the probe touching an obstacle). This is a from–to relation: we are aware of the subsidiaries in the act of focusing our attention *from* the subsidiaries *to* the focal target. Two kinds of awareness are therefore involved in skilful action: focal and subsidiary in that it is not watched in itself. The second aspect is the *phenomenal transformation*. We feel the end of the probe whilst the sensation of the probe in the hand being guided by

194   *Job Redesign*

muscular action is lost. The third is the *semantic* (meaning giving) aspect. The information obtained from the act of probing builds up a mental picture of what it is that we are observing. Such a picture is a tacit creation which does not exist in itself. Polanyi's description reminds us that underlying any human activity is a complex series of perceptions and responses. 'All sensations are assisted by some (however slight) *skilful* performance, the motions of which are performed with our attention focused on the intended action so that our awareness of the motions is subsidiary to the performance. From–to structures include all skilful performances, from walking along a street to walking a tightrope, from tying a knot to playing a piano' (1975: 36).

3. In Polanyi's terms, 'focal awareness is always fully conscious activity but subsidiary awareness, or from-awareness, can exist at any level of consciousness, ranging from the subliminal to the fully conscious' (Polanyi and Prosch 1975: 39).

4. Polanyi expresses this by explaining that the worker no longer sustains the integration from subsidiaries to a fixed target as new situations arise. Awareness is focused on the specific motion(s) required to deal with the new situation – awareness is then focused on what were the subsidiaries. Once these new motions have been learnt the 'from awareness' of the subsidiaries is re-established.

5. Gramsci too, understood that this kind of social skill bound the work force together to form an organic whole. 'In a sense every firm is to a greater or lesser degree "unique" and will form a labour force with qualifications proper to its particular requirements. Little manufacturing and working secrets . . ., practised by this labour force, which in themselves seem insignificant, can, when repeated an infinite number of times, assume immense economic importance' (Gramsci 1971: 312).

6. This has important implications for dual labour market theory. According to Doeringer and Piore (1971) internal labour markets in the primary sector are created to develop and retain workers' job specific skills; the grading of wage structures reflects the hierarchy of such skills. For radicals, such as Edwards (1975), such grading structures of internal labour markets are the creation of employers intent on dividing and ruling their workforce, there being no basis in the skill content of workers for such structures; conflict is presupposed and analysis of it avoided in their model. This paper implies that employers will be intent upon retaining workers for their skills, but that there is no *necessary* hierarchy of job specific skills thrown up by the 'progressive' development of capitalist production. Further, employers may not need to establish elaborate wage grade structures to retain workers. There may be a number of constraints on the choice which workers may exercise in deciding where to work, such as the awareness of the operation of 'last-in/first-out' redundancy procedures, which confer a limited job security upon long-stayers. In the case of women, the pressures of domestic responsibility may further limit their 'choice'. Such constraints may mean that even in firms where there is a recognised hierarchy of skill specific to that firm, it will not be reflected in the wage structure. Indeed, the existence of hierarchical grading structures may be more a reflection of the organisational status and product market position of the firm than the internal logic suggested by the skills required in the labour process; for example, small monopolists operating in extremely competitive product market environments may require a range of skills but cannot afford a high wage in terms of the going labour market rate because of the constraints placed on prices.

References

r>r>iteful performances, from walkingiful performances, from walking
Armstrong, P. (1982), 'If it's only women it doesn't matter so much', in J. West (ed.), *Work, Women and the Labour Market*, London: Routledge and Kegan Paul, 27–43.
Aronowitz, S. (1978), 'Marx, Braverman and the logic of capital', *Insurgent Sociologist*, 8, nos. 2 and 3, 126–146.
Beechey, V. (1982), 'The sexual division of labour and the labour process', in S.J. Wood (ed.), *The Degradation of Work?*, London: Hutchinson, 54–73.

Blackburn, R.M. and Mann, M. (1979), *The Working Class in the Labour Market*, London: Macmillan.

Blackler, F.H.M. and Brown, C.A. (1978), *Job Design and Management Control*, Farnborough (Hants.): Saxon House.

Bradley, K. and Hill, S. (1983), '"After Japan": the quality circle transplant and productive efficiency', *British Journal of Industrial Relations*, **XXI**, no. 3, November, 291–311.

Braverman, H. (1974), *Labour and Monopoly Capital*, New York: Monthly Review Press.

Burawoy, M. (1978), 'Towards a Marxist theory of the labor process', *Politics and Society*, **8**, nos. 3–4, 247–312.

Burawoy, M. (1979), *Manufacturing Consent*, Chicago: University of Chicago Press.

Burawoy, M. (1981), 'Terrains of contest', *Socialist Review*, no. 58 (vol. 11, no. 4), 83–125.

Cochrane, S. (1982), 'Consciousness, control and the capitalist labour process', CSE Conference Handbook, 67–71.

Coombs, R. (1978), 'Labour and monopoly capital', *New Left Review*, **107**, January–February, 76–96.

Cressey, P. and MacInnes, J. (1980), 'Voting for Ford: industrial democracy and the control of labour', *Capital and Class*, **11**, 5–33.

Doeringer, P. and Piore, M. (1971), *Internal Labour Markets and Manpower Analysis*, Lexington, Mass.: Heath.

Edwards, P.K. (1983), 'Control, compliance, and conflict: analysing variations in the capitalist labour process', unpublished paper, Coventry: ESRC Industrial Relations Research Unit, University of Warwick.

Edwards, R.C. (1975), 'The social relations of production in the firm and labour market structure', in R. Edwards *et. al.* (eds.), Lexington: Lexington Books, 3–26.

Edwards, R. (1979), *Contested Terrain*, London: Heinemann.

Edwards, R., Reich, M. and Gordon, D. (eds.) (1975), *Labour Market Segmentation*, Lexington, Mass.: Heath.

Elger, A. (1982), 'Braverman, capital accumulation and deskilling' in S. Wood (ed.), *The Degradation of Work*, London: Hutchinson, 23–53.

Friedman, A. (1977a), *Industry and Labour*, London: Macmillan.

Friedman, A. (1977b), 'Responsible autonomy versus direct control over the labour process', *Capital and Class*, **1**, Spring, 43–57.

Galjaard, J.M. (1981), *A Technology Based Nation*, International Institute of Management, Delft, Netherlands.

Gramsci, A. (1971), *Selections from Prison Notebooks*, London: Lawrence and Wishart.

Heckscher, C. (1980), 'Worker participation and management control', *Journal of Social Reconstruction*, **1**, no. 1, 77–102.

Jones, B. (1982), 'Destruction or Redistribution of Engineering Skills? The Case of Numerical Control', in S. Wood, (ed.), *The Degradation of Work?* London: Hutchinson, 179–200.

Kelly, J.E. (1982), 'Economic and structural analysis of job redesign', in J.E. Kelly and C.W. Clegg (eds.), *Autonomy and Control at the Workplace*, London: Croom Helm, 21–50.

Kelly, J. and Wood, S. (1984), 'Le taylorisme en Grande-Bretagne', in M. de Montmollin and O. Pastré (eds.), *Le taylorisme*, Éditiano La Découvert, 257–272.

Knights, D. and Roberts, J. (1983), 'Understanding the theory and practice of management control', *Employee Relations Monograph*, vol. 5, no. 4.

Koestler, A. (1976), *The Ghost in the Machine*, London: Picador.

Koestler, A. (1977), *The Act of Creation*, London: Picador.

Kusterer, K. (1978), *Know How on the Job*, Boulder, Cal.: Westview Press.

Lee, D. (1982), 'Beyond deskilling, skill, craft and class', in S. Wood (ed.), *The Degradation of Work?*, London: Hutchinson, 46–62.

Littler, C.R. (1982a), *Control and Conflict: The Development of Modern Work Systems in Britain, Japan and USA*, London: Heinemann.

Littler, C.R. (1982b), 'Deskilling and changing structures of control', in S. Wood (ed.), *The Degradation of Work?*, London: Hutchinson, 122–145.

Littler, C.R. and Salaman, G. (1982), 'Bravermania and beyond – recent theories of the labour process', *Sociology*, **16**, no. 2, May, 251–269.

Mackenzie, G. (1977), 'The political economy of the American working class', *British Journal of Sociology*, **28**, no. 2, 244–252.

Manwaring, A. (1984), 'The extended internal labour market', *Cambridge Journal of Economics*, **8**, no. 2, 161–187.

More, C. (1982), 'Skill and the survival of apprenticeship', in S. Wood (ed.), *The Degradation of Work?*, London: Hutchinson, 109–121.

Nichols, T. and Beynon, H. (1977), *Living with Capitalism*, London: Routledge and Kegan Paul.

Nolan, P. (1983), 'The firm and labour market behaviour', in G.S. Bain (ed.), *Industrial Relations in Britain*, Oxford: Basil Blackwell, 292–310.

Penn, R. (1982), 'Skilled manual workers in the labour process, 1856–1964', in S. Wood (ed.), *The Degradation of Work?*, London: Hutchinson, 90–121.

Polanyi, M. and Prosch, H. (1975), *Meaning*, Chicago: University of Chicago Press.

Roberts, C. and Wood, S.J. (1982), 'Collective bargaining and job redesign', in J. Kelly and C.W. Clegg (eds.), *Autonomy and Control at the Workplace: Contexts for Job Design*, London: Croom Helm.

Rubery, J. (1978), 'Structured labour markets, worker organisation and low pay', *Cambridge Journal of Economics*, **2**, no. 1, 17–36.

Stark, A. (1980), 'Class struggle and the transformation of the labor process: a rational approach', *Theory and Society*, **9**, January, 89–130.

Thompson, P. (1983), *The Nature of Work*, London: Macmillan.

Tomlinson, J. (1982), *Unequal Struggles*, London: Methuen.

Wood, S. (1982), 'Introduction', in S. Wood (ed.), *The Degradation of Work?*, London: Hutchinson, 11–22.

Wood, S. (forthcoming), 'The flexibility of recruitment systems', *British Journal of Industrial Relations*.

Wood, S. and Kelly, J. (1982), 'Taylorism, responsible autonomy and management strategy', in S. Wood (ed.), *The Degradation of Work?*, London: Hutchinson, 74–89.

Zeitlin, J. (1979), 'Craft control and the division of labour engineers and compositors in Britain, 1890–1930', *Cambridge Journal of Economics*, **3**, no. 3, 263–274.

Zimbalist, A. (1979), *Case Studies on the Labor Process*, New York: Monthly Review Press.

9 Redesigning Work on the Shopfloor: A Question of Control or Consent?

D. Knights and D. Collinson

(1) Introduction

Until comparatively recently both the theory and practice of job redesign was dominated by industrial psychologists, human relations sociologists, socio-technical theorists and management consultants. With minor exceptions their respective interests led them to prescribe moral and/or technical changes to working arrangements at the point of production. Since the development of labour process theory, following the seminal work of Braverman (1974), the debate has broadened considerably. As is clear from the chapters in this volume, it has resulted in descriptive and critical accounts that seek to understand and explain the redesign of jobs from historical, structural and international perspectives as well as in terms of the more domestic matters of humanising the workplace or increasing the productivity of labour. In particular, the book has concentrated its attention upon external and internal product and labour markets as stimulants of job redesign.

Of recent times these markets have been subject to severe economic recession which has resulted in an intensification of competition where production has been forced to adjust rapidly to changes. In these circumstances, a prime concern of job redesign is that of increasing the flexibility of labour. Such an exercise is facilitated by conditions of mass unemployment and tight labour markets as workers are generally more amenable to the demands for increased flexibility when it can be seen to enhance their job security. But, as Ramsay (chapter 4 in this volume) and Kelly (1982: 50) have pointed out, the role of financial incentives and the wage-effort bargain has been underplayed in analyses of the conditions and consequences of job redesign.

This neglect, we would argue, is largely a function of the predisposition of job redesign theorists to subscribe either to *technicist* or *humanistic* ideologies. Both tend to neglect the social organisation of production concentrating their attention respectively on the productive power of technology and the psychological benefits of job satisfaction.

Others have looked at the importance of extrinsic economic rewards in securing the commitment of workers as individuals to the production process (cf. Marriott 1968; Goldthorpe *et al.* 1969; Lawler 1971; and Locke *et al.*, 1980). But in none of these studies has the full extent of the economic incentive been recognised as also stimulating a *social* commitment to production. For although the technicist and the humanist may acknowledge the importance of economic incentives they do so only in relation to labour as an aggregate of separate individuals.

What is missing from analyses that focus on individual motivation is the way in which production is organised very much like a game embodying internally generated rules and regulations. Shopfloor responses to bonuses, incentives and production targets cannot be understood simply at the level of the individual. For, as has been known every since the publication of the Hawthorne experiments (Roethlisberger and Dickson 1939), the response of individuals to targets and incentives is mediated through a complex informal, yet socially organised, set of shopfloor games, rules, interpretations and controls. Generally, the literature has concentrated on how shopfloor games serve primarily to restrict output below the level of management's expectations. Numerous studies of output restriction have been conducted over the years (cf. Roy 1952; Brown 1965; Lupton 1963; Klein 1964) but only recently has the replication of Roy's (1952) research revealed the production expansion aspects of informal shopfloor control (Burawoy 1979). Burawoy's research has made clear that the socially organised or game-like control of production on the shopfloor can just as much stimulate as restrain increases in output. Leaving aside some of the contributions of this volume, the job redesign literature has on the whole failed to acknowledge, let alone incorporate into its analyses, the undoubted significance of shopfloor games and their potential to sanction socially either an expansion or a limitation of productive output. Part of this failure must be traced to the influence of neo-human relations within the job redesign literature. For there has been a complete antipathy to economistic interpretations of human behaviour and hence a neglect of the role of financial incentives in job redesign schemes. As Kelly (1982) has suggested, job redesign theorists have attributed improvements in worker performance almost entirely to increases in individual *intrinsic* motivation and therefore not to any connection with either the *social* character of production relations or the material and economic conditions in which they prevail.

The significance of Burawoy's study is to demonstrate how production is a socially organised activity embodying worker-generated norms and rules which are just as likely to facilitate as to impede productivity. In so far as job redesign theorists and practitioners treat the worker as if he or she related only individually to the work task, the social character of production remains unexamined. Most of the papers in this volume have focused upon the structural dynamics of competitive capitalism thus shifting the debate on job redesign away from an over-preoccupation with the psychological well-being of the individual worker. Now in the final chapter we want to re-assert the contribution of the previous authors in directing attention to the wider economic and technological forces that surround employment but not at the complete expense of neglecting the social-psychological and structural conditions and consequences of job redesign at the point of production. Consequently, whilst taking account of national and international economic, market and technological conditions, our attention is directed towards an empirical focus upon the design or redesign of jobs as a medium and outcome of industrial relations and social organisation on the shopfloor.

Although refocusing analysis on social relations at the point of production, clarification of our departure from conventional neo-human relations approaches to job redesign must precede the main substance of the paper. Accordingly, this chapter begins by distinguishing our perception of the *social* character of production from what might appear to be an equivalent understanding in the conventional job redesign literature. Having drawn out the distinctive features of our conception of the social character of production, these are illustrated further by examining Burawoy's (1979) account of self-organised consent on the shopfloor consequent upon the design of jobs around financial and target incentives. Before turning to our own empirical research which parallels yet raises certain doubts about Burawoy's conclusions, a brief summary of what we consider to be the main limitations of *Manufacturing Consent* is provided. The report on our case study research at Slavs[1] is introduced in section (2) through a short synopsis of the study wherein job redesign can be seen in one sense to involve an increase, and in another a relaxation, of management control. At the same time, Slav workers often resisted being controlled, but they did so in such a defensive manner as to result in a compliance to the conditions of their own subordination. After describing the rationale underlying, and some of the consequences resulting from the reorganisation of work, section (3) compares and contrasts 'making out' in Slavs with Burawoy's account of its practice at Allied. The section concludes by arguing that although reflecting a certain degree of consent, 'making out' at Slavs also represented an expression of worker resistance. This, and its implications for job redesign, are elaborated through an examination of the mistrust of management. Quite clearly, resistance and mistrust undermined the promise of labour flexibility expected of the job redesign programme. However, it also had severe contradictory consequences for labour itself. Section (4) explores first, the way in which resistance reflected workers' attempts to preserve their dignity and second, how this resistance took the form of pursuing narrow economic self-interests. This was seen to weaken the collective solidarity and resilience of workers to defend jobs against management's rationalisation once the recession began to bite. The chapter concludes by coming full circle, with an account of management's abandonment of many of the changes that characterised the reorganisation of work in the earlier expanisionist phase.

1.1 *Contrasting our perspective with neo-human relations*
There are a number of reasons why it is important to indicate how our approach to job redesign is distinct from neo-human relations' perspectives. First, the theory and practice of job redesign has unjustifiably been dominated by the neo-human relations literature in recent years. Second, as a result of this, analyses of job redesign in terms of the social relations of production are assumed to flow from a similar perspective. Since our approach does not, it is vital to discount false parallels. A third and final reason is our concern to demonstrate the inadequacy of neo-human relations accounts of job redesign even on its own terms. Clearly, as the chapters in the volume have shown, an understanding and explanation of job redesign has to extend beyond the immediate social or psychological context of the worker. Nonetheless, the broader critique is enhanced when the conventional approach to job redesign is shown to be equally inappropriate in its failure to conceptualise production as a fully social activity.

Now in as much as neo-human relations theorists reject narrowly economic explanations of worker behaviour, it may appear that they take seriously a conception of production as a social phenomenon. However this is not so except in the rather mechanical way in which they perceive social relations as a resource from which workers extract what is necessary to satisfy their individual 'needs'. In effect, then, the so-called humanistic strain within the job redesign literature subscribes more to an *individualistic* than to a social conception of the worker. Most critiques have been concerned to identify the managerial technicism that is to be detected behind the false humanism of this literature (cf. Baritz 1960; Silverman 1970; Braverman 1974: Watson 1980). Few difficulties are placed in the way of exposing the managerialism of this approach to job redesign especially when one of its leading exponents sums up job enrichment as follows:

If you have someone on a job use him. If you can't use him on the job, get rid of him either via automation or by selecting someone with lesser ability. If you can't use him and you can't get rid of him, you have a motivation problem.

(Herzberg 1968: 125).

However, the concern here to disassociate ourselves from this literature is not simply an objection to its dissembling of a spurious humanism.[2] Rather, our criticism is more substantive. Broadly, the problem with such approaches to job redesign is that, in subscribing to an individualistic conception of the worker, they are unable to grasp fully the social character of production. This would not necessarily be disturbing except that the job redesign strategies proposed often have the effect of reinforcing the individualism which informed their construction. It is not that worker individualism is a false or inaccurate description. Clearly, the whole of modern culture places a premium upon the pursuit of material and symbolic individual self-interests. What is problematic is the treatment of a partial truth as an ontological principle or as an exhaustive description of what it is to be human. A consequence is that by concentrating on an appeal only or principally to the individual self-interests of workers, job redesign theorists and practitioners can actually undermine rather than strengthen the productive potential of an organisation (Knights and Roberts 1982; 1983). This was precisely what happened at Slavs which is discussed below. Paradoxically, the individualistic character of these instrumental managerialist approaches to job redesign leaves them vulnerable to precisely the same criticisms that they directed against the 'economistic' assumptions of Taylor and scientific management. The common problem is to represent and reproduce work organisations as mere aggregates of separate self-interested individuals. For, at root, the threat to cooperation and interdependence in production is not economic instrumentalism per se so much as the individual self-interest that underlies 'economism', but yet can manifest itself in other ways.

Burawoy's study of the shopfloor, examined in the next section, provides a welcome departure from the individualistic accounts of the workplace reflected in the more psychological descriptions and prescriptions within the job redesign literature. For, in *Manufacturing Consent* (1979) the collective and social character of production is clearly exhibited in the pursuit of targets and bonuses that constitute a complex game governed by self-generated and socially sanctioned rules and norms. What is distinctive about Burawoy's contribution to the literature on job redesign, as has already been intimated, is his demonstration of how production is a socially organised affair in which workers reconstruct their job tasks and related reward structures in terms of a game which can just as easily coincide as conflict with the interests and objectives of management. Theorists and practitioners of job redesign clearly cannot afford to ignore the socially organised character of production within which reconstructions of tasks, rewards and relations continually take place on the shopfloor as well as in the formal corridors of managerial power. Although the social relations at the point of production reflect and are circumscribed by all sorts of forces in and outside of work, they have an importance in their own right in constituting the immediate conditions, and in their turn shaping the actual consequences, of job redesign. While the contribution of Burawoy has been to focus upon these issues, there is a danger in his reading too much *consent* into the social game of 'making out' (see also Manwaring and Wood, chapter 8 in this volume). For in our own study, participation in the redesign of jobs reflected and reproduced a cynical *compliance* with the demands of management. Before drawing out the implications of our respective researches for the theory and practice of job redesign, we provide a brief summary, then critique, of Burawoy's study.

(2) Manufacturing Consent

In his participant observation of shopfloor culture, Burawoy resists the objectivism in contemporary Marxism where wage labourers are reduced 'to objects of manipulation; to commodities bought and sold in the market, to abstractions incapable of resistance; to victims of the inexorable forces of capitalist accumulation' (1979: 77). Rejecting this deterministic derogation of the subject, Burawoy displays how the labour process develops in and through the relative and limited autonomy of shopfloor workers to engage in the social organisation of production. As he indicates, 'these changes do not seem to support theories of intensification of the labour process or increase of managerial control through separation of conception and execution. What we have observed is the expansion of the area of the "self-organisation" of workers as they pursue their daily activities' (p. 72). Here Burawoy points to the active participation of labour in the production process which can be explained neither in terms of economically instrumental prior orientations to work (Goldthorpe *et al.*, 1969) nor simply as the product of the external agencies of socialisation (e.g. family, school, previous employment, etc.). In place of these interpretations, he draws out an analysis from his empirical research of how workers collaborate with one another to reconstruct the conditions of their labour as a game in which they view their participation as 'freely chosen'. As Burawoy argues (1979: 27):

Within the labour process the basis of consent lies in the organisation of activities as though they presented the worker with real choices, however narrowly confined those choices might be. It is participation in choosing that generates consent.

The form and content of the productive system that Burawoy investigated lent itself to the development of output targets, piecework rates and individual bonus incentives which readily provided the conditions for treating work as a game. Workers both individually and collectively perceived the targets, rates and bonuses as a legitimate challenge around which an elaborate culture of 'making out' emerged. Within this culture, consent was socially manufactured such that the rules and resource constraints of the game were legitimised. As Burawoy notes 'the significance of creating a game out of the labour process . . . extends beyond the particularities of making out. The very activity of playing a game generates consent with respect to its rules . . . one cannot both play the game and at the same time question the rules' (1979: 81). In this way, labour contributed to the reproduction of the conditions of its own subordination within a complex system of capitalist exploitation. In effect, the social organisation of consent to the rules of a game fabricated around production targets, established by management, secured as it obscured the expansion and expropriation of surplus value.

Burawoy's analysis of informal shopfloor culture reveals this not as a form of labour resistance that threatens management control, as the accounts of output restriction suggest, but as a facilitator of socialised production which is the necessary condition of private appropriation. The informal shopfloor culture, then, provides for a meaningful existence within the parameters of underlying relations of exploitation which are obscured in and through the very process of 'making out'. To be sure, the eclipse of the exploitative social relations of capitalism is not a directly intended accomplishment. Rather, it follows almost inevitably as a result of the relaxation of management controls which are a condition and consequence of the social organisation of shopfloor consent which develops through participation in the game of 'making out'.

To elaborate, self-organised forms of control on the shopfloor embody their own internal status hierarchy within which individual workers are assessed. Burawoy clearly reveals how 'making out' is not just a means of increasing earnings; it is a complex social institution through which workers qualify for group acceptance, a sense of purpose, significance and achievement (1979: 89). Personal significance on the shopfloor necessitates developing practical and verbal skills in order to accomplish a competent manipulation of the piecework system colloquially described as 'making out'. So dominant is the cultural significance of 'making out' that those apprentices not yet having acquired the knowledge and practical skills required to meet production quotas and targets are the objects of scorn, derision and ostracism. However, labouring within such a 'coercive cultural system' (1979: 65), they do not take long to realise that 'making out' is the main criterion of interpersonal evaluation and the medium through which relationships with fellow workers are established and maintained.

2.1 The limitations of manufacturing consent

Burawoy's empirical analysis provides a counter to the tendency within the conventional job redesign literature to view management's power narrowly in terms of its direct control over labour and to believe that workers can only be motivated by redesigning jobs in such a way as to increase intrinsic or non-economic rewards. *Manufacturing Consent* demonstrates that, given the appropriate framework of incentives linked to a set of production targets, there can be a relaxation of management control associated with the development of a system of self-organised shopfloor consent in which workers achieve high standards of production. Moreover, the internal policing of these standards are much more effective than any controls that management might apply directly to the shopfloor. The implications of this for job redesign are considerable. For if a bonus scheme can generate a self-organised system of worker consent, then job redesign may in some circumstances be seen as a relaxation, not an extension, of control. This quite clearly contradicts the claims of a number of labour process theorists who perceive little but management control in job redesign. For the present we turn to an examination of certain limitations in *Manufacturing Consent*. Burawoy's description of Allied workers' mutual collaborations to reconstruct the conditions of their labour as a game cannot be faulted. A critical evaluation can only be brought to bear upon the subsequent interpretations Burawoy places on his data.

As we will demonstrate shortly, the surface features of collective collaboration and consent that secure and obscure the production of surplus value may themselves conceal an undercurrent of conflict, resistance and dissent. But Burawoy denies the existence of hierarchical conflict or resistance. Maybe there was no latent conflict at Allied but the structural conditions of capitalist production and other studies of the shopfloor would lead one to suggest otherwise. There are two possible explanations for Burawoy's emphasis upon the consensual character of production relations – one methodological, the other theoretical. *Methodologically*, Burawoy was unable to engage fellow-workers in general conversation about work because, as a fully participant member of the workforce, he was tied to his own machine which precluded much social intercourse. Moreover, there is no indication in his analysis that any attention was paid to symbolic meaning as opposed to observable action. Consequently, the very real distinction between compliance and consent could not have been ascertained.[3] However, Burawoy would appear also to have had a *theoretical* reason for perpetrating a view of consensus on the shopfloor at Allied. For it fits more neatly into assumptions about the historical transformation of capitalism from a competitive to a monopoly stage of development. Briefly, Burawoy's view is that competitive capitalism is characterised by 'anarchy in the market [which] leads to despotism in the factory' whereas the monopoly situation allows for a 'subordination of the market leading to hegemony in the factory' (1979: 194). Because the latter enables corporations to secure their profits through monopoly pricing, they can afford to relax previous coercive controls over labour thus creating the conditions in which management and workers may perceive their interests as mutually compatible. Work organisation is then described as hegemonic since workers absorb into their culture the very values and practices that reproduce the system of their own subordination.

What has to be questioned is not the applicability of this thesis to Burawoy's own case study, although even here we are suspicious as to whether the interpretation was not convenient in terms of his broader conceptions of the development of capitalism. Rather, the issue concerns the extent to which the data is generalisable. That it may not be so is suggested by research material of a parallel kind presented below where the conclusions diverge considerably from those drawn by Burawoy. Part of the problem,[4] we think, revolves around the unique circumstances at Allied. For although it was an operating unit of a multinational corporation organised along multi-divisional lines, the plant Burawoy studied enjoyed a secure product market by supplying other plants internal to the larger corporation. The multi-divisional structure is ordinarily adopted for purposes of reinstating competitive pressures upon the separate production units of a corporation that would otherwise experience monopoly control over its markets (cf. Chandler 1962; Williamson 1975). Untypically, in guaranteeing secure markets for Allied, the corporation was not taking advantage of its multi-divisional structure to restore competitive pressure upon its units. Instead, as a service division for the wider organisation, any losses made by Allied did not immediately rebound on labour, but were absorbed by the corporation or passed on to the customer. Necessarily, in such circumstances, Allied workers were not suffering the full consequences of their structural position within the labour process and may therefore have collaborated partly to preserve an advantageous situation. This provides at least part of the explanation for the divergence in interpretation of Burawoy's research and our own empirical investigation of Slavs where 'making-out' manifested a wholly different spirit from that displayed at Allied.

(3) Control, Consent and Resistance at Slavs

Job redesign involves aspects of control, consent and resistance. Relatedly, labour process theory has demonstrated how control frequently stimulates the resistance it seeks to eradicate (Edwards 1979) and how a relaxation of control can generate forms of self-organised consent on the shopfloor (Burawoy 1979). In a way not dissimilar from Burawoy's account of Allied, our research at Slavs[5] shows how workers in the context of job redesign draw upon and contribute to the reconstruction of organisational structures of exploitation and domination.

Unlike the situation at Allied, the case study at Slavs provides evidence of a culture of 'making out' which reproduces the conditions of the workers' own subordination even when consent is replaced or accompanied by active resistance. Slav workers appeared to play a strikingly similar game to those at Allied. However, a closer analysis of the cultural meanings that informed and were reproduced by shopfloor action suggests significantly different conclusions. In neglecting to investigate the *meaning* of the actions he observed, Burawoy failed to consider in any detail the symbolic aspect of 'economic struggles' (1979: 177) over the effort bargain at Allied.

The transformation of work into a game at Slavs was informed by understandings which served to expose the instrumentality of management's exploitative intent. Although the game reflected a comparative relaxation of management control, the redesign of jobs that occurred after the company had been taken over by an American multinational was also seen as a form of manipulation which provoked shopfloor opposition. It may have facilitated higher returns to labour and a certain degree of self-organised consent to achieving production targets but it in no way diminished the polarisation of conflict reflected in the 'them' and 'us' mentality of the shopfloor. The contradictions of control remained despite the greater commitment to output created by the redesign of jobs, but the defensive character of the workers' resistance also embodied its own contradictions. In a modified form, the resistance reproduced the conditions that actually facilitated management control. Workers sought to resist by emphasising their 'commodity status', whilst denying or minimising their interdependence with management. Seeking to retain a measure of personal dignity in conditions of subordination, they distanced themselves mentally from the organisation. For Slav workers believed that the most effective means of maintaining a defensive control over daily existence was to limit any interest in work to the price and terms of their commodified labour.

On the one hand, by treating their labour power as a fixed but highly priced commodity they were able to maintain a distance from an ultimate dependency on management. On the other hand, this commodity status reflected and reinforced their disposability should the market turn against them. In short, the defensive resistance to subordination had the consequence of facilitating management's tendency to treat labour as a replaceable and disposable commodity. Far from overcoming job and status insecurity, their defensive resistance actually contributed to reproducing the conditions of labour's own subordination. When translated into rank and file economic instrumentalism within the union, this negative defensiveness generated tensions which undermined internal shopfloor solidarity. Partly as a result, the union representatives had to negotiate deals which exchanged wage increases and job security for a guarantee to management that they would control the shopfloor. In sum, the paradox of shopfloor resistance was its contribution to the reproduction of labour's subordination. To explain these processes and the contradictions they embodied, we will now consider in more detail the effects of the recent job redesign changes at Slavs. This is followed by a description of both 'making out', and then the wider shopfloor culture through which workers expressed their mistrust of management but in ways that only served to reproduce the conditions of their own subordination.

3.1 Work re-organisation

After the American multinational takeover of Slavs in 1974, a new approach to management based upon a human relations perspective began to be pursued. A team of managers from the parent company were installed at Slavs with the task of placating widespread shopfloor anxieties about 'the faceless men in Chicago' who were now to decide the workers' fate. Whilst employees at Allied enjoyed advantages from their employment in a multinational corporation, Slav workers felt threatened by the financial strength of the company under its new ownership. The shopfloor feared that the corporation could absorb and diffuse worker dissent over a sustained period of time simply by virtue of the increased inequality of power. Most of the workers felt that, in contrast to the previous family owners, the multinational was less vulnerable to shopfloor resistance and could be more 'ruthless' in disposing of labour if acceptable profits were not forthcoming. Against this background of anxiety, the Americans tried to generate trust by promising to eradicate 'outdated' status differentials, and by improving the quantity and quality of 'personal' communication to the shopfloor. 'Call me Barney' was the managing director's front page message in the first edition of the newly created house magazine in 1978. However, this new 'open' policy was not intended merely as an internal exercise in nurturing employee goodwill but was an integral part of a wider strategy designed to improve distributor and customer confidence in the company and its products.

Under a campaign banner of 'quality and image' the American managing director argued repeatedly that the only answer to 'fierce competition' from foreign imports and internal state subsidised firms was to develop and differentiate product models in terms of their quality and reliability. In addition, it was recognised that there had to be considerable improvements in the aftersales service and the spare parts distribution system. With the help of an aggressive marketing and public relations policy aimed both at customers and employees, the Americans hoped to become 'Number One in Europe' by penetrating more deeply into their various product markets. The way to achieve this was through a massive increase in sales and productivity.

In addition to extending and improving the product range, the new emphasis on marketing demanded increased effort to ensure that communications between the company, distributors and customers were both visible and effective. Buyer satisfaction was held to be the key to repeat sales, so top management declared their objective as one of 'providing greater satisfaction than any of the twenty main competitors'. Although the success of the new aggressive marketing venture would depend partly on the flexibility and commitment of labour, consultation was restricted almost exclusively to communications with customers. The outcome of this consultation was that management had to try and improve the quality of product design and production methods, which involved, for example, the introduction of quality control audits and other test inspection services. Combined with this was a series of new managerial post appointments, a new parts centre and the opening of a service training school. All of these innovations were accompanied by a fanfare of publicity in the recently introduced house magazine. Produced largely to improve internal communications, this publication also became the major medium through which the various new product models were announced to the trade.

By 1979 the Slav basic range had reached 26 standard models and these were supported by strong managerial assurances that variations were possible to meet individual customer specifications. Inevitably, this preoccupation with marketing, product differentiation and more personalised customer services demanded a flexibility and commitment to production of considerably greater proportions than previously. In an attempt to stimulate shopfloor commitment to the new strategy, attention was given to improving communications and physical conditions on the shopfloor. The major part of this reorganisation of work, however, was one of emphasising the interdependence of departments and the sense of harmony that could be achieved through an integration of internal production and external marketing. An important strand of the marketing strategy was to build up customer confidence by stressing that, unlike many of their competitors, 'Slavs were small enough to work well together.' This increasingly close interrelationship between product and labour markets was summarised in the following statement by the managing director,

> Quality is an image our customers view not only from the finished product but as they walk through our plant. If they see dirty floors and paper cups lying everywhere, our image is less than satisfactory . . .
> We have a tremendous amount going for us but one thing that is frequently mentioned is a lack of communication. We will change that. We plan to keep everyone informed, but I also expect everyone to keep me informed.

Like marketing, training was also given high priority in this new campaign. An Employee Development Manager was appointed, who subsequently concentrated his efforts on managerial and supervisory skills in communication.[6] By drawing upon neo-human relations theory, especially the 'need' hierarchy of Maslow, communication skills were perceived as the means whereby confrontation in industrial relations could be avoided. In order to secure the voluntary and flexible commitment of labour, there was a continuous appeal for teamwork and cooperation. Management repeatedly emphasised the cooperative and interdependent character of production at Slavs. In a way not dissimilar to Burawoy's description of changes at Allied, hegemonic power was replacing despotism as jobs were designed so as to build cooperation, commitment and interdependence into the very structure of production.

Behind the publicly expressed concern to improve communication, the prime interest in securing and sustaining management control, as part of the process of stimulating higher productivity, was not difficult to detect. Expressing the matter openly, the personnel manager argued:

> There's two ways of getting people to do what you want, the mail fist or the soft soap method. You should treat people as people, that's the best way.

In terms of the technical facilities for expansion, the company was well placed at the time of the take-over. For the Americans inherited a production system which had already been partially streamlined to facilitate an expansion in production and some product differentiation, consequent upon a previous merger in 1970. A flowline assembly system, introduced in 1973, had already made an impact upon labour productivity. Indeed, it had been a significant factor in the take-over decision since it provided the production facilities with which to exploit the market for purposes of securing a position of leadership. But the multinational parent company had not envisaged a 'free ride' on the financial front for a great deal more re-organisation of working arrangements and operations was still required. This was clearly going to be costly so the corporation backed up its faith in Slavs' potential by making a £3½ million loan available for purposes of funding the re-organisation.

It has been repeatedly argued that the new marketing strategy depended for its success on securing greater labour productivity and flexibility. As part of an attempt to secure this kind of commitment from its employees, the American management demonstrated their goodwill by conceding in 1976 to pressure from the shop stewards committee to introduce a collective bonus scheme. This was particularly attractive to the labour force since it allowed for a circumvention of the pay restrictions which were being rigidly enforced by the then Labour government. As at Allied, this decision contributed to the continuing relaxation of hierarchical control whilst also increasing employee wages and benefits. Once negotiated the scheme allowed for the elimination of overtime which the union had seen as capable of being exploited through the arbitrary decisions of foremen and the tendency for employees to ingratiate themselves to secure managerial favour. When the union pressed for higher wages, management saw the advantages in the implementation of a productivity agreement. By tying blue collar wages to production and white collar salaries to sales, management hoped to coordinate their own interests in financial and productive expansion with the economic interests of their employees. Even as soon as the beginning of 1979, the campaign had achieved a measure of success. The previous year had been a 'record for Slavs' with company turnover reaching £80 million for the first time. Popular new product models combined with an aggressive marketing style and the new productivity scheme had resulted in annual production output exceeding 5000 chassis – the highest in the company's history. By December 1978 Slavs was in a 'strong position' in the heavy vehicle market after a year when production had risen by 30% as a result of the re-organisation of work in both the production and marketing spheres. In the first six months of the following trading year the number of sales rose to 2527 product units and included a record 664 in just 23 working days of one month. Reporting this as 'headline news' in the house magazine, the managing director commented:

We've moved from a position of being 'one of the other guys in the vehicle business, to being the company that the other guys watch'. It's a good feeling.

For the shopfloor, increases in productivity of 20–30% per day made Slavs the highest paid set of engineers in the locality. At the same time, they could add a possible maximum bonus of £30 to their 'basic' of £80 per week. And yet, even at this stage, behind the public rhetoric and images of success which surrounded the company, a high degree of mutual cynicism and a polarised distance existed between management and shopfloor workers. Despite their public expression of confidence in the company's teamwork, management privately recognised the narrow economic concerns of the workforce. Still, managers remained ignorant of how their policies, especially the bonus system, contributed to the reproduction of narrow economic self-interest on the shopfloor. Moreover, management were only partially aware of how this made a mockery of all the propaganda about cooperative teamwork and employee commitment. Interestingly management's preconceptions were revealed implicitly in the personnel manager's initial reaction to our original research proposal,

> Why do you want to find out what they work for? The meaning of work, that's a bit esoteric, isn't it? I can tell you now to save your time, it's money, nothing else.

Since economic self-interest was considered to be unalterable, management collaborated with the union to re-organise production so as to appeal to the workers' instrumental pursuit of money. The bonus scheme confirmed management's preconceptions about workers' economic instrumentalism whilst reducing the necessity for a more directly coercive system of control and discipline. Yet, despite their comparatively favourable economic position, workers demonstrated their cynicism about the merits of the re-organisation programme quite explicitly. So, for example, on the machine room noticeboard a newspaper article extolling this success story of 'Anglo-American cooperation, never seen to better advantage than at Slavs' where 'wages swell as output rises yearly', had the additional comments of:

> Bullshit from Barney

written over it by the union convener. Here was a typical example of how the campaign to improve the quality of product design and production had not been matched by advances in the quality of company communication and teamwork. This becomes clearer as we examine the workers' attitudes to making bonus.

3.2 'Making out' at Slavs

As Burawoy found, the bonus at Slavs established and emphasised a network of shopfloor interdependencies which, in certain instances, reinforced tensions between individual workers. A part of our research data supports Burawoy's claim that making a bonus becomes a game which generates self-control and socially organised consent on the shopfloor. For example, some of the workers played the game believing in their common interest with management, whilst negatively evaluating and sanctioning those workers who failed to 'make out'. A typical complaint of this minority of workers was:

> There's certain blokes day in, day out, don't make bonus. They're bloody idle. I don't believe in scrounging but some people find it harder hiding than working the machine. The best workers are the skilled men. The semi-skilled fellas are lazier.

Here we see how the redesign of jobs at Slavs, just as at Allied, diverted tension ordinarily directed at management into lateral divisions and internal conflict on the shopfloor. Expressed in the form of internally generated shopfloor discipline, these divisions actually reduced the necessity for direct management control. Reflecting a recurring sense of being victimised by this 'coercive cultural system' (Burawoy 1979: 65), one driller argued:

> The men are the gaffers now, they watch one another like hawks. The nature of the blokes is such that they turn on each other. You're more worried about what the men think than the gaffers.

However, this lateral conflict embodied a dissatisfaction with management's failure to coordinate and control production. Whilst 'making out' facilitated the relaxation of management control, many on the shopfloor complained of the resulting problems of coordination. These problems created and sustained a credibility gap since the cooperative ideology supporting management's reorganisation of work sharply contradicted the experience of shopfloor production. Many workers felt less involved because of the increasing, rather than decreasing, distance between themselves and management. As one skilled man said,

> We want to respect authority, that's very necessary. But people on the shopfloor don't feel that management are giving as much effort as them. Job satisfaction suffers because of the communication breakdown. Newman (the manager responsible for payment systems and negotiations) said three years ago, 'I'll be walking round the shop, so stop me if you've got a problem.' But you never see him! If management are not interested, why should we be?

Nearly every worker had a story to tell about the inefficiencies of those 'higher' in the organisation. In particular, the increasing specialisation of the technical division of labour, instigated by the American parent company to improve product design and production methods, created problems about which the shopfloor continually complained. Typical of such complaints, the previous respondent argued:

> With the planners, the drawings they send are often miles out. I have to make a book of my own and work to that. The one thing they won't do is come down here and ask the operator who knows more about the job than anyone. The planners decided to increase the size of this part, but not the size of the hole inside, so it seized up. I'd warned them, then they tried to blame me. To ask us is 'Too much trouble' we're told. They want to make all the decisions.

Systematic change in work practices and the tightening up of written communication and procedures had consequences for people at all levels of the company. These developments in bureaucracy had increased the distance experienced by foremen whose job responsibility had been largely divided up and placed in the hands of the more specialised departments, for example, purchasing, stock control and personnel. Pointing to the forms and sheets scattered on his desk, one objected bitterly,

> Look at this bloody lot. I used to keep the stock going with a simple system. I had it all in my head. If yours is a Slavs' system they don't want it. I don't like pen pushing, it's American bullshit. Yanks like qualifications and their offices looking nice for visitors. Same with these planners and extra staff. It's the American disease 'too many Chiefs and not enough Indians' and once they're in, they pass the buck for their own survival. I bet in the last two years the overheads have gone up three or four hundred per cent.

Whilst impersonal bureaucratic procedures encroached upon him from above, this foreman's role had also been eroded by the increasing involvement of the shop stewards in the management of production now that the bonus system was in operation. This collapse of the 'foreman's empire' inevitably reinforced the relaxation of hierarchical control at Slavs since the bonus scheme had replaced more direct or personal forms of management supervision. Yet workers exploited the complexities surrounding the construction of targets and bonuses as a means of expressing their resistance and opposition to many of the work re-organisation changes at Slavs. A majority of the workers interviewed refused to leave managerial prerogative unchallenged and the bonus scheme, involving complex social processes of 'making out', provided them with the space in which to mobilise their dissatisfaction and express a sense of opposition to the company. Although some evidence was found to support Burawoy's findings about the reduction of battles with management, lateral conflict between workers at Slavs certainly did not *always* replace hierarchical conflict. This may have been because, in contrast to Allied's individual incentives, Slavs had adopted a collective bonus scheme. A collective arrangement conceals to a larger degree the extent of any individual's contribution or shortfall to the overall bonus whereas under an individual scheme a weak link will be seen as directly affecting a worker's level of pay. Moreover, the complexity of calculating bonuses under a collective scheme will always leave room for worker suspicion that management are fiddling the figures. Nevertheless, lateral conflict might be expected, and was in evidence to some degree at Slavs, since workers can demand more of each other in order to ensure the attainment of maximum collective bonus.

Before turning to an analysis of the amount of mistrust in industrial relations at Slavs, it will be useful to provide a few examples of how the bonus scheme served to limit as well as to extend workers' commitment to production. In the axle department, for example, by collaborating with each other to work 'flat out' in the morning, assemblers were able to cease work at 2.30 in the afternoon having secured maximum pay. Many of the men then retired to the toilets where they played their preferred 'games' of cards, lotteries, crosswords, football pools, gambling and trading. Here group solidarity was facilitated by a strong collective sense of 'working the system' (Goffman 1968). The bonus scheme provided a majority of manual workers with the legitimate space in which to oppose and actively subvert management's control, especially its demand for continuous production. Once bonus had been maximised, their willingness to continue work was limited to the 'private' production of 'foreigners' for personal consumption. Many workers remained sufficiently distant from the social organisation of production to be constantly aware that management were always ready to manipulate the bonus scheme when it suited them. Their cynicism was compounded when the lorry drivers strike of 1978–9 led to the incentive first being reduced to a 'mini-bonus' and then abandoned altogether as the supply of components and the demand for finished goods took a downturn. On the shopfloor, production consequently fell dramatically. Clearly, any reduction in bonus rates had the effect of encouraging the shopfloor to adopt 'go slow' tactics, and in some cases led to absenteeism and even resignations as individuals left in search of higher or more stable earnings elsewhere. Viewing their relationship with management as an impersonal economic exchange, workers resisted by maintaining the inflexible attitude that 'management can't have what they don't pay for'.

Whilst management had been attracted to the scheme because of its promise of production flexibility, the bonus scheme simply reinforced a rigid economic self-interest on the shopfloor that resulted in an avoidance of work whenever there was no further financial incentive to produce. The bonus scheme enabled Slav workers to redefine the terms (effort bargain) of the sale of their labour, without questioning the sale itself. At the individual level workers also played the game of 'systematic soldiering' (Taylor 1911) in the face of management's demands for ever more production. A driller in the top machine shop expressed pride in his capacity to use his skill against management:

> You can't tell 'em what you can do, or else you'd be doing three men's jobs for one man's wage. So you play yourself down a bit. The time I got for the job was eight minutes but I can do them in two. See it pays to know your job.

Slav workers used their own 'discretionary knowledge' (Clegg 1979: 124) as a resource to facilitate the defensive management of their output. They consented to game playing not, as Burawoy suggested, merely to avoid boredom, to secure group acceptance, or because of the attraction of the game itself. In addition to all this, 'making out' highlighted workers' resistance and/or indifference to management. Consent on the shopfloor (Burawoy 1979: 85), developed through the process of 'making out' within Allied, was limited for many at Slavs by a sense of opposition which was not 'obscured' but expressed through participation in the game. It became completely legitimate for men on the shopfloor to argue, as indicated above, that 'management can't have what they don't pay for'.

3.3 The mistrust of management

We acknowledge that many similar complaints concerning managerial 'cheating' (Burawoy 1979: 83) in the games at Allied were also to be heard at Slavs,

> It doesn't matter what you produce, management fiddle the figures to suit themselves.

However, these criticisms did not merely legitimise the 'rules and values' of 'making out', as Burawoy (1979: 83) suggest. Rather management's manipulation of the bonus was treated as further confirmation of the untrustworthiness of the new American owners. Fuelled by violent oscillations in the weekly bonus payments and the widespread failure to understand how the figure was calculated, enormous shopfloor tension and suspicion was generated. Often individual departments would reach their necessary production targets yet would rarely receive full bonus after the collective payment had been averaged out with the other sections of the plant. Paradoxically, and in marked contrast to Burawoy's account of Allied, the relaxation of controls in the guise of the bonus scheme at Slavs rebounded on management. For it brought into sharp relief management's instrumental interests thus heightening rather than dampening worker suspicion and defensiveness. Management's attempts to sustain an ideological hegemony by emphasising the socialised and harmonious character of production merely exacerbated the cynicism of many workers who readily penetrated the manipulative and superficial declarations and assertions passed down to them through the formal hierarchy. As a steward in the bottom machine shop expressed it:

> All management are worried about is production. So all we're worried about is wages. You can't trust them because they'd shit on you from a dizzy height if it wasn't for the unions here. They tell us a pack of lies so we have to check the time sheets so that they don't fiddle us. Their interests are for profits so it's up to us to get as much as we can. They'll not give you anything.

Regardless of management's concern to manipulate an appearance of harmony and consent in industrial relations, the workers' experience of the bonus scheme at Slavs actually intensified the reality of conflicting interests. Much of the time, this conflict remained simmering, expressed only in the form of joking, ribaldry and the negative stereotyping of management. Occasionally, though, the clash of economic interests surfaced, as for example when workers were accused of producing below the 'minimum required' in the period when the bonus scheme was inoperative because of the lorry drivers' strike. Immediately on claiming that the axles department 'owed' management a number of hours, a 'lightening downer' or stoppage of work occurred which lasted all afternoon. In this instance, management eventually apologised once the shop steward explained that production had fallen because parts were unavailable. Relating this incident, the axle steward complained:

> See, you can't trust them bastards, can you? They know the more we turn out, the more they'll get. So they're there all the bloody time devising schemes to get us to work. They try these things on 'cos they've nothing to lose.

In disclosing management's exploitative intent, workers saw themselves as victims, whose economic instrumentalism was a justified defensive response.

A second incident during the summer of 1979 confirmed the validity of worker suspicion and suggested that far from constituting a relaxation of control, the bonus scheme was being used as a mechanism through which management could manipulate production in a more subtle way. In the two months prior to the 'Wakes Week' holidays, the flow of production and thus the capacity to maximise bonus became increasingly uneven. Stewards, at least, were convinced of management's attempt to generate a stock of axles to maintain a continuous flow of production to the other plant in North Lancashire whose summer vacation did not coincide. By managing the flow of production so that some departments on site had no work outstanding whilst others, like the axle department, were suddenly overloaded, it was clear that management's aim was to avoid having to pay a higher average bonus. On the advice of the stewards, and in the face of some opposition from members who wished to protect their wages, the union retaliated by dispensing with the incentive altogether and reducing production accordingly, so as to force management to offer work for all, and thus to create the possibility of collectively maximising bonus. Management's attempt to generate flexibility for themselves was being met by 'rigid' resistance.

The shopfloor sense of vulnerability to manipulation in work was compounded by the knowledge that management's interest in profit and production was a constant threat to job security. The 'Yankee hypnosis and bullshit' displayed in the company magazine contrasted with the old family management who at least could be remembered for their brutal honesty, as the union convener (AUEW) recollected:

> You knew where you stood with the Greens. But these Yanks are nice when it suits them. They give the impression we work together but when the going gets rough its always the working man who suffers. Two months ago they wanted people to work overtime. It's the American greed wanting more all the time. But if we're losing money, they say 'let's hit the fellas on the shopfloor'.

Workers resisted management demands for total flexibility and treated the bonus virtually as a necessary condition of, and limit upon, their productive cooperation. So, although the bonus scheme did stimulate higher productivity, it also reinforced a purely economically instrumental attitude to work. Reciprocating management's instrumentalism, workers restricted their output and the amount of responsibility they were prepared to accept. As one welder in the fabrication department explained:

> There's no longer any team spirit in here. So we don't tell them the problems anymore. It's management's right to manage. They get paid to know what the problems are. I'm paid to do nothing else, why should I help anyone?

Far from improving cooperation, flexibility and interdependent commitment, job redesign at Slavs encouraged conflict, labour rigidity and individual economic self-interest. Whilst this was the opposite of management's intentions, it also had contradictory consequences for the shopfloor.

3.4 Contradictions of control and resistance at Slavs

We have observed how Slav workers expressed their resistance to the work reorganisation demands of management through an equally stringent, reciprocally instrumental pursuit of economic returns to labour as a commodity. Employees restricted their commitment and cooperation to that which was necessary to maximise wage income. In this way, they experienced a sense of independence and freedom from the conditions of subordination. Contrasted favourably against those who had hierarchical responsibilities and whose lives therefore resulted in too many 'compromises, anxieties, and heart attacks', subordination was re-interpreted by many workers as a form of freedom:

> I leave here at 4.30 and I'm not taking my work home. I'm not leaving at 7.30 p.m. with a briefcase full of notes.

But this distancing from management and responsibility was not sufficient to compensate for the structural subordination experienced by Slav workers. For although they might feel a sense of freedom in not having responsibility for the long-term viability of the company, Slav workers could not ignore the reality of their vulnerability as dispensable commodities in times of recession. Nor was it easy to obliterate the experience of numerous formal and informal hierarchical inequalities in the terms and conditions of employment (e.g. wages, hours, pensions and sickness schemes, holidays, and canteen and car park facilities). Despite management's commitment to reorganising and humanising the workplace, none of these material and symbolic disadvantages of working on the shopfloor had been removed.

The only way of retaining a measure of dignity, in these circumstances, was to invert the conventional status hierarchy by negating management and those in white collar jobs. As Sennett and Cobb (1977: 21) also discovered, many workers saw themselves as honest and trustworthy, unlike the middle class in the offices who were 'good with their mouths':

> Fellas on the shopfloor are genuine, they're the salt of the earth. They're all twats and nancy boys in the offices. When it comes to practical things they're bollocksed.

The American personalistic style of management self-defeatingly heightened the shopfloor sense of difference, as the chairman of the shop stewards' committee insisted:

> Management manage, workers work. You can't play two sides like the Yanks try to. The further away they are the better. They live in a different world to

us, think differently and act differently. They don't want to understand us, so I don't think it will ever change.

On the shopfloor there was a strong sense of 'knowing better', that workers' practical knowledge borne of experience led to greater efficiency than the abstract theoretical conceptions and academic qualifications highly valued by management. The elevation of 'practice' over 'theory' incorporated a self-confirming ideology of 'common sense'.

There's more common sense on the shopfloor than anywhere else. The shopfloor is more practical.

The practical skills of engineering not only provided the basis for 'conning the rate fixer' but also formed a central plank of cultural self-respect,

Engineering is the backbone of this country. The working man is producing and paying for all those silly cunts in the offices. We're keeping the rest!

The macho elevation of manual work over that of managers, office staff and women had consequences that both strengthened but also weakened labour's power of resistance. At one level, it had a solidifying effect on the shopfloor since their collective identity had to be continually secured as a counter to the conventional material and symbolic hierarchy. But, at the same time, the romanticising of macho shopfloor culture expressed in their reversal of the status hierarchy removed or at least weakened the major stimulus for challenging class inequalities. In a sense, the shopfloor's preoccupation with identity provided for a convenient accommodation to labour's subordinate material and symbolic status.

However, this manipulation of symbolic reality through asserting a sense of independence and reversing the official hierarchical evaluations of self-worth or social identity could not in itself justify coming to work every day. In many senses, the reorganisation of work and the redesign of jobs at Slavs had been introduced to generate on the shopfloor a more positive identification with work and production. The problem, of course, was that management was attempting this largely to reduce the unpredictable element of workers' behaviour. Yet management's public assertions, couched in the language of improving communications, teamwork and the interdependence of the social relations of production, reinforced rather than weakened shopfloor mistrust and cynicism. Far from stimulating a commitment to and identification with work, the contradiction between the ideology of the job redesign programme and its practice limited workers' interests instrumentally to production only as a means of maximising bonus payments. Although the satisfaction of these economic interests depended upon workers complying to some extent with management's demands, this compliance was extremely precarious as a result of the refusal to identify with the company. In so far as we have interpreted workplace collaboration and compliance at Slavs as highly precarious, our analysis contrasts sharply with Burawoy's stress upon the stable and positive productive features of jobs and work organised around bonus systems. The precariousness at Slavs was a result not simply of a prevailing indifference amongst the workers. It was also reinforced by management's failure to maintain a steady supply of materials and to fulfil the promise of the work reorganisation programme. For the discrepancy between propaganda and practice generated a good deal of tension on the shopfloor, not least because it jeopardised bonuses. In order to ensure smooth supplies of materials to an economically instrumental workforce, shop stewards had to step in to plug a management vacuum. Stewards effectively redesigned the work so that they had a greater control over supplies.

As one shop steward complained when assuming this new job responsibility:

> Nobody's bothered. We had to order the parts yesterday. The blokes don't give a fuck and management give less.

Concerned to protect jobs and secure bonus, the stewards had to control the self-defeating consequences of their members' indifference and of management's inefficiencies. In effect, they were becoming incorporated into the management process as a means of protecting the narrow economic interests of their members. But when the economic factor had to be sacrified for a longer term principle such as the protection of jobs or the demand that management re-organise its work to eliminate inefficiency, workers would turn against their stewards. For example, in April 1979, the stewards suspended the bonus scheme in protest at the inadequate supply of parts due to management inefficiencies. They were vigorously attacked by sections of the rank and file for reducing the size of the wage packet. Similarly, in 1980 as a result of a deepening recession and management's announcement of the need for redundancies, the membership resisted the shop stewards' solution of dispensing with the bonus as an alternative to losing jobs. The shopfloor rancour, division and fragmentation when narrow economic interests were at stake was expressed in the following typical response to a reduced wage packet:

> I'm twenty quid down thanks to that cunt (the convener of shop stewards).

Clearly, labour's economic instrumentalism forces union representatives to collaborate with management in controlling the shopfloor.

This necessarily involves the union in sanctioning any worker 'not pulling his weight in terms of earning bonus'. For without delivering to management a disciplined and productive labour force, union wage demands would rarely be met. As long as the union is responding directly to the immediate economic interests of workers, shop steward control is tolerated. But once the union considers that short-term economic interests have to be subordinated to the long-term preservation of jobs and the survival of the company, workers resist the union every bit as much as management control. When their resistance is seen to have little impact, shopfloor indifference is reinforced with a consequent further weakening of a precarious collective potential to defend jobs. Sooner than anyone expected, this proved to be the case demonstrating the self-defeating character of workers' indifference to anything but their short-term economic interests. For this indifference created and sustained a level of labour rigidity that prevented the company from responding adequately to fluctuations in the market and left workers vulnerable to the alternative strategy of corporate retrenchment.

(4) The Decline of the Work Reorganisation Programme
Although the redesign of jobs and the work reorganisation programme had been carried out at an enormous financial cost, it had not apparently secured the levels of productivity which might have enabled the company to ride the recession. Far from stimulating 'team-work', labour flexibility and a commitment to work, the redesign of jobs had reinforced individual economic self-interest, worker rigidity and an indifference to the company and its activities. Literally only months after the achievement of record sales and production figures, a massive rationalisation scheme was pressed on Slavs by the parent company. As a consequence of a 30% drop in sales in 1980 due, management argued, to a strong pound, high interest rates, cheap imports and poor productivity, various small operations were closed down, the nightshift was eliminated, and first a three then a one-day week introduced. Work methods were also changed to accommodate an American labour-saving technology for producing axles. 'Man hours' were reported to be reduced from 35 to 5 per productive unit as a consequence. But these rationalisations proved insufficient and in 1981 one-third of the 1000 strong labour force at Slavs were made redundant.[7] Of less immediate concern to the workforce but indicative of the comparative superficiality of the company's interest in improved communications in the previous job redesign programme, the house magazine was withdrawn as part of the cost-cutting exercise. As one of the stewards remarked cynically:

They can't find any good news to tell us!

Despite management's previous claim to have instituted a re-organisation of work so as to stimulate worker cooperation and commitment, fluctuations in product demand led immediately to the coercive practice of shedding labour. The absence of shopfloor solidarity rendered the union impotent to protect its members from redundancy. The only time that the union had any power was when product demand was high. As the shop steward convener described it:

> As long as they had a good order book management was no trouble. You can get the moon when they want more production. Well half the moon. They'll never concede the full moon! Your bloody worries come when the order book flops. They take advantage; of course, they deny it.

Paradoxically then, union power was weakest when most needed to protect jobs and only in situations where product demand was expanding could shop stewards begin to assert themselves.

Strangely enough, in spite of the deepening recession and the mass redundancies, by 1982 there was a re-expansion of demand partly as a result of the product differentiation policy. A re-assertion of union power in the form of a go-slow over an unacceptable wage offer resulted in the suspension of three workers provoking a two-day strike. An improved offer was rejected since management, responding to the upsurge in product demand, sought to tie certain departments to an overtime commitment. The stewards had to reject such an agreement on labour flexibility since it would create intense interdepartmental resentment because one person's overtime might mean another's lost bonus. Here was a further example of the failure of the whole re-organisation of work programme over six years to have secured a greater measure of labour flexibility. Instead, management had re-designed jobs so as to reinforce the economic instrumentalism of workers rendering them vulnerable to oscillation in the demand for labour but completely inflexible and intransigent when changes in work patterns were required to accommodate market pressures.

(5) Summary and Conclusions

In contrast to the other chapters in this volume which have primarily explained work re-organisation strategies in terms of broader economic and market forces, we have concentrated on the consequences of job redesign for workplace relations. More particularly, we have sought to emphasise the contradictions that result from a redesign of jobs where the social character of production is subordinated to individualistic conceptions of worker behaviour. Research at Allied and at Slavs partially confirms the empirical validity of these individualistic assumptions. However, at Slavs worker individualism was not seen as independent of specific job redesign strategies but often a consequence of them. Only from a perspective which focuses upon the social character of production can the assumptions informing job redesign be seen as reproducing the very individualistic behaviour it takes-for-granted. There is no doubt that complex socially organised games, where workers readily consented to secure production targets, developed as a consequence of redesigning jobs around a set of incentives. Nevertheless, cooperation was quickly withdrawn whenever individual economic benefits were not directly available.

As we saw, management's determination to change working practices and attitudes was part of a package designed to support an aggressive new marketing strategy imposed upon Slavs by the American multinational. Because of this, it was not difficult for Slav workers to recognise the instrumentalism of management's redesign of jobs. They demonstrated to their own satisfaction that far from dispaying a genuine concern for workers as people, job redesign at Slavs was just a gimmick perpetrated as a means of securing labour productivity and flexibility. Accordingly, they complied with the re-organisation of work only in so far as concrete economic rewards were the result of so doing. In other words, they responded with the same degree of economic instrumentalism that they detected in management. Work re-organisation at Slavs contributed nothing to the development of cooperative teamwork for which it was designed. Instead, it further bureaucratised the employment relationship leaving individual employees tied to their jobs and the company principally through the cash nexus. The majority of employees cynically distanced themselves from any concern other than the instrumental rewards of work. However, their defensive responses provided them with no protection against the subsequent employment surgery. Although the negation of management may have upheld labour dignity whilst in employment, the symbolic security it provided was soon eroded by redundancy and perpetual job insecurity. As a postscript to the research, in July 1983 the components division in which our study took place was completely closed down. The ineffectiveness of economic instrumentalism was again demonstrated here in the union's incapacity to stimulate opposition. For, against the stewards' advice, the labour force chose short-term redundancy benefits in preference to collectively struggling to maintain employment.

Clearly, in terms of stimulating labour flexibility, the costly job redesign programme at Slavs could not be described as a success. For even though productivity and sales increased when buoyant product markets facilitated high bonus payments, workers were completely intransigent to demands for their flexibility in periods of economic downturn. This individualistic inflexibility worked against both management and employees in that it reduced the company's adaptability to the market but also increased workers' vulnerability to management rationalisation. However, it is also important to recognise that larger-scale forces were operating to render the whole of Slavs vulnerable. As part of an American multinational corporation which had suffered worldwide setbacks in the early 1980s, Slavs was under tremendous pressure to generate *continuous* profits. Precarious markets disrupted this possibility leading the multinational, which was itself still fighting for survival, to offer Slavs up for sale. In a matter of only seven years, the multinational had moved full circle from its determination to make Slavs the 'number 1 producer in Europe' to abandoning it altogether. These broader forces indicate how, despite reproducing the conditions of their subordination, Slav workers (and management for that matter) were not exclusively the authors of their own destiny.

As a majority of papers in this volume have indicated, an adequate understanding of job redesign must embrace an analysis of the interrelationship of product and labour markets. Our contribution has confirmed the significance of this interdependence of markets and its implications for relations at the point of production. The impetus for job redesign at Slavs was quite clearly a consequence of a multinational corporate strategy designed to penetrate the product market. Yet, when translated into everyday practices on the shopfloor, the job redesign programme stimulated a socially organised pursuit of individual self-interest, the consequences of which were self-defeating for both management and worker alike. For in addition to the built-in inflexibilities, the absence of any collective solidarity rendered Slavs completely vulnerable to the 'faceless men' from Chicago who eventually were to decide the company's fate.

Where an understanding of the social interdependence of production is limited to reproducing instrumental relations of mutual exploitation, job redesign generates its own contradictions. For when introduced as a form of management control, any reorganisation of work undermines the development of mutual trust thus reinforcing personal and collective insecurity.

Whilst this analysis has focused upon social relations at the point of production, parallel contradictions can be discerned in the state's management of the economy. In taking-for-granted individual self-interest as the dominant characteristic of human beings, governments develop institutions designed to constrain such interests along channels that are considered orderly and socially productive. But, in doing so, they have to appeal to the very self-interest they seek to constrain. As a result, the state not only reproduces self-interest but also distorts rather than facilitates the moral as well as the material benefits of social interdependence. State or corporate control, then, is both a condition and consequence of individual self-interest. By stimulating an interest in protecting self, control reproduces individual self-interest. But this individual self-interest is drawn upon to justify the necessity for, and legitimacy of, control. Only if job redesign can undermine these vicious circles is it likely to expand both the social interests and the productive power of labour.

Notes

1. Slavs is a fictitious name used to preserve anonymity.
2. Nonetheless, we do believe that the disguising of technicist or managerialist objectives behind a humanistic facade results in a theoretical atrophy of the moral dimensions of the social relations of production. Accordingly, practices guided by such theory reflect and reinforce social relations distorted by an assumption that they are devoid of morality.
3. In our view, Burawoy misuses the concept of consent and would, therefore, have been better speaking about socially organised compliance. As we demonstrate throughout this chapter, what on the surface appears to be consent is more often an unintended consequence of a defensive resistance which reproduces rather than undermines the contradictions of control.
4. Indeed, Burawoy recognises that if consent collapses and/or profitability is threatened, capital will draw upon reserve powers that are extended as a result of its monopoly-corporate status in the economy.
5. The research was conducted in one of two lorry-making Lancashire plants which had at one time constituted separate companies, but were merged in 1970. Immediately after the merger the unions were able to secure a closed shop agreement and an eradication of status and pay differentials between skilled and semi-skilled workers. At Slavs when the research began there was a workforce of just over 1000 people of whom around 700 were male manual workers. Over 60 of these workers were interviewed, each on several occasions. The research was concentrated in the 250-man components division in the departments of fabrication, axle assembly, toolroom, loading bay, paint spray and top and bottom machine shops. In addition, managers at various levels of the hierarchy were interviewed from foremen, who incidentally proved to be the most reluctant and mistrustful group, to plant manager and personnel manager. The research combined depth interviews with non-participant observation over a period of twelve months. Essentially the focus of the research was shopfloor culture but a major concern was to examine its impact on, and its conditioning by, the conduct of industrial relations in the factory. See Collinson (1981) for further details.
6. Ironically, three of the supervisors were absent from one course on communications because no one had told them about it!
7. This 'streamlining' was part of a wider rationalisation scheme encompassing all three of the plants in Lancashire. In total, of the 2000 people employed by Slavs, 810 lost their jobs as a result of management's dramatic change of policy.

References

Baritz, L. (1960), *The Servants of Power*, New York: Wiley.

Braverman, H. (1974), *Labour and Monopoly Capital*, New York: Monthly Review Press.

Brown, R. (1965), *Social Psychology*, New York: Free Press.

Burawoy, M. (1979), *Manufacturing Consent*, Chicago: Chicago University Press.

Chandler, A.D. (1962), *Strategy and Structure*, Cambridge, Mass.: MIT Press.

Clegg, S. (1979), *The Theory of Power and Organisation*, London: Routledge and Kegan Paul.

Collinson, D. (1981), Managing The Shopfloor, unpublished MSc Thesis, Department of Management Sciences, UMIST.

Edwards, R. (1979), *Contested Terrain*, London: Heinemann.

Goffman, E. (1968), *Asylums*, Harmondsworth: Penguin.

Goldthorpe, J.A., Lockwood, D., Bechofer, F. and Platt, J. (1969), *The Affluent Worker in the Class Structure*, Cambridge: Cambridge University Press.

Herzberg, F. (1968), *Work and The Nature of Man*, New York: Crowell.

Kelly, J.E. (1982), *Scientific Management, Job Redesign and Work Performance*, London: Academic Press.

Klein, J. (1964), *The Study of Groups*, London: Routledge and Kegan Paul.

Knights, D. and Roberts, J. (1982), 'The power of organisation or the organisation of power', *Organisation Studies*, 3, no. 1.

Knights, D. and Roberts, J. (1983), 'Understanding the theory and practice of management control', *Employee Relations Monograph*, 5, no. 4.

Lawler, E.E. (1971), *Pay and Organisational Effectiveness*, New York: McGraw-Hill.

Locke, E., Feren, D., McCaleb, V.M., Shaw, K.N. and Denny, A.T. (1980), 'The relative effectiveness of four methods of motivating employee performance', in K.D. Dureau, M.M. Gruneberg and D. Wallis (eds.), *Changes in Working Life*, London: Wiley.

Lupton, T. (1963), *On the Shop Floor*, Oxford: Pergamon.

Marriott, R. (1968), *Incentive Payment Schemes: A Review of Research and Opinion*, London: Staples.

Roethlisberger, F.J. and Dickson, W.J. (1939), *Management and The Worker*, Cambridge, Mass.: Harvard University Press.

Roy, D. (1952), 'Quota restriction and goldbricking in a machine shop', *American Journal of Sociology*, 57.

Sennett, R. and Cobb, J. (1977), *The Hidden Injuries of Class*, Cambridge: Cambridge University Press.

Silverman, D. (1970), *The Theory of Organisations*, London: Heinemann.

Taylor, F. (1911), *The Principles of Scientific Management*, New York: Harper and Row.

Watson, T. (1980), *Sociology, Work and Industry*, London: Routledge and Kegan Paul.

Williamson, O.E. (1975), *Markets and Hierarchies*, New York: Free Press.

Summary and Conclusion

To a quite significant degree the practice of job design or redesign during the last half century has developed on the basis of theories of scientific management and/or human relations. Although critical of one another's detailed prescriptions on the redesign of jobs, what each theoretical perspective shares is a managerialist commitment to improving labour productivity. In spite of their divergences, both approaches subscribe to a view that technical solutions can be found to the managerial problems of motivation and control through an appeal to the individual economic or psychological self-interests of labour.

More recently, as the chapters in this volume have made clear, an alternative approach has shown job redesign to be a far more complex phenomenon than is revealed by these dominant technical-managerial perspectives. By exposing the social and politico-economic dimensions of work organisation, this new approach challenges the assumption that redesigning jobs is merely a technical exercise or is fully understood through an examination of the attributes and attitudes of individual workers at the point of production. In moving away from a technical-managerial position of prescription towards a more descriptive and/or critical approach to job redesign, the papers in this volume have sought to understand and explain job redesign through a broader range of analyses. More specifically, attention has been focused upon examining job redesign in the context of technological innovation, changing product and labour markets in a period of the intensification of competition both at home and internationally, socio-political developments within and between organisations, as well as a re-appraisal of social relations at the point of production.

Before outlining in more detail this emerging alternative approach, let us briefly summarise the key features and limitations of the technical-managerial perspective on job redesign. The classicial application of this perspective, exemplified in scientific management and its developments in work study, concentrates upon 'rationalising' the division of labour, job techniques, task performance, training and incentive payments systems. According to human relations theorists, the major shortcoming of this classical approach to job redesign is the over-emphasis upon a standardisation and routinisation of work tasks combined with a narrow assumption that workers are motivated exclusively by economic reward. Arguing that such mechanistic arrangements create worker dissatisfaction and low productivity, human relations recommend a redesign of jobs in ways which fulfil individual worker's needs (or expectations) for social recognition, self-esteem and personal achievement.

Two fundamental criticisms have been levelled against each of these prevailing technical-managerial approaches to job redesign. The first criticism concerns their common tendency to treat organisations as 'closed systems'. Completely neglected is the significance of 'external' or environmental contingencies – such as changes in the structure of markets – that condition and support work reorganisation. The second, less prominent but equally important criticism has been directed at the assumptions about human nature underlying the dominant perspective on job redesign. The objection has been that it treats people as atomistic, self-interested units who behave individualistically to secure their personal needs, be they economic (scientific management) or social (human relations). This model of human nature is criticised because it abstracts behaviour from social structures – structures that are the medium as well as the outcome of individual action (Giddens 1979).

What is particularly problematic about the technical-managerialist projection of economic or social needs upon individuals is that it can result in job redesign prescriptions which stimulate precisely the kind of behaviour assumed. That is to say, where the job is designed principally to maximise economic self-interest or the social benefits of group membership, workers may concentrate their efforts on securing these rewards to the exclusion of everything else. In effect, they limit their horizons to objectives that are realisable but, in doing so, confirm the assumptions about human nature implicit in the technical-managerial perspective which informed the redesign of jobs in the first place. This character of technical-managerialism, where assumptions can become self-fulfilling prophecies, is rarely considered in the conventional theory and practice of job redesign. However, in failing to reflect upon how their prescriptions reproduce the behaviour they assume, these theorists and practitioners also are unable to identify many of the unintended consequences of job redesign which may undermine its purpose.

These criticisms strike at the heart of existing technical-managerial approaches to job redesign. For, on the one hand, the adequacy of the theory of organisation that underpins conventional wisdom is questioned. In particular, the failure to relate job redesign to the development of corporate strategy in response to environmental opportunities and constraints is exposed (cf. Thurley and Wood 1983). And, on the other hand, the dominant perspectives on job redesign are found to embrace a theory of human nature that reduces the social dimension of work to the individualistic satisfaction of material or non-material needs. Disregarded in this formulation is the socially organised and interpreted character of individual actions. As a result, consequences of job redesign that may be wholly unproductive often are ignored or actually reinforced by technical-managerial theory and practice.

It may be argued that the overall critique emanating from the papers in this volume reflects the emergence of an alternative perspective on job redesign. In contrast to the human relations approach, it does not merely recommend a revision of the scientific management approach to job redesign. Rather, it involves a *rejection* of the theoretical assumptions about human nature and organisation that informs the technical-managerial perspective. In other words, it embodies a radically different way of making sense of work reorganisation and the redesign of jobs.

What, then, are the defining features of this alternative perspective. First and foremost, it is not directly governed by an interest in increasing productivity. Instead, the concern is to examine the conditions and consequences associated with changes in the organisation of work. From this perspective job redesign is a significant social phenomenon that is worthy of investigation not merely as a by-product of an interest in improving the technologies of organisational control. Put at its simplest, the concern is to study *how* and *why* work is reorganised, and not with advancing rationales or prescriptions which are attractive to management because they appear to facilitate their control over labour productivity.

In breaking with the technical-managerial tradition, the alternative perspective highlights the significance of the politico-economic conditions and processes both outside and inside the workplace. On the one hand, attention is directed to the connection between changes in the structure of product and labour markets and the introduction of new technologies and working arrangements. And, on the other hand, the alternative perspective on work organisation attends to the social and political processes involved in the redesign of jobs. In both cases, the political nature of job redesign is exposed. Gone are the references to 'regaining managerial control', 'organisational needs' and to 'humanisation' as the primary motive for job redesign. In their place are references to pressures from the environment to maintain or secure a competitive advantage and to 'work humanisation' as a management strategy for sugaring the pill of labour intensification, or de-manning. Similarly, instead of accounting for employees' behaviour in terms of the satisfaction of individual needs, it is seen as a medium and outcome of a structure of social relations in which management and workers pursue interests that in some senses or circumstances overlap and yet in others are fundamentally opposed. From this standpoint, the integration of individual and managerial interests can neither be taken-for-granted nor assumed to be an entirely realistic objective of job redesign within a capitalist structure of production relations. Where industrial conflict fails to manifest itself, this is not regarded as indicative of collective harmony. Rather, it is seen to indicate a precarious but presently undisturbed balance or 'stalemate' in the power relations between management and labour.

Finally, it is worth commenting upon the practical implications of the alternative perspective. So far we have tended to present this volume as exhibiting 'just' another, more scholarly and perhaps impartial way of making sense of job redesign. However, it is a mistake to assume that theoretical perspectives are either developed or received within a political vacuum. At the very least, the alternative perspective has political significance because it poses a challenge to the authority of conventional thinking on job redesign. Moreover, in doing so, it does not merely seek to remedy minor omissions but implicitly shows established wisdom to be seriously compromised by its prior and largely unacknowledged grounding in managerial ideology. Beyond this, the alternative perspective may provide a frame of reference for both managers and workers alike whereby they can envisage forms of work reorganisation which transcend the limitations of technical-managerialism. For the critical exposure of the underlying manipulative intentions, the polarisation of conflicting sectional interests and the unproductive consequences of technical-mangerial strategies of job redesign could lead to a recognition of the importance of seeking *social* or fully participative solutions to the problems of production and its organisation.

To conclude, as we stressed in the introduction, job redesign is a phenomenon shrouded in ambiguity. In large part, this is because there is no politically neutral way either of accounting for job redesign or or interpreting such accounts. It can therefore be anticipated that some researchers will attempt to accommodate the insights of the alternative perspective within the conventional wisdom. In certain cases this has occurred where 'open system' contingency theory has been adopted in the study of job redesign. At the same time, it is probable that more attention will be paid to the social and political enactments and processes through which the redesigning of jobs is conceived and executed. But it is also to be expected that other researchers will seek to promote the independent development of the alternative perspective on job redesign. To this end, they will be inclined to draw more heavily upon labour process theory and to advance a highly critical account of the role of conventional job redesign methods in the subordination of labour to management control. Some practitioners may penetrate the significance of such critique, recognising that production involves far more than the relationship of discrete individuals to jobs and the detailed construction of tasks. In those circumstances they may encourage a genuinely participative approach to job redesign consistent with the inescapable socially interdependent character of production relations. However, not all practitioners will be 'open' to the potential of transforming the structure of relations at work so that it becomes more compatible with the social character of production. Many will reject the alternative perspective precisely because of a fear that it would threaten their material and symbolic privileges; others might resist its implications in order to preserve the polarisation of sectional interests which invests them with a legitimate role in negotiating compromises. Similarly, it can be anticipated that some practitioners will reject the alternative perspective for being 'academic' or 'political', whereas others will seek to incorporate elements of it within their strategic thinking. Whatever the response, and this is of course unpredictable, the papers in this volume must be seen not merely as scholarly descriptive and critical accounts which indicate the ambiguous character and contested nature of job redesign. Their significance for the practice of job redesign can also be understood as extending beyond, and overcoming some of the limitations in, the technical-managerial approach which has dominated the literature over recent years.

References

Giddens, A. (1979), *Central Problems in Social Theory*, London: Macmillan.
Thurley, K. and Wood, S. (eds.) (1983), *Industrial Relations and Management Strategy*, London: Cambridge University Press.

Index